The Cunard Line's second *Mauretania*, although not as famous as her distinguished namesake, was a fine example of the beautiful style of the great Atlantic liners of the 1930s. (CA/ME)

Liners of the Golden Age
A Pictorial Record of Passenger Ships in the 1930s

CARMANIA PRESS

This book is for Laurence Dunn,
who has been such an inspiration
to generations of shiplovers

All rights reserved.
No part of this publication may be reproduced
or transmitted in any form or by any means
without the prior permission of the publisher

© **2004 Carmania Press**

If not otherwise credited, photographs are from the Maurizio Eliseo Collection;
photographs from the Cronican-Arroyo Collection, now part of the Maurizio Eliseo Collection, are indicated as C-A/ME.

A Catalogue Record for this book is available from The British Library

Art Director: Maurizio Eliseo
Printed by: Tisak Zambelli, Rijeka
First published: May 2005

Carmania Press
Unit 212, Station House,
49, Greenwich High Road,
London, SE10 8JL,
Great Britain
email: CarmaniaPress@transatlantici.com

ISBN 0-9543666-2-X

Front endpaper. *The United American Lines' Resolute, dressed overall, steams up the Hudson River on April 24th, 1922 at the end of her maiden voyage from Hamburg. At the time, she was registered in New York but after a few months she became one of the very first ships to be transferred to the Panamanian flag of convenience together with her sister ship Reliance. This was not done for tax reasons but to overcome the ban on the sale of alcohol imposed by the American Prohibition legislation.*

Back endpaper. *The Nieuw Amsterdam was not the largest or fastest liner of the inter-War years but she was nevertheless one of the most handsome passenger ships of her time.* Photograph: C-A/ME

Background. *Southampton, April 7th, 1935: the 'Old Reliable', White Star's Olympic, is manoeuvred by tugs into her lay-up berth astern of her old rival on the Atlantic, the Mauretania, which had also been laid up. Both of these famous ships would soon fall victim to the demolition crews.*

William H. Miller

Anthony Cooke Maurizio Eliseo

LINERS
of the Golden Age

A Pictorial Record of Passenger Ships in the 1930s

CARMANIA PRESS LONDON

The German liner *St. Louis* during her last call at New York just days before the outbreak of the Second World War. A few months earlier, in May, 1939, she had made a tragic voyage to Cuba with 937 Jewish refugees. When they reached their destination, the authorities refused to allow them to disembark. This episode was immortalised in 'Voyage of the Damned', a dramatic British movie of 1976.

(C-A/ME)

CONTENTS

Acknowledgements	9
Preface	11
Foreword	13
Already Sailing	16
The First Post-War Liners	32
A New Generation, A New Style	93
The Glamorous 'Thirties	125
Clouds of War	200
Afterword	210
Fleet List	212
Bibliography	237
Statistics	238
Ships Index	239

The glorious *Conte di Savoia* symbolised Italy's newly won position as a major power in the world of passenger shipping, together with her rival and running-mate, the record-breaking *Rex*. *(Enrico Repetto Collection, Genoa)*

ACKNOWLEDGEMENTS

It takes quite a crew to compile a book such as this. Selecting the ships to be included, gathering the photos, collecting anecdotes and then sorting them both. Fortunately, I am blessed with many very kind and extremely generous friends, acquaintances and shipmates.

One of the most special, when it comes to these ocean liner books, is Richard Faber, the internationally known maritime memorabilia collector and dealer. Repeatedly, he has opened his glorious collection, the vast files of photographs, post cards, brochures, sailing schedules and newspaper clips, and made them available for these projects. They are often several years in the works. Following publication and once the photos are returned, they often go on the open market and finish up in some private collection, locked away in a file cabinet or picture album. Therefore, I am especially grateful to Dick for allowing this precious material to be shared first, seeing the light of day, so to speak. We always need to see new and fresh views of ocean liners, both the big and famous 'stars' and the smaller, lesser-known ships.

I am also highly indebted to Ernest Arroyo, another dear and longtime friend, who rescued the Frank Cronican collection from oblivion - in fact, from being trashed. Mr. Cronican had died and his heirs had little interest in several drawers full of vintage photographs, all alphabetically catalogued. I made two hauls, actually, and after I had used them they were sold to Dick Faber. The ones used in this book, and many more, have since become part of the Maurizio Eliseo collection.

Besides being a talented young shipping historian, Maurizio has also made a huge contribution to the production of this book in his capacity as the business partner of Anthony Cooke in the running of his brilliant Carmania Press. There is so much to be told about ocean liners and possibly no one does it better than Cooke and Eliseo and their Carmania these days! Indeed, both Maurizio and Tony have added so much to my original project, contributing extra text and photographs. They are also responsible for the fleet list at the end of the book, which has added many unknown details to the history of the vessels featured.

The late Everett Viez was a World-class ocean liner collector and historian who lived in Southern Florida. We used to spend hours on the 'phone. Our conversations often included anecdotes and remembrances of passenger ships as far back as the late 'Twenties. Busily, I jotted it all down. Great portions of his recollections appear herein.

Grand appreciation also goes to other dear friends who have given me valuable help: Frank Braynard, Tom Cassidy, Dr. Richard Gottlieb (the well known Art Deco expert and collector who wrote a detailed and evocative foreword), Arnold Kludas, Hisashi Noma and Mario Pulice. Enormous praises as well to Abe Michaelson, my ever-devoted, ever-busy business partner. Often deep into the night, he despatches books to the four corners of the earth.

I would also like to thank many other great sources, both for anecdotes and insights as well as yet more photos and other printed materials: Frank Andrews, Captain Helge Brudvik, Stephen Card, Michael Cassar, Philippe Cazade, Colonel Norman Dodd, the late Alex Duncan, Laurence Dunn, the late John Gillespie, the late Jacob Goldstein, Lewis Gordon, Andres Hernandez, Alice Keppel-Thomas, Peter Knego, Richard K. Morse, Todd Neitring, Paolo Piccione, Frank Pichardo, Sal Scanella, Der Scutt, Roger Sherlock, Bianca Shorr, the late Captain Ian Tompkins, Dr. Horst Uppenberg and V. H. Young.

Organizations that have assisted include: Crystal Cruises, Cunard Line, French Line, Hapag-Lloyd, the Ocean Liner Council at the South Street Seaport, P&O, Real Photographs, the Steamship Historical Society of America (especially the Long Island Chapter) and the World Ship Society (particularly the New York branch). Please forgive any oversights.

Last but not least, on behalf of Carmania Press, a word of sincere gratitude to the printers, Messrs Zambelli, and their staff, and to Norman Spiler, Tomislav Uhac, Francesco Fegitz, Tamar Stock, Roberto Fazi, Ippolita Tolja and Marina Grego for their much-appreciated support.

Repeated thanks, warmest regards and three very special blasts to 'the crew' for this latest book.

Bill Miller
Secaucus, New Jersey
Fall, 2004

Sleek, glamorous and speedy, the French Line's *Normandie* was one of the great icons of the 'Thirties. Technically, she was one of the most advanced ships of her time.
  (Richard Faber Collection, New York)

PREFACE

When first planning this book, I thought mostly of the 'Thirties and, in ways, I still do. They were, of course, the time of the Great Depression and they saw the seeds sown of the devastating Second World War. But they were also a glamorous period of sleek skyscrapers and streamlined trains, lavish Hollywood musicals and stylized Art Deco furniture. Those times have always fascinated me. The Empire State Building and the Rockefeller Center, the *Normandie* and the *Hindenburg*, Garbo and Dietrich.

That early plan for the book was to include only ships built in the 'Thirties, perhaps balanced between two British liners, White Star's *Britannic* (1930) and then a Cunarder, the second *Mauretania* (1939). It was Anthony Cooke of Carmania Press who, soon after the manuscript reached his London office, thoughtfully recommended that the book be expanded and reshaped. The 'Thirties were a great vantage point from which to see the development of the ocean liner. So many older ships overlapped – earlier-built ships that sailed on, often with continued popularity and at least some financial success. Germany's *Imperator*, completed back in 1913, was still active, for example, but for Cunard as the beloved *Berengaria*. So were the likes of the famous first *Mauretania* (1907), *Olympic* (1911) and *Aquitania* (1914). Then, of course, there was another large fleet built after the First World War, in the 'Twenties, with ships such as the splendid *Paris*, the charming *Statendam*, the *Augustus*, the *Cap Arcona* and, most notably of all, the *Ile de France* of 1927. With her startling Art Deco interiors, she singlehandedly revolutionized ocean liner decoration forever.

The 'Thirties, of course, did produce some of the most important and thrilling liners ever created – the *Empress of Britain*, *L'Atlantique*, *Rex*, *Conte di Savoia*, *Queen Mary*, *Queen Elizabeth* and, almost in a class by her luxurious self, the *Normandie*. Nothing would surpass these great ships for decades, until the 1990s, the age of the seemingly ever-expanding cruise business with its mega-ships. And although the 'Thirties were a time of economic depression, of great losses and political and social uncertainties, they ended for passenger liners in the high pitch of 1939. That year gave us the likes of the *Andes*, *Dominion Monarch*, *Oranje*, *Pasteur*, second *Mauretania*, *Wilhelm Gustloff* and several that were still under construction, such as the *America* and *Queen Elizabeth*.

So we cover an astonishing range of ships, starting with those of the pre-World War I generation which were still sailing some twenty years later. They had been built in the twilight of the Edwardian era for a different age and even for different trades. But, by the mid-'Twenties, the massive migration from Europe to the United States had been slashed to a fraction of its booming, revenue-producing, pre-1914 level. On the North Atlantic, at least, these old liners were now carrying a very different kind of passenger in their cheaper accommodations. And most of them had been converted from coal-burning to more efficient oil-fired furnaces.

Most of the liners created in the first half of the 'Twenties were much more moderate, more conservative, certainly less flamboyant than those earlier "floating palaces". However, the second half of the 'Twenties marked a significant turning point, particularly with the appearance of the superb *Ile de France*. Not only did her décor change home office thinking but she was the first of a new generation of bigger and grander ships being planned on the shipyard drawing boards, the *Bremen* and the *Europa* for instance. Finally, we come to the 'Thirties, an age that not only reached new heights and distinctions with the likes of the *Normandie* and the *Queen Mary* but gave us so many other fine ships: the *Empress of Japan* (for speed), the *Orion* (for decoration) and the *Noordam* (for high standards on a smaller ship) as examples. The age ended with the biggest liner yet built, the mighty *Queen Elizabeth*.

There was a sadder side to the 'Thirties, of course. Because of the very worrisome financial times and the resulting drop in trade (North Atlantic traffic slumped from 1 million to 500,000 voyagers between 1930 and 1935, for example), some famous liners went to the breakers, often prematurely. Between 1935 and 1938, ships such as the *Homeric*, *Majestic*, *Olympic*, *Belgenland* and *Leviathan* finished their sailing days. The *Aquitania* was suddenly the last of the "four stackers", those "floating palaces" from pre-World War I days.

Tragedies in the 'Thirties included the wrecks of the *Monte Sarmiento* and the *Highland Hope* in 1930 and a quartet of disastrous fires: the *Bermuda* (1931), the *Georges Philippar* (1932), *L'Atlantique* (1933) and the *Morro Castle* (1934). The *President Hoover* was wrecked in 1937 and then two prominent French liners, the *Lafayette* and *Paris*, burned out in 1938 and 1939 respectively. But despite these sad events, the 'Thirties were undoubtedly the Golden Age of the Ocean Liner.

I began watching liners in the 'Fifties. There was still a sizeable collection then, coming and going at New York and every day, with the possible exception of Sunday, included some activity. But to have been an onlooker in the 'Thirties, to have been at the Battery Park seawall or aboard a shuttling Staten Island ferry and to have seen the *Normandie*, the *Rex* or the *Aquitania* underway, and the smaller *Batory*, *Stavangerfjord* or *Morro Castle*, would have been perfection. A now deceased friend once told me of seeing the heavily floodlit, oversized buff-yellow funnels of the *Empress of Britain* on a very cold, but very clear winter's night at the end of West 21st Street in Chelsea. Silent, but so majestic and imposing, she seemed almost to overtake the sheds of the pier itself. She left an indelible impression and began his lifelong interest in passenger ships. He also recalled the maiden arrival of the *Champlain* – "exciting, cheerful, very noisy, a mass of escorting tugs around that sparkling inbound ship." And he made midnight sailings aboard the *Empress of Australia* and the *Transylvania*.

Another friend, of similar vintage, recalled a Saturday morning when six outbound liners slipped past Battery Park in less than an hour. "It was like a procession of royal elephants," he noted. "The *Kungsholm* was followed by the *Veendam*, which was followed by the *Saturnia*, then the *Washington* and still more!"

And so, here is another nostalgic pictorial review – the great liners and something of their fabulous interiors – coupled with short biographies, historic notations and occasionally with personal recollections. Sentimentally, we look back to a Golden Age and, in this procession of ships, we see a clear and obvious evolution: from the cluttered, four-funnelled top decks of the *Mauretania* and *Aquitania* to the sleek, cleaner lines of the *Nieuw Amsterdam* and *America*; from the Old World splendor of the Smoking Room onboard the *Columbus* to the sleek modernity of the Grand Salon on *L'Atlantique*, a ship completed a mere seven years later, in 1931. It is an exceptional collection of names – many of them well-remembered to this day.

But now it is time to begin our voyage of pure and total nostalgia, a trip through an age of great passenger ships. Sit back. Hear the steam whistles. Set sail for New York or Liverpool or Rio or Sydney or even some colonial outpost. *Bon Voyage!*

FOREWORD

Bill Miller's "Liners of the Golden Age" hardly sailed on the Sea of Tranquility. The mood of the 'Thirties varied from technological marvels and elegance to economic collapse and despair, accompanied by political and social upheaval as well as extreme nationalism and the looming of war. The singular decade of the 'Thirties properly began on October 24th, 1929 – Black Thursday, the day of the Stock Market Crash, which was followed by the Depression. Bank closings, unemployment, soup kitchens, hardship and delays of all kinds ensued in every field of endeavor. Hardship was met with Hope and Optimism, combined with Futurism. The 'Thirties ended as an era on September 3rd, 1939 when World War II began.

In between those dates were a myriad of influences and historical events that fashioned the world behind the ships. The motifs of those ten years were dynamic 20th Century visions of machines, jazz and speed. Key words were Larger, Taller, Longer, Streamlined and Faster. Style for all this began with the 1925 Exposition Internationale des Arts Décoratifs et Industriels Modernes in Paris . i.e.: Art Déco.

By 1930, the Chrysler Building in Manhattan, soaring to 1,064 feet but to be surpassed by the 1931 Empire State Building of 1,250 feet, was remarkable for its sheer record height and established Skyscraper Style. Symbolic 'Speed Stripes' were applied to buildings, as well as to furnishings, radios, toasters. The designs of the Streamlined Decade in transportation, for faster more efficient travel, were evident in the 1934 Chrysler Airflow automobile, all curves and teardrop shape, and the smooth continuous profile of the legendary all-metal, low-wing twin-engined DC3 plane of 1935.

A threat to the Ocean Liners was the advent of the large Flying Boats such as the Martin M-130 *China Clipper*, which heralded a new era of travel – seven days, instead of several weeks, from San Francisco to Manila in 1935. By June, 1939, the Pan Am Boeing 314 started mail and passenger service across the North Atlantic from New York to Western Europe in little more than a day. But World War II curtailed both these Pacific and Atlantic clippers.

The chief rival for the Ocean Liner, however, seemed for a time to be the elegant cigar-shaped lighter-than-air dirigible, a German creation. The 775-foot *Graf Zeppelin* made a spectacular, safe round-the-World flight in 1929. In 1936, the 803-foot *Hindenburg*, carrying up to 70 passengers, made 34 crossings with the logo '2 days to Europe'. Since it flew at a ceiling of 1,000 feet, the 80 mph airship looked immensely impressive from the ground. It briefly captured the imagination for inter-continental travel but the disaster of the *Hindenburg* explosion in 1937 brought the airship era to an end, as being romantic, impractical and technically flawed. The Ocean Liner remained firmly in control of inter-continental travel.

Long distance overland travel was predominantly by steam train. The burgeoning automobile and bus on the inter-state highways were met by the attractive, streamlined appearance of the exotic 1934 *Burlington Zephyr* and the Union Pacific M-10,000. Trains remained paramount on land until the 1950s when super-highways, cars and planes took over.

The human voice on radio became perhaps the most important factor in moulding political choices in the 'Thirties: in the United States, where Franklin Delano Roosevelt's smooth Fireside Chats brought the message of his New Deal to the American people; while Adolf Hitler's strident voice hypnotized Germany into preparation for world domination via military conquest. The human voice also featured when sound was added to the movies – 'the talkies' and the Golden Age of

The *Georgic*, the last ship to be ordered by the White Star Line, was a fine example of the 1930s motorliner. Of more moderate size and speed than the express turbine steamers, she was a very steady, comfortable ship. (CA/ME)

Hollywood. Superstars such as Garbo, Gable, Fred Astaire and Ginger Rogers, Shirley Temple, the Marx Brothers and others were idolized as America's 'royalty'. 1939 was Hollywood's quintessential year, with movies such as *Gone With The Wind* and *The Wizard of Oz* (including color). Hollywood and radio reciprocated each other when the film stars reprised their movies with radio scripts and many radio personalities made movies. Also, sports and radio worked together with baseball, boxing and football reportage. The 1936 Olympics in Berlin produced African-American track hero Jesse Owens' unprecedented four gold medals and in 1938 Joe Louis knocked out the German Max Schmeling in one round, all of which was reported on radio to millions around the World, as black athletes achieved hero status for the first time.

Radio played a large role as the rhythms of the Jazz Age gave way to the Swing Era of the Big Bands. Maestro Benny Goodman, the Dorsey brothers and Glenn Miller performed in the hotel ballrooms, theaters and studios, while their records were played by Martin Block and the first disc jockeys. The music of the time was composed by Irving Berlin, Cole Porter and the Gershwin brothers for Broadway and Hollywood musicals. Kate Smith, Rudy Vallee and Bing Crosby sang these songs on their own radio programs and in recordings and in movies.

Movie palaces such as Radio City Music Hall of 1932 were huge architectural fantasies with exuberant interiors. An exciting visual experience was also included in lobbies, banks, public buildings and stores, with chrome, marble, mirrors and exotic lighting.

The New York World's Fair of 1939, 'The World of Tomorrow' was a brave attempt at optimism for the future, with its 728-foot tall Trylon and the Perisphere, a huge white globe. But while President Roosevelt ('FDR') opened the Fair in April, 1939, Hitler was completing plans for the invasion of Poland.

The most intense rivalry occurred in the 'Thirties for the capture of the Blue Riband speed record at sea across the Atlantic. This was the last and most glorious decade for this type of international competition. These were essentially 'Ships of State', subsidized by governments for reasons of national pride and for military use in war as troopships or hospital ships, but mostly because they were cultural statements for each nation in those beleaguered economic times – i.e. Germany, Italy, Great Britain and France. The 938-foot *Bremen* (1929) and 937-foot *Europa* (1930), sister ships, both broke the venerable British *Mauretania*'s record, which she had set in 1909. In 1933, the 880-foot Italian *Rex* took the record from the Germans but in 1935 the 1,029-foot *Normandie* did even better and competed with the 1,019-foot *Queen Mary* until the latter established supremacy in 1938. (America did not participate in the Blue Riband contest until 1952, when the 990-foot *United States* broke the *Queen Mary*'s 14-year old record with a crossing of 3 days 10 hours 40 minutes, an average of 35.59 knots. It has never been challenged by a conventional liner.) Incidentally, the *Queen Mary*'s consort, the 1,031-foot *Queen Elizabeth* of 1940 never made an attempt at a record run.

Finally, at this writing, there are still a few vintage style passenger liners, vessels which have operated as true liners rather than solely as cruise ships. Three of them are particularly notable. One is an authentic original, the beloved *Queen Mary*, miraculously preserved at Long Beach, California, as a non-operating, tethered exhibition ship, hotel and convention center since 1968. There are also Cunard's 963-foot *Queen Elizabeth 2* (1969) and the 1,035-foot *Norway*, formerly the *France* (1962), for many years the longest passenger ship ever built. The layout, appointments, size and ambience make these last two ships direct descendants of, respectively, the Cunard *Queen Mary* and *Queen Elizabeth* and the French Line *Normandie*. They are about to be joined by the new *Queen Mary 2*, at 1,128 feet, the longest passenger ship yet built.

Dr. Richard Gottlieb
Miami Beach, Florida
Spring, 2004

ALREADY SAILING

Many of the ships sailing into the 'Thirties had, of course, been built long before that era and had served in the First World War. They were liners of the 'Belle Epoque' and it was a quite different World. They were impressive, often with three or four tall funnels and heavily paneled lounges. They had been built for speed, with countless boilers and with giant and spectacular steam expansion engines or experimental direct-driven turbines which consumed massive quantities of coal. One of them, the venerable *Mauretania*, had been specifically conceived to conquer the coveted Blue Riband. Others, such as the *Olympic* or the *Imperator*, were built to gain for their owners the distinction of the largest and most luxurious liner afloat. But by the 'Thirties, they seemed like old dinosaurs, and could hardly meet the new needs of the market. The Great Depression and the entry into service of new and modern vessels sealed their fate, but not before they made an honourable and urgently needed contribution to re-establishing commercial service on the intercontinental routes.

MAURETANIA (31,938 grt; 1907 - 1935)

She was the most famous and popular liner of her day, and the ultimate in engineering genius. She remained the fastest ship in the World from 1909 to 1929. Earlier, in 1907, her sister, the *Lusitania*, had wrested the Atlantic's cherished Blue Riband from Germany's *Kaiser Wilhelm II* but the *Mauretania* soon proved to be slightly the faster of the two new Cunard flyers. Astonishingly, she held the record until 1929, when she finally lost it to another Teutonic superliner, the *Bremen*.

Unlike her sister, which came from the John Brown yard, the *Mauretania* had been built by Swan, Hunter & Wigham Richardson of Newcastle. The two ships were designed for the Cunard Line's Liverpool – New York express service as well as for use as armed merchant cruisers in the event of war. They were the first really big liners to be powered by steam turbines rather than the earlier reciprocating

"All 'dolled up' for her cruises" was the caption for this news photo of the classic *Mauretania* as she arrived in New York harbor in July, 1933. The great Atlantic speed champion was given an all-white hull in readiness for cruise service in the lean years of the Depression. (*CA/ME*)

Sentimental farewell: To the sound of a band, the beloved *Mauretania* leaves Southampton Docks for the last time, watched by a sizeable crowd and filmed by a newsreel camera. It is July 1st, 1935 and, rust-streaked and wreathed in smoke, the old liner is on her way to be broken up at Rosyth in Scotland. (CA/ME)

engines. Their first class interiors were highly stylized, ranging from English country house to French Renaissance.

There was a Palm Court and the bathroom fixtures were silver-plated. Known affectionately as the "Maury", the *Mauretania* did yeoman service during the First World War as a trooper and as a hospital ship. Afterward, she resumed commercial service as one of Cunard's "Big Three" with the newer and larger *Aquitania* and *Berengaria*. (The *Lusitania* had been torpedoed and sunk off the Irish coast in May, 1915.)

By the 'Twenties, the line's express service was being run from Southampton and, in the depths of winter, there were more and more cruises to warm weather areas such as the Caribbean and the Mediterranean.

When, in July, 1929, the *Mauretania* lost her prized Blue Riband distinction to the brand new *Bremen* which crossed the Atlantic westward at 27.83 knots and eastward at 27.92 knots, the captain of the aged Cunarder radioed congratulations to the sleek new German flagship.

But the following month, the *Mauretania* responded to the challenge. There were valiant efforts on the part of her engine department and she registered 26.90 knots

Last remains: the final days of the *Mauretania's* demolition. This view is dated May 15th, 1936, shortly before the World's attention was turned to a new, far larger and much faster Cunarder, the great *Queen Mary*. (CA/ME)

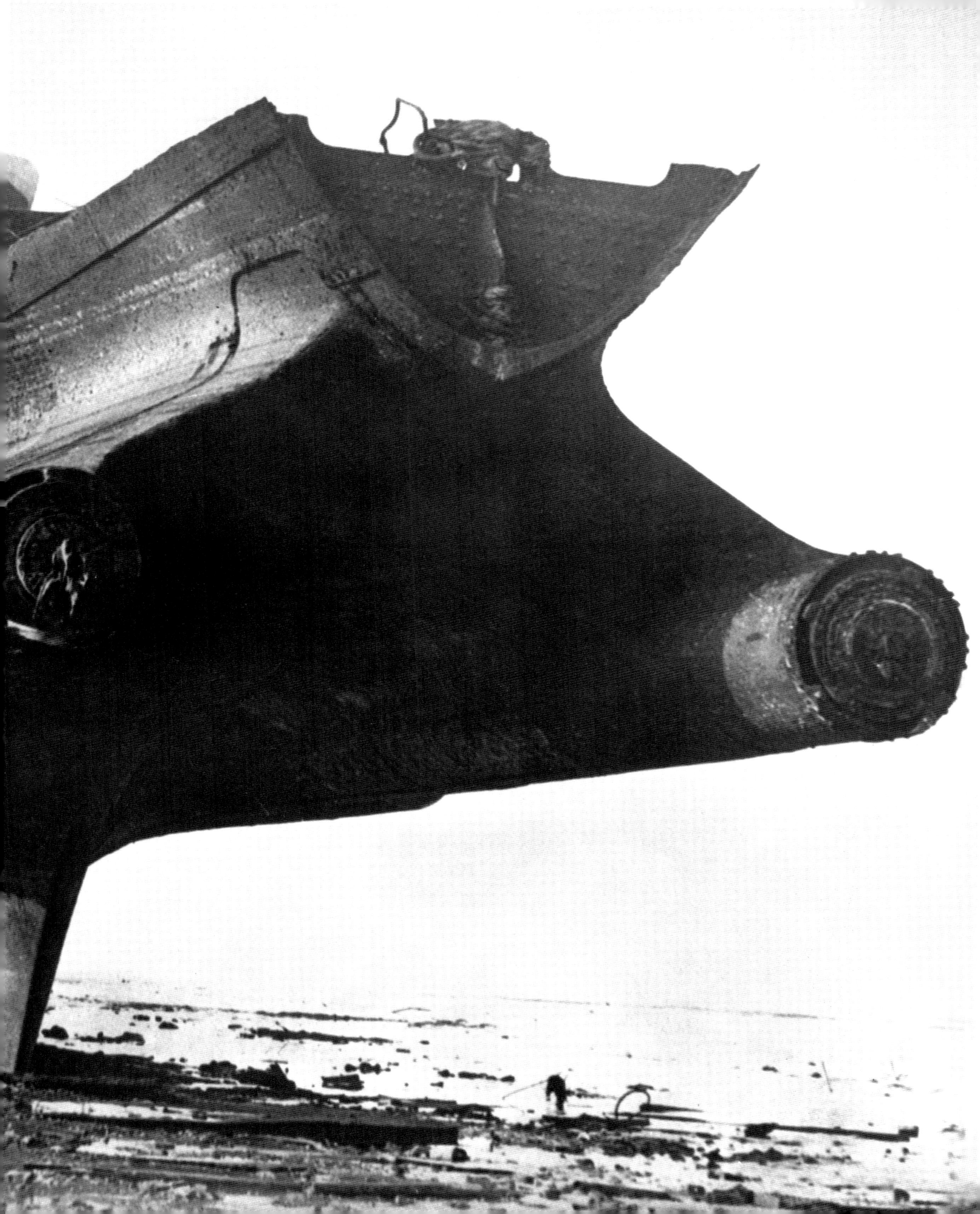

Already Sailing

The *George Washington*, still looking very German but now flying the Stars and Stripes, is seen in drydock at the Philadelphia Naval Shipyard in this view dated July 15th, 1929. She was one of many German liners that had been seized by the Americans when they entered the War in 1917. (CA/ME)

and 27.22 knots, not quite enough to beat her younger and much more modern rival but an amazing achievement.

Beginning in 1930, the *Mauretania*, hard hit by the Depression and by increasing age, was sent mostly on one-class cruises. Three years later, her hull was painted entirely in white, which denoted her more tropical tone as well as being heat-resistant.

But the end came in September, 1934, soon after the cost-cutting Cunard-White Star merger. On the same day that the *Queen Mary* was launched (September 26th), the *Mauretania* left New York for the last time. For a few months, she sat forlornly at Southampton. She was a perfect candidate for a museum ship but the times were quite wrong.

With her furnishings going for auction, she was scrapped in Scotland in the spring of 1935.

GEORGE WASHINGTON (23,788 grt; 1909 - 1951)

When she was built for North German Lloyd back in 1909, the *George Washington* was one of the largest ships of her day and followed the German tendency of using American names in order to recruit more of the westbound European emigrant trade. It was widely believed that arriving onboard a ship with such a name would ease the entry procedures at Ellis Island in New York harbor, where incoming migrants were screened. When the First World War started in the summer of 1914, North German Lloyd left her for safety at their Hoboken terminal on the River Hudson. Then, however, America entered the War in 1917 and she was seized by the US government for use as an Allied trooper. Afterwards, she sailed in peacetime service between New York and Bremerhaven for the United States Lines. A victim of the Depression and of increasing age, the "Big George" was laid-up for most of the 'Thirties on the Patuxent river. She was, however, restored for military service in 1940, briefly as the *Catlin* but then reverting to *George Washington*. She was damaged in March 1947 while at New York and was then towed to Baltimore and laid up. A new and more violent fire set her ablaze on 17th January 1951. By then, she was far too old to be repaired and so was scrapped.

OLYMPIC (45,324 grt; 1911 - 1935)

The *Olympic* is mainly remembered as a sister to the legendary *Titanic*. But she was a great liner in her own right. In fact, when built, she was the largest ship afloat. She was also noted for the elegance and luxury in which she carried her first class passengers and she became known as "the old reliable" for the punctuality of her transatlantic service and also because, after her sister ship went to the bottom, she underwent a long refitting, making her one of the safest vessels afloat. The White Star Line, her owners, preferred to build their liners for comfort rather than record-breaking speed. Nevertheless, with a 22 knot service speed, the *Olympic* was a fast liner and in the 'Twenties she ran in White Star's express service between Southampton and New York together with the ex-Germans *Majestic* and *Homeric*. Before being converted to

A victim of the Depression, the *Olympic*, one of the most famous luxury liners of her day, leaves Southampton for the last time, in October, 1935. She might have been sold to Mussolini's government for use in their East African campaign but, instead, she went to be scrapped at Jarrow in northeast England. *(CA/ME)*

Already Sailing

Final remains of a great liner: largely scrapped and now merely an empty husk, the lower hull of the Olympic was towed from Jarrow to Inverkeithing in September, 1937 for demolition to be completed. (CA/ME)

oil firing and returning to the passenger service in Summer 1920, she had honourably performed her war duties as troop transport. A war episode which made her famous happened on May 12th, 1918, when she was attacked by the German submarine *U-103*. With a brave manoeuvre, her master not only avoided the torpedoes, but also followed, rammed and sank the U-Boat.

Like so many other ships of her age, however, she was a victim of the Depression. The Cunard-White Star merger in February 1934 sealed her fate. Laid-up in April 1935 at Southampton, she was soon sold for scrapping at Jarrow.

FRANCE (23,666 grt; 1912 - 1935)

She had been the first of the big French liners and took over the name of an old steamer belonging to the same owners, which had been sold for scrap in 1910. The new liner was ordered from the Chantiers et Ateliers Penhoët yard at Saint Nazaire, on the Loire river. She left on her maiden voyage Le Havre - New York on 20th April 1912, with the celebrations marred by the sinking of the *Titanic* just a few days before.

She sailed in that pre-First World War era with other four-stackers such as the *Mauretania* and *Olympic*, although her funnels had to be much shorter to reduce her top weight;

FRANCE

The *France* had a long, very Gallic profile but was the sole four-stacker in the French Line fleet. After years of distinguished service as a luxurious Atlantic express liner, she finished her career mostly as a cruiseship. (CA/ME)

the *France* was indeed a heavy roller, in part owing to the weight of her rich interior décor; indeed she was dubbed 'Le Château de l'Atlantique' being not only one of the most lavish liners on the Atlantic, but also one of the best fed. She was the French challenge to the British and German liners on the Atlantic, and indeed, with her 24.5 knots, when she entered service she was second in speed only to the *Mauretania* and *Lusitania*.

Her success prompted an era of even larger French Line passenger ships, with the likes of the *Paris* and the *Ile de France*. During the First World War, she sheltered at first in the bay of Brest, to escape the German U-Boats, and later served as a troop transport and hospital ship. Between November 1915 and May 1917, she carried about 25.000 troops wounded on the Eastern front of Salonica and Corfu. At the end of the War, the *France* repatriated many American troops before resuming her passenger liner duties in August 1919. By the early 'Thirties, with the Great Depression raging, the *France* was relegated more and more to cruising and to periodic lay-ups. As the oldest of the line's ships and being fitted with direct driven turbines, she was also the most expensive to operate. Withdrawn from service in September 1932, she was sold to scrappers at Dunkerque in April 1935, when her mighty new fleetmate *Normandie* was ready to run her sea trials.

The grand staircase and the two-level dining room of the *France* anticipated a popular lay-out of future liners.

23

ALREADY SAILING

The Norwegian America Line's *Bergensfjord* arrives in New York's Lower Bay on April 15th, 1940. She had left Norway only the day before the Nazis invaded the country. Note the neutrality markings along her side. Later, she took up duties as an Allied trooper. *(CA/ME)*

BERGENSFJORD (10,666 grt; 1913 - 1959)

"This rather ordinary-looking ship added to Atlantic liner history on at least three occasions," said Frank Braynard. "Built for Oslo – Copenhagen – New York service, she was one of the first two ships (the other being her sister *Kristianiafjord*) for the recently-formed Norwegian America Line. In 1946, she was sold to become the first ship of the new Home Lines fleet and then, in 1953, she became the first large liner in the Israeli fleet, sailing trans-Atlantic between Haifa and New York for Zim Israel Lines." Built by Cammell Laird at Birkenhead, she ran for the Norwegians until 1940 and then began Allied war duties under British (Furness Withy) management. Too old for her owners by 1946, she was sold to become the *Argentina* on Home Lines' emigrant route between Italy and South America. When bought by the Israelis, she was renamed *Jerusalem* and, in 1957, *Aliya*. Laid-up in 1958 after 45 busy years of service, she was said to become a hotel ship at Brussels for the World's Fair but instead went to Italian shipbreakers a year later.

BERENGARIA (52,117 grt; 1913 - 1938)

One of the great favourites of 'Twenties travel on the North Atlantic, the *Berengaria* was Cunard's largest liner until the *Queen Mary* appeared in 1936. She had been awarded to the company after the First World War as compensation for the loss of the *Lusitania*. Built as the *Imperator*, she had been the first of the three large liners which the Hamburg America Line planned for the North Atlantic run. But all three were seized by the Allies in 1918, the slightly larger *Vaterland* becoming the American *Leviathan* and the uncompleted *Bismarck* eventually entering service as the *Majestic* of the White Star Line. Cunard placed the *Berengaria* in their express service from Southampton to New York, where she was partnered by the *Mauretania* and the *Aquitania*. She was, however, greatly affected by the lean Depression years. Cunard began sailing her on short, inexpensive cruises from New York down to Bermuda and on long weekends up to Halifax. With her luxurious Atlantic days almost a thing of the past, she was dubbed the "Bargain Area". Everett Viez was aboard one of her earliest

BERGENSFJORD and BERENGARIA

Cunard's *Berengaria*, one of the greatest of all trans-Atlantic liners, was a prize of war. She had been built as the *Imperator*, the first of the Hamburg America Line's trio of huge superliners, and, indeed, for a short time had been the World's largest vessel of any kind. (CA/ME)

Splendor at sea: the sumptuous Palm Court aboard the *Berengaria*. One of the legends surrounding this great ship concerned the number of her wealthy passengers who were ruined by the Wall Street Crash of 1929 while they were crossing the Atlantic. (CA/ME)

BERENGARIA

short cruises, a 4-day trip to Bermuda and back in 1930. His fare was $50.

"She still rode with a slight list (a problem from her German days) and could manage about 19 knots, down from her 23 on the Atlantic run," he recalled. "She also vibrated very badly. But she was a charming ship, surely one of the great liners of her time. Her German heritage was evident in just about all the public rooms and the first class suites were very Teutonic. There was still a great 'heaviness' about the ship."

After Cunard merged with the rival White Star Line in 1934, the old *Berengaria*'s fate fell into greater question.

For a time, she sailed with the new *Queen Mary*, but only as a temporary running-mate. She might have lasted until the *Queen Elizabeth* was due to come into service in 1940, but old age accounted for her first. In 1938, she was plagued by small fires, caused mostly by aged wiring.

The U.S. Coast Guard refused her sailing permit from New York at one point. She was sold to shipbreakers in Scotland soon afterward, but her final pieces were not cut up until 1946.

Already stripped of most of her lifeboats, the *Berengaria* leaves Southampton on December 6th, 1938. Her demolition will provide much needed work for the unemployed in the Jarrow area. Her scrap value was approximately £100,000. (CA/ME)

The mighty *Leviathan*, built as the second of Hamburg America's trio of huge luxury liners but now the flagship of United States Lines, is here seen outbound off Spithead in the early 'Thirties. Never a commercial success for the Americans, she was soon to be laid-up. *(Richard K. Morse Collection)*

LEVIATHAN (54,282 grt; 1914 - 1938)

She had been the *Vaterland*, the second of the Hamburg America Line's projected trio of magnificent Atlantic liners, after the *Imperator* and before the *Bismark*. When she entered service on May 14th, 1914 on the express line Cuxhaven - New York, at 54,282 grt, she ranked as the largest liner yet built and she would remain such until the 'Thirties. She was also the fastest of the trio, thanks to several thousand extra horsepower: on speed trials she managed 25.8 knots, 2 nautical miles per hour more than the *Imperator* and one more than the *Bismarck*.

But the First World War quickly disrupted her commercial career and, in a great miscalculation, her owners left her in the neutral safety of her Hoboken berth when the hostilities started.

On April 3rd, 1917, just hours before she was seized by America, now a combatant, her German crew wrecked her engines. She was eventually repaired but only in August was she ready to take up her new duties as a U.S. Army troop transport, with the new name of *Leviathan*. She made ten round voyages across the Atlantic as a trooper, the first starting from New York on Christmas Day, 1917. In all, she carried 96,804 servicemen to the European front. In September 1919, her repatriation duties accomplished, she was laid up.

At the beginning of 1922, it was decided to put her back into commercial service for the United States Lines, but

The magnificent entrance to *Leviathan*'s First Class grand salon. On the right is her coat of arms as flagship of The American Evacuation Fleet, while on the left is a plaque dedicated to the passengers she carried home at the end of the conflict, 98,749 men and officers in nine transatlantic voyages. *(CA/ME)*

In the sad last days of her long lay-up at Hoboken between 1934 and 1938, the *Leviathan*'s masts and rust-streaked funnels were shortened. She had been sold to scrappers at Rosyth in Scotland and she would have to clear the Forth Bridge. (CA/ME)

When refitted in the U.S.A., the *Leviathan* had been given this modern-looking Art Déco nightclub, very different in style from her original German décor. (CA/ME)

only on July 4th, 1923 did she set sail on her first voyage from New York to Southampton. Despite being the largest liner afloat (now remeasured at almost 60,000 grt) and the fastest together with the *Mauretania* (the Americans further increased her power and she could now average 27.5 knots), she was also, unfortunately, one of the least successful. She suffered from high American costs, Prohibition laws (which kept her "dry") and the general belief by the travelling public that European ships were both better run and better served. In 1926, when she carried 36,479 passengers in 25 one-way crossings of the Atlantic, she was on average sailing only half full.

Then, once the Depression began, her losses became staggering. At a certain stage, her gross register tonnage was re-calculated to under 50,000 grt, in order to save on harbor dues and taxes. This measure was not enough.

She was laid-up in 1932, but was revived for several sailings in 1934. But these were as unsuccessful as ever. The US Government allowed United States Lines to withdraw her provided a running-mate was built to join the new *Manhattan* and *Washington*.

The *Leviathan* was moored at Hoboken and spent the next three years there, silent, rusting and neglected. Eventually, she was cleared for sale and on January 26th, 1938 she left for Rosyth in Scotland to be broken-up.

AQUITANIA (45,647 grt; 1914 - 1949)

On the North Atlantic, she was one of the grandest, most palatial liners of all time. Her first class interiors were sumptuously stunning in the style of the times – indeed, she was one of the legendary "floating palaces". She was also one of the biggest ships afloat until the 1930s. Later, she survived as the last ocean liner with four funnels.

She was the grand old *Aquitania*. Building at the John Brown shipyard at Clydebank when the *Titanic* went to the bottom in April, 1912, she was completed in the spring of 1914 but was soon to go into gray-painted duties in the First World War. Towards the end of that conflict, she served as a huge hospital ship. In the 'Twenties and 'Thirties, she was one of Cunard's great express liners – 6 days from New York to Cherbourg and Southampton. In 1938, first class fares started at $219, tourist at $130 and third class from $85. That same year, Lewis and Ruth Gordon went off on the first of their many liner crossings to Europe. "We went over on the *Aquitania* and came back on the *Berengaria*. We travelled third class and were locked out of first and tourist. But one evening, I found the fire stairs that led into first class. I saw great cheeses on the bar tops and the beef being carved alongside the dining room tables." In the 'Thirties, the *Aquitania* could carry over 3,200 passengers – 618 in first class, 614 in tourist and 1,998 in third. "There was no running water in third class cabins back then," recalled Mr. Gordon. "You had a container called a Lavebo, which was round, ceramic and had a little spigot from which water dropped out. Each day, it was refilled by a steward. There were no private bathrooms, either. You made an appointment with a special bath steward for the use of a little room with a tub. You were allowed thirty minutes. A steward would knock on your cabin door and announce when your bath was ready."

The veteran four-stacker was due to go to the scrappers in 1940, just as the brand new *Queen Elizabeth* was readied, but she endured to serve in another World War, travelling all over the globe – to Sydney, Singapore, San Francisco, Cape Town. Afterwards, in the late 'Forties, she resumed trans-Atlantic service but she was used for austerity service, subsidized by the Canadian government and carrying mostly migrants, troops and some fare-paying passengers between Southampton and Halifax. In December 1949, after 35 years, 443 sailings, 3,000,000 steaming miles and 1,200,000 passengers, she was sold to shipbreakers at Faslane in Scotland.

During the Depression, and in particular after the entry into service of the *Queen Mary*, the venerable *Aquitania* was occasionally used for cruises. Here we see her at Naples, with Vesuvius in the background, during a pleasure voyage in the Mediterranean.

THE FIRST POST-WAR LINERS

The mammoth liners running in the early 'Twenties were all survivors from the pre-War years or had been laid down just before the conflict. Times had changed and owners were no longer placing orders for large express ships. The pre-War 'floating palaces' had been famous for pampering their First Class passengers in amazing luxury but most of their profit had come from carrying huge numbers of migrants in much less comfortable conditions. Now, laws passed by Congress imposed strict limits on immigration into the United States. There were still many people emigrating from war-devastated Europe but relatively few were going to America. It seemed that the days of the big North Atlantic liner were over. Instead, the first newbuildings of the early 'Twenties were 'intermediates', less glamorous but more economical and flexible to operate. They were of 15 or 20,000 tons and had speeds of around 18 or 20 knots. Some of them were fitted with oil engines instead of the traditional steam reciprocating engines or turbines. The new diesels could not develop the power needed for higher speeds but they were more economical to run and proved extremely successful.

Although the migrant trade was still the core business on many routes, post-War optimism encouraged a new type of passenger, the middle class tourist (mainly American) who demanded more comfort than the migrants but did not expect First Class luxury. Ships were now given Tourist Class accommodations for those who were travelling for pleasure. But they had more to offer these passengers. The ship herself could become the background for their vacation. More and more, passenger liners were used for pleasure cruising. In between their liner voyages, they became floating resorts taking their passengers to exotic and historic places.

On May 21st, 1932 no less than eleven liners with a total gross tonnage of 403,859 were in the port of Southampton. The *Aquitania* is in the foreground of this aerial view of the Ocean Dock. Ahead of her is the *Mauretania*, while the rival *Majestic* lies on the other side of the dock. Looking tiny in comparison, a typical example of the cruise liner of the 'Twenties, the *Arandora Star*, can be seen to the far right. (CA/ME)

The *Belgenland*, noted for her long winter cruises, is docked at San Diego, California on December 31st, 1930. A small crowd has gathered to greet the famed scientist Albert Einstein who has arrived from Germany with his wife. The ship has come from northern Europe via New York, the Caribbean and the Panama Canal. Below, she is seen as the Panama Pacific Line's *Columbia*, departing New York on a short cruise in 1935. (CA/ME)

BELGENLAND (27,132 grt; 1917 - 1936)

"She was a popular trans-Atlantic liner on the Red Star Line's Antwerp – New York service, but she was even more famous as a world cruise ship," according to Everett Viez. "She had a very, very loyal following."

Built by Harland & Wolff, she was actually launched in 1914 but remained incomplete owing to the First World War. Eventually, in 1917, she entered service for the White Star Line as a large, two-funnel cargo ship, the *Belgic*. Rebuilt in 1922-23 as a three-stack passenger liner, as originally planned, she became the *Belgenland* and began Atlantic service for the Red Star Line. She had quarters for as many as 2,600 passengers – 500 in first class, 600 in second and 1,500 in third.

"By the early 'Thirties, however, she seemed to have too few conveniences," continued Viez. "She was of an old

THE FIRST POST-WAR LINERS

The popular Stavangerfjord *lying at Pier 4 in Brooklyn's Bush Terminal in the fall of 1939. After returning to her Norwegian homeland, she was seized by the invading Nazis but survived the War and resumed her trans-Atlantic service. Still sailing in the early 'Sixties, she became known as "the dowager of the Atlantic".*
(Richard Faber Collection, New York)

style with lots of woodwork. Too many cabins – about 75% of them – were without private facilities. This was a drawback, especially in the American cruise trade." Laid-up in 1933, she was transferred two years later to an associated American company, the Panama Pacific Line, and renamed *Columbia*. According to Viez, "The Americans tried to upgrade her, but she was too old, too dated. Making mostly cheap, short cruises, she lasted but a year before being laid-up at Hoboken, nested alongside another out-of-work American liner, the *Leviathan*. Both were sold for scrap in Scotland in the end.

The day the *Columbia* was due to sail, she was undocked into the Hudson River, but then couldn't go forward. She had to be re-docked and repaired. She finally made the voyage across the North Atlantic, under her own power but at a very slow 8 knots. The large builder's model of her, which was kept on the ship herself, was supposed to go to the Smithsonian Institute in Washington, D.C., but the shipbreakers wanted it and so it too went to Scotland."

STAVANGERFJORD (12,977 grt; 1918 - 1963)

"The *Stavangerfjord* was a delightful old ship," said Everett Viez. "She was quite small and very old-fashioned in so many ways. The corridors, for example, were very narrow and you could feel the roll of the decks. She was very home-like, very cozy. Only the few de luxe staterooms in first class had private bathroom facilities: all the other cabins did not. On the outside, she had a cruiser stern, unique for her time when she came out. She had the reputation of being very solid, a great 'sea boat' for the often stormy North Atlantic. The Norwegian America Line ships were unusual in sailing into Brooklyn and, no doubt as a result, a large Norwegian colony developed there."

Built by Cammell Laird at Birkenhead, this sturdy-looking twin-stacker was one of the Atlantic's most durable ships. She sailed for 45 years, until late 1963, when she was finally retired and sold off to Hong Kong scrappers.

STAVANGERFJORD and RELIANCE

RELIANCE (20,200 grt; 1920 - 1938)

This fine-looking three-funnel ship, and her twin *Resolute*, were very similar to the Canadian Pacific *Empress of Australia*, and had rather interesting careers. They were ordered by the Hamburg America Line in 1913, before the First World War started, but their construction was staggered and then they were sold to the Dutch, to the Royal Holland Lloyd, for Amsterdam – East Coast of South America service.

The Germans had intended them as the *Johann Heinrich Burchard* and *William O'Swald*, respectively, but they became the Dutch *Limburgia* and *Brabantia* instead. In 1922, however, they were sold to the United America Lines, using American and later Panamanian registry, and were now called *Reliance* and *Resolute*. United America Lines ran a New York – Hamburg service in conjunction with Hamburg America but in 1926 they sold the two ships outright to that company. The *Reliance* and *Resolute* therefore returned to their original owners. After 1928, they were used as full-time cruiseships.

According to Everett Viez, "They were very beautiful, with gorgeous public rooms. With their three funnels, they looked much larger than they actually were. They had a great following in the early 'Thirties for cruises out of New York, especially short voyages to Bermuda. They were always full."

The *Reliance* survived until she burned out at Hamburg in August, 1938; the *Resolute*, however, had been sold to the Italian government in 1935 for use as a troop transport, becoming the *Lombardia*.

She was sunk during an Allied air raid on Naples in the summer of 1943. Her remains were salvaged and scrapped three years later.

The Hamburg America Line's *Reliance*, which became a well-known cruising liner, is here seen in Hamburg harbor in the late 'Twenties. She had previously belonged to American owners and had been one of the very first passenger ships to use Panamanian "flag of convenience" registry. (*CA/ME*)

35

THE FIRST POST-WAR LINERS

EMPRESS OF AUSTRALIA (21,498 grt; 1920 - 1952)

"We sailed at midnight and hundreds of people were at the New York pier to see us off. A British band in full uniform played on deck as we tossed streamers and cheered and cried," remembered Alice Keppel-Thomas. She was a passenger on a 1935 winter cruise aboard the *Empress of Australia*, a luxury liner owned by the giant Canadian Pacific transportation combine. With three tall stacks painted in golden yellow, the ship carried about 500 passengers on these cruises and had a superb reputation and a loyal following in her day. "Then, the sailings were gala affairs," added Mrs. Keppel-Thomas. "My whole family, sixteen in all, had come aboard and squeezed into our stateroom. All of us drank champagne and ate canapés and little sandwiches off huge, crested silver serving trays." Mrs. Keppel-Thomas was on a three-week West Indies cruise. "We had eleven days of sea travel – leisurely and restful," she wrote in her journal. "We'd have deck games in the morning, a big lunch in the columned dining room and then the whole ship napped from about 2 o'clock until 4. There wasn't a sound or even a knock on the stateroom door. Tea was next, a big event in itself. Men were in shirt, jacket and tie, ladies in day dresses and the waiters in immaculately starched jackets with polished brass buttons. While a string quartet played and the passengers danced,

In this May, 1939 view at Southampton, Canadian Pacific's white-hulled *Empress of Australia* is awaiting the start of a notable trans-Atlantic crossing. She will be carrying King George VI and Queen Elizabeth on the first leg of their Canadian tour. (CA/ME)

Smoking Rooms were once an essential amenity. Elegantly furnished in the Louis XVI style, with oak panelled walls and a moulded ceiling, the first class Smoking Room on the *Empress of Australia* was described by Canadian Pacific as "dignified and comfortable". (CA/ME)

those waiters pushed trolleys and carried large trays laden with cakes, cookies and sandwiches."

"For dinner, we dressed in full evening clothes – long gowns and fur wraps and the men in tails. There were fourteen formal nights altogether. As we dined, an orchestra played on a balcony. Afterward, there was dancing, sometimes a quiz, occasionally a film in the main lounge. But there wasn't really much to choose from. You enjoyed the ship itself, the far-off ports and lands and those extraordinary star-filled tropic nights. The ship was usually 'dark' by midnight."

Sometimes, the *Empress of Australia* would embark on much longer, more expensive cruising itineraries, often from New York. Seventy days from one end of the Mediterranean to the other, for example, had a minimum cost of $600, or just a little more than $8 a day! According to Everett Viez, "She was well-known in New York travel circles for her very spacious public rooms. Her cruises were very popular." In the peak, summer months, however, when the Atlantic routes were busy, she would sail in the service between Southampton and Quebec City, carrying traditionally class-divided passengers: 387 in first class, 394 in tourist and 358 in third.

She was another of the big German liners which had passed into Allied hands after the First World War. She had been launched at Stettin at the end of 1913 as the *Tirpitz* for the Hamburg America Line but work was halted by the War. She was completed in 1920 and given to the British as reparations. The following year, she raised the Canadian Pacific houseflag and initially sailed on their trans-Pacific route between Vancouver, Victoria and the Far East. She made history when she rescued hundreds of people at Yokohama during the Great Earthquake of 1923. Some years later, in May, 1939 – by which time she had long since been transferred to the Atlantic route – she carried Britain's King George VI and Queen Elizabeth to the start of their goodwill tour of Canada. During and after the Second World War, she was used as a troopship until going for scrap in 1952, by which time she had seen 32 years of service.

THE FIRST POST-WAR LINERS

Canadian Pacific's *Montcalm*, one of three sisters built for intermediate service across the Atlantic, is seen leaving Montreal in May, 1937, carrying 300 Canadian officers to attend the Coronation of King George VI in London the following month. *(CA/ME)*

MONTCALM (16,418 grt; 1921 - 1952)

"It was £1 a day for 15 days – £15 for a complete cruise in 1933," remembered Colonel Norman Dodd. "Ships such as the *Montcalm* were cruising just to stay in service, especially as her trans-Atlantic sailings for Canadian Pacific were virtually empty in those Depression years. So she took lots of youngsters like me to the sunshine - to Madeira, Lisbon, Vigo." Ordered from yards on the Clyde by Canadian Pacific just after the First World War, the *Montcalm*, and her sisters *Montrose* and *Montclare* were intended for the Liverpool - Montreal run, carrying over 1,800 passengers, but by the 'Thirties they were being used almost entirely as cruise ships. None of them would return to Canadian Pacific service after the War. When the conflict started, the *Montcalm* became the armed merchant cruiser HMS *Wolfe* and was later sold outright to the British Admiralty for use as a depot ship. She was broken-up in 1952. The *Montrose* became the HMS *Forfar* but was sunk off the Irish coast in December, 1940. The *Montclare*, on the other hand, retaining her name until the very end, was sold to the Admiralty and converted into a depot ship. She lasted until going to the scrappers at Inverkeithing in Scotland in 1958, the last of her class.

PARIS (34,569 grt; 1921 - 1939)

The *Paris* was another big liner whose construction was interrupted by the First World War. She had been launched in 1916 but was not ready to enter service on the French Line's Le Havre - New York route until 1921. Although her first class quarters were sumptuously decorated, she is not nearly as well remembered as her later running-mate, the *Ile de France*, which introduced Art Deco to the oceans of the World. Not everybody preferred the new style. Everett Viez commented, "The *Paris* was really better in ways than the *Ile de France*, which was, of course, more innovative. The *Ile* was the more solid of the two ships, however. The *Paris* was more French in style, the *Ile* more European international. The three stacks on the *Paris* appeared to be too close and too straight, so the *Ile* was slightly better looking." The *Paris* was one of several French liners that fell victim to fire. She burned at her Le Havre berth in April, 1939 and capsized. The wreckage was not finally removed until 1947. The previous year, the still submerged *Paris* had been involved in another mishap when the *Liberté*, the former German speed champion *Europa*, crashed into her wreck and sank. Fortunately, the *Liberté* was raised and eventually entered service.

38

One of the most favored of all Atlantic liners, the splendid *Paris* is attached by a web of ropes, nets and gangways to her New York berth on the north side of Pier 57, at the foot of West 15th Street. Although not the largest or the fastest, the French Line ships had a fine reputation in the 'Twenties. (CA/ME)

THE FIRST POST-WAR LINERS

The ornate, two-tiered, three deck high Dining Room in which first class passengers on the *Paris* enjoyed her celebrated cuisine. This photograph was used for a postcard bearing the company's slogan: "French Line. The Longest Gangplank in the World" *(Richard Faber Collection, New York)*

French Line ships were more prone to fire than those of many companies. Having already suffered one serious blaze, in 1929, the *Paris* caught fire at her Le Havre berth while preparing for another Atlantic crossing on April 18th, 1939. The following day, she capsized. *(CA/ME)*

SCYTHIA and ARUNDEL CASTLE

Winter sailing: Cunard's intermediate liner *Scythia* departs from New York's Pier 56 on an icy January afternoon. She was one of a series of sturdy ships built in the early 'Twenties to replace the losses which the line had suffered in the First World War. (CA/ME)

SCYTHIA (19,730 grt; 1921 - 1958)

After the First World War, Cunard Line built two groups of single-stackers. There were the 14,000-ton *Andania* sisters and the larger (19,500 grt) *Scythia*, *Samaria*, *Laconia* and the later *Franconia* and *Carinthia*. The *Scythia* came from the Vickers yard at Barrow-in-Furness, where she was launched on March 22nd, 1920, although one year later she had to be transferred to a French yard at Lorient to be completed, owing to a workers' strike in Great Britain. She could carry 337 first class passengers, 331 second and 1,538 in a simple third class. She and her sisters ran a variety of Atlantic services to New York, Boston and Montreal, as well as cruises. Three of them survived the Second World War: the *Scythia*, *Samaria* and *Franconia*. They resumed Cunard service until scrapped in the late 'Fifties.

ARUNDEL CASTLE (18,980 grt; 1921 - 1959)

The *Arundel Castle* was completed by Harland & Wolff in 1921 after a lengthy, war-interrupted construction. Her sister, the *Windsor Castle*, followed from the John Brown yard in 1922. They were the largest liners to date for Britain's Union-Castle Line. They were also the only four-stackers built for a service other than the North Atlantic route. They plied the "mail run" between England and South Africa. In 1937, they were re-engined and modernized in order to fit them for the faster service required by a new mail contract. They now had two funnels and a less stately profile.

The *Windsor Castle* was sunk by German aircraft in Mediterranean waters in 1943 but the *Arundel Castle* survived the War, later resuming South African sailings until she was broken up at Hong Kong in 1959.

THE FIRST POST-WAR LINERS

Union-Castle Line's *Arundel Castle* and *Windsor Castle* were the only four-stackers built for a line service other than the North Atlantic. Re-engined and extensively rebuilt in 1937 (below), they now had two funnels and a new raked bow. (Above: Laurence Dunn Collection; below: CA/ME)

MAJESTIC (56,551 grt; 1922 - 1939)

She was intended to be the Hamburg America Line's *Bismarck* but her construction was interrupted by the First World War and afterward she was allocated to the British, to the White Star Line. She began sailing as their *Majestic* in 1922. She was launched in Hamburg by the Blohm & Voss yard on June 20th, 1914, but the following August the outfitting of the new pride of the German merchant marine came to an abrupt halt owing to the Great War. When, on June 28th, 1919 Germany had to sign the Treaty of Versailles, the idle *Bismarck* went into the list of War prizes. As the majority of the fittings and furnishings of the vessel where ready and in stock in Hamburg warehouses, it was decided to bring her to completion at Blohm & Voss, instead of towing the giant liner to a UK yard. British surveyors from the new owners went to Hamburg to supervise her completion. One can only imagine the atmosphere which surrounded the ship, and indeed, when in Fall 1921 she was almost ready, an arson attempt delayed her completion by six months. "She was the best looking of the three Hamburg America Line giants", according to Everett Viez. "The *Majestic*'s main lounge was the best of all. It was more ornamental. Even so, in the 'Twenties and early 'Thirties the 'British' *Olympic* was always the favourite ship in the White Star fleet. Also, the *Majestic* suffered from hull fractures. White Star was slipping in the early 'Thirties, at the beginning of the Depression. They needed to reduce their fleet, including the *Majestic*. In 1934, they were forced into a merger with Cunard, creating the Cunard-White Star Line. Otherwise, they would have folded on their own."

Laid-up in 1936, the 2,145 passenger *Majestic* was sold to scrappers but then resold to the British Admiralty and refitted as the naval cadets' training ship *HMS Caledonia*. She burned and sank while berthed at Rosyth on September 29th, 1939. Her remains were scrapped during the War, in 1940-43.

In the twilight of her career, the *Majestic* arrives in New York harbor on January 21st, 1936 with her flag at half-mast. King George V had died the previous day. Several weeks later, with the new *Queen Mary* soon to enter service, the *Majestic* was laid-up. (CA/ME)

THE FIRST POST-WAR LINERS

The White Star Line's *Majestic*, the World's largest liner from 1922 until 1935, looks even more imposing as she stands high and dry in the giant floating dock at Southampton. She had been laid down before the First World War as the final member of Hamburg America's projected trio of superliners. *(Richard Faber Collection, New York)*

HOMERIC (34,351 grt; 1922 - 1936)

Intended to be the *Columbus* of North German Lloyd, she was launched in December, 1913 but lay uncompleted throughout the First World War. She was handed over to the British as reparations and, like the *Bismarck*, she was allotted to the White Star Line, who renamed her *Homeric*. Completed by 1922, she ran on the Southampton – New York express service along with the *Majestic* (ex-*Bismarck*) and *Olympic*. Although a fine, beautifully appointed ship, she was overshadowed by the two larger liners.

She became an early victim of the Depression, being assigned to fulltime cruising in 1932 and then, after less than fourteen years of service, she went to shipbreakers in Scotland in 1936.

By then part of the Cunard-White Star fleet, she joined the likes of *Majestic*, *Mauretania* and *Olympic* in enforced retirement.

VOLENDAM (15,434 grt; 1922 - 1952)

"It was September, 1939. The War had just started in Europe and everything changed very suddenly. It all grew very perilous, very unsafe. My parents decided that we should flee, leaving our home in Vienna. We left in the middle of the night. We walked away from everything, carrying nothing more than a small suitcase and having no more than the equivalent of $20 between the four of us – my parents, my sister and myself. Through relatives, we made our way to Antwerp and across the Dutch border to Rotterdam. We were very lucky. My uncle obtained tickets for my sister and me onboard the liner *Volendam*. She was bound for the United States and for freedom!" So remembered Bianca Shorr, by then retired and living in southern California.

We were fellow passengers on a luxury cruise in the

HOMERIC and VOLENDAM

Another former German liner, the *Homeric* became the third ship in White Star's express service. Here she enters the floating dock at Southampton in October, 1932 to be prepared for her winter cruise program. Note the rival Cunard Line's *Mauretania* in the background. (CA/ME)

Mediterranean some fifty-five years later. "The *Volendam* was very crowded as we went aboard. Everything seemed hectic, almost chaotic. We were told that she was completely full, about 2,000 passengers in all, booked with anxious tourists returning to America and with children and refugees running from the threatening Nazi forces. We sailed in the darkness of night," added Mrs. Shorr. "Many people were on deck, however. Many cried. Some looked back in fear, on Holland and on all of Europe. Some felt that they might never see their European homelands again or, worse still, might not even reach the safe shores of America. As we entered the North Sea, the ship became very solemn, very tense. There were no exterior lights and thick steel covers had been placed over the portholes. The windows on the upper decks had been overpainted in a dark colour. There seemed to be no daylight. Even the lights onboard had been

The First Post-War Liners

It is September, 1939. War has been declared between Britain and Germany and Holland America's *Volendam* makes a hurried departure from Hoboken, returning to Europe to collect anxious tourists and refugees. In the distance is Eastern Steamship's *Saint John*, temporarily chartered to the United States Lines for the same purpose.

(CA/ME)

English Channel where, it was said, many Nazi mines had been laid. And there were U-Boats around as well. A British ship (the *Athenia*) had just been sunk with considerable loss of life. No European ship was safe any longer. The *Volendam* traveled onwards, sometimes very slowly. I seem to recall that it took 9 or 10 days to reach New York. But each day brought greater hope and lessened the fears. We tried to amuse ourselves but it was often quite difficult. The Dutch crew were very kind and tried to make us as comfortable as possible. Although the ship was over-booked, she was well-provisioned. We once again saw foods that had disappeared in occupied Austria."

Along with such other passenger ships as the French Line's *De Grasse* and Cunard's brand new *Mauretania*, the *Volendam* reached New York in early October. "We landed at the 5th Street pier in Hoboken. It was our first steps on American soil," concluded Mrs. Shorr. "Passengers came ashore with old trunks, battered cases and many with nothing more than the clothes they were wearing. The immigration procedures took hours and hours, but the sight of some cousins, who lived in nearby Brooklyn, behind the wooden partitions on the dock made it all worthwhile. We shall never forget that voyage on the *Volendam*. It was literally our trip of a lifetime."

Just months later, the *Volendam* was torpedoed and nearly sunk off the Irish coast but, after repairs, she served for the remainder of the War as a troopship. She had been built for the Holland America Line in 1922. She and her twin sister, the *Veendam*, sailed the North Atlantic route between Rotterdam, the Channel ports in England and France and then over to New York. (The company's terminal was actually located in Hoboken in New Jersey, just across the Hudson River from the more famous New York City piers.)

In the early 'Thirties, as the Depression deepened, both ships spent more and more time on cruises to Bermuda, Havana, other Caribbean ports, eastern Canada and sometimes on long four- and six-week voyages. Conservative looking liners with two tall smokestacks, they had typically Dutch interiors for that period – lots of dark wood panelling, heavy furniture, real fireplaces in some of the public rooms and the smell of strong tobacco. During warm-weather cruises, a canvas pool would be erected on deck and filled with sea water.

After her war service, the *Volendam* resumed Holland America sailings but was broken-up in 1952.

dimmed, mostly by using smaller bulbs. Reading was often difficult.

"Tensions among the passengers rose as we entered the

The First Post-War Liners

Navigazione Generale Italiana's *Duilio* sailing from Pier 97 in New York on November 20th, 1923. Although they did not match the Atlantic express liners of other countries in size, Italy's prestige liners of the 'Twenties were famous for their exuberant décor. (CA/ME)

GIULIO CESARE (21,848 grt; 1922 - 1944)
DUILIO (24,281 grt; 1923 - 1944)

In 1915-16, a company called Transatlantica Italiana planned Italy's largest liners to date, two 20,000-tonners of over 25 knots, which were to be called *Andrea Doria* and *Camillo di Cavour*.

They were intended to compete with Navigazione Generale Italiana's *Duilio* and *Giulio Cesare*. The *Duilio* was launched in early 1916 at the Ansaldo shipyard at Genoa and the *Giulio Cesare* was under construction at the same time, but at Swan, Hunter & Wigham Richardson at Newcastle. Also in contention would be the *Conte Rosso* of the Lloyd Sabaudo, under-way in the First World War. The lost plans for the intended *Andrea Doria* and *Conte di Cavour* were found in a Rome antique shop in the 1990s. One set of plans was for a three-funnel design and another had a fourth dummy one. Unfortunately, Transatlantica Italiana went bankrupt before the ships could be built. The *Giulio Cesare* and *Duilio* were used on the Genoa – New York and Genoa – South America runs until 1934, when they began sailing from Italy to South Africa. They made a great impression in comparison with the Union-Castle ships also running into South African ports. But both were war casualties: the *Duilio* was sunk near Trieste in July, 1944 and the *Giulio Cesare* was sunk nearby two months later. Both were raised but were scrapped.

The luxurious writing gallery of the *Giulio Cesare*; she and her sister ship *Duilio* were the first Italian palatial ship and marked the start of their nation's challenge to British, German and French companies on the Atlantic.

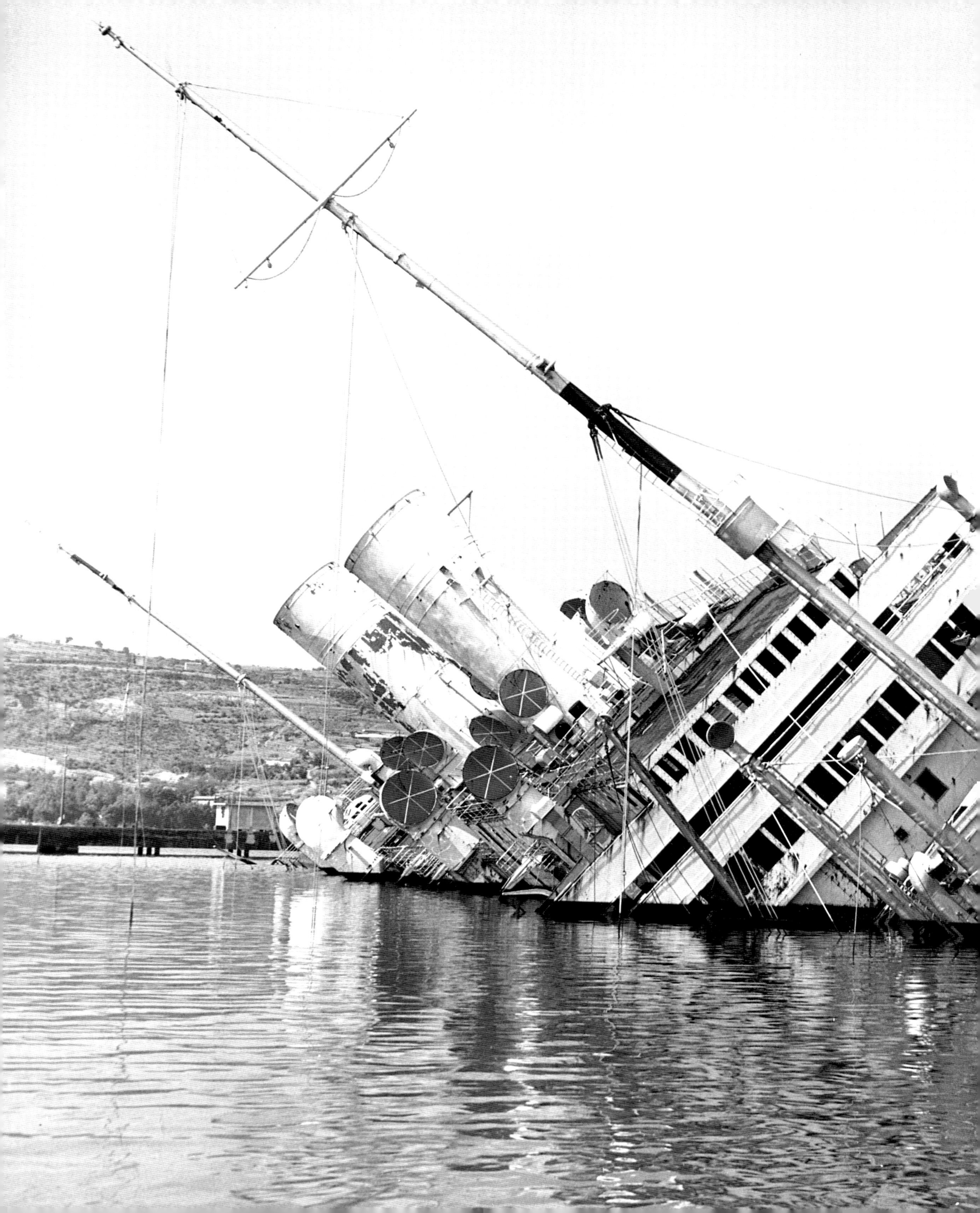

The Italian passenger fleet suffered grievous losses in the Second World War. The *Sabaudia*, former *Stockholm*, the *Duilio* and the *Giulio Cesare* (pictured) were sunk by Allied warplanes in 1944 in Muggia Bay, near Trieste. *(CA/ME)*

The First Post-War Liners

The *Conte Verde* pictured in Lisbon in the early stages of her career, sporting the traditional Lloyd Sabaudo livery. The original funnel colors of the Italian company were curiously the same as those of the Holland America Line, but later the thin green bands were repainted blue. The upper ends of the stacks were a distinctive mark of her Scottish builder, Beardmore of Dalmuir.

CONTE ROSSO (18,017 grt; 1922 - 1941)
CONTE VERDE (18,765 grt; 1923 - 1944)

One of the most prolific and interesting Italian shipping companies of the beginning of the 20th century was the Lloyd Sabaudo, founded in Turin (the first - far from the sea - capital of united Italy) in June, 1906. Few people know that this company, at the climax of its expansion in the 'Twenties, was headed by the scientist Guglielmo Marconi.

He became honorary president of the company at the eve of First World War, thanks to his personal friendship with Lloyd Sabaudo's general manager, Marquis Renzo Durand de la Penne, a prominent character in the history of the Italian merchant marine, who prompted the building of the famous five Counts: *Conte Rosso, Conte Verde, Conte Biancamano, Conte Grande* and *Conte di Savoia*.

Marconi and de la Penne met for the first time on board the *Principessa Mafalda* sailing to South America. Marconi was a passenger, while de la Penne was the master. As the latter studied the science of telecommunications, he obviously was a great admirer of the world-famed scientist who in turn, fond of music, appreciated the *Mafalda*'s master's great skill in playing piano and entertaining the passengers.

In 1913, Marconi brought another friend, William Beardmore, owner of the Scottish shipyard bearing his name, into the Lloyd Sabaudo venture, persuading him to build a large passenger liner for the company at a bargain price in exchange for a seat on the board and a share of the dividends of the Italian firm. The vessel, laid down in 1914 and named *Conte Rosso*, was a near sister to Beardmore's latest ocean liner, the *Alsatian*, but during the War, while on the stocks, she was sold to the British Admiralty and completed as the *H.M.S. Argus*, the first aircraft carrier in history.

At the end of the hostilities, a new *Conte Rosso* and, this time, also a sister ship, the *Conte Verde*, were ordered, but they were quite different from the original liner which became the *Argus*: they had a clipper stern instead of a counter one and only two propellers, with double reduction geared turbines, instead of four directly coupled to the turbines as originally foreseen. *Conte Rosso* and *Conte Verde* were intended to become the direct com-

CONTE ROSSO and CONTE VERDE

petitors to the new *Giulio Cesare* and *Duilio*, ordered by the rival company NGI on the eve of First World War. Other interesting vessels intended to compete with NGI's and Lloyd Sabaudo's new flaghsips were the superliners *Andrea Doria* and *Camillo di Cavour* (ordered by Transatlantica Italiana) and the steamear *Savona* of Italia S.A. di Navigazione a Vapore (not to be confused with Italia Flotte Riunite founded in 1932). Eventually, the newbuilding programs of these two companies were wound up: they were both backed by German interests and the eruption of the First World War, with Italy opposed to Germany, caused the companies' demise and subsequent closure.

At the end of the War, Lloyd Sabaudo insisted that the design of the their new 'Contes' was to be from scratch, fulfilling their desire to have the most technologically advanced and beautifully appointed vessels possible. Indeed, when the *Conte Rosso* was finally delivered in early March, 1922, sailing on the 29th on her maiden voyage to Buenos Aires, she was the first merchant ship in the world to sport double reduction geared turbines (much more efficient in comparison to the direct driven turbines envisaged for the first *Conte Rosso*) and also an advanced electrical supply system by means of a main switchboard and local substation, derived from those on the latest generation of British Navy battleships. Inside, the hotel area for first class was equally thought on a grand scale: the opulence of the fittings on the two sister ships, designed by the Coppedè brothers of Florence, took inspiration from the deeds of Amedeo VI of Savoy, known as the 'Conte Rosso' ('Red Count'), and his son Amedeo VII, known as the 'Conte Verde' ('Green Count'). In contrast to the austere tones found on English or German ships, great use was made of polychromatic decoration, with gaily coloured floors, wallpaper and upholstery as well as bright stuccoes and large oils on canvas narrating the life of the two Savoy Counts, painted by Carlo Coppedè. Maria Cristina Marconi, wife of Guglielmo, launched the *Conte Verde* on October 21st, 1922;

The *Conte Rosso* and the *Conte Verde*, conceived for the warm weather route from Mediterranean ports to South America, were among the first trans-Atlantic liners to be fitted with a open-air restaurant. In the 'Thirties, when they were transferred to the Far East line, a lido and pool were added to the open deck.

The First Post-War Liners

In early 1932, the *Conte Verde* joined the new Italian Line for only a few months, adopting their colors on her funnels, to run three Summer cruises from Venice, before joining her sister *Conte Rosso* on the Far East service of Lloyd Triestino.

the following April the new liner left on her maiden voyage, but in order to attract the rich North American clientele she was not sent to Buenos Aires, like her sister ship, but to New York; actually, the *Conte Rosso* herself, after only two voyages to the River Plate ports, had been rerouted to North America. Both 'Counts' were moved to the Genoa-Buenos Aires line in 1928, after the entry into service of their larger fleetmates *Conte Biancamano* and *Conte Grande*.

In January, 1932, when Lloyd Sabaudo merged with NGI and Cosulich to form the Italian Line, the *Conte Rosso* was transferred straight to Lloyd Triestino to run a new express service to Shanghai; she never sported the Italian Line colours on her funnels. The *Conte Verde*, however, before joining her sister on the Far East line in October, 1932, made three Mediterranean cruises from Venice for the Italian Line.

Both ships had been revamped for their new service: the heavy Coppedeian décor was partly removed to give the vessels a brighter and fresher style, more suitable for the hot climate of the Far East route, and an open air swimming pool was added. After sailing for a while with the black funnels and hulls of Lloyd Triestino vessels, a new, more solar livery was adopted: at first, the funnels were repainted yellow and at a later stage the hull white, with a blue boot-topping and a green band.

When Italy entered the Second World War, the *Conte Rosso* was in her mother country and was converted into a troopship, while the *Conte Verde* was in Shanghai and, after a period of idleness, was chartered to Japan for the exchange of war prisoners. *Conte Rosso* was sent to the bottom by torpedoes fired by the British submarine *Upholder* on May, 24th 1941, with a heavy toll of lives, while the *Conte Verde*, scuttled by her crew after Italy's armistice, was recovered by the Japanese and transformed into their troopship *Kotobuki Maru*. Bombed in the Bay of Nakata by the U.S. Air Force just days before Japan surrendered and the end of the hostilities, her wreck was put at disposal of the Italians. Far too damaged to be worth repairing, the remains of the old steamer were sold to a local shipbreaking firm.

The Conte Rosso steaming at full speed in the Indian Ocean heading to Bombay and Shanghai, seen from one of her running-mates on the Far Eastern service of Lloyd Triestino, the famous motorship *Victoria*.

The *Conte Rosso*, wearing the Lloyd Triestino livery, sails from Naples in January, 1937 for Bombay. Among her passengers she carries Cardinal Pacelli (later Pope Pius XII) going to the Indian Eucharistic Congress; the Vatican flag flies from the vessel's mainmast.

THE FIRST POST-WAR LINERS

Hamburg America Line's large, four-masted combination passenger-cargo liner *Hansa*, the former *Albert Ballin*, is seen loading freight at Pier 86, New York on August 28th, 1937. Seized by the Russians at the end of the War, she had a career spanning 58 years. *(CA/ME)*

ALBERT BALLIN (20,815 grt; 1923 - 1981)

At the turn of the century, the great Hamburg America Line, Hapag to many, had the biggest passenger ship fleet in the World. They owned some of the largest, fastest and grandest liners then afloat. But the absolute high point came in 1910 when they announced a trio of successively larger "superships". The first was the 52,000-ton *Imperator*, a full 6,000 tons bigger than the ill-fated *Titanic*. She was commissioned in May, 1913, a year after that ship's tragic sinking. Next came the 54,000-ton *Vaterland*, delivered in the summer of 1914, and then there was to have been the 56,000-ton *Bismarck*. But, because of the outbreak of the First World War, the *Bismarck* never entered German service. By 1919, Hamburg America was in ruins with barely any ships flying its flag. Of the big passenger liners, only the cruiseship *Victoria Luise* remained. She was demoted to become the all-third class

Hansa. Restrictions placed by the Allies on the rebuilding of the German merchant marine, together with financial limitations and the reduced state of the North Atlantic passenger trade, led the slowly reawakening Hamburg America Line to think of much more moderate tonnage. And so, their first full-scale passenger ships after the War were the 20,000-ton *Albert Ballin* and *Deutschland*. They were built by Blohm & Voss of Hamburg for the Hamburg – New York service via Southampton and Cherbourg.

"The *Albert Ballin* was actually a very large passenger-cargo ship, a big combo with huge holds and four masts," noted Everett Viez. "All the accommodation (for 1,551 passengers in three classes) was amidships. The two sisters were said to be very fine, very solid ships that rode well at sea. They were beautifully appointed, especially in first class. They were very German, of course, and always clean as a whistle. Along with their near-sisters, the *Hamburg* and *New York* of 1926-27, they were well known for their mid-

ALBERT BALLIN and MALOJA

They were P&O's largest liners in the 'Twenties: the good-looking 20,000-ton sisters *Maloja* (seen here) and *Mooltan* were the most important ships in the company's UK - Australia service for ten years until the advent of the 'Straths'. (CA/ME)

night sailings from New York's Pier 84." Re-engined and extensively refitted in 1930 and then lengthened in 1934, the *Albert Ballin* was renamed *Hansa* in 1935 at the insistence of the Nazi government.

Herr Ballin, the great shipping entrepreneur who had been responsible for Hamburg America Line's amazing growth before the First World War, had been Jewish and in Nazi Germany it was no longer acceptable for him to be commemorated by having a ship named after him.

Left virtually untouched in German waters during the Second World War, the *Hansa* was mined off Warnemünde on March 6th, 1945.

Salvaged by the Soviets in 1949, she then began a long and tedious rebuilding before re-entering passenger service as the *Sovietsky Sojus* out in the Far East, sailing out of Vladivostok. The largest passenger ship ever to fly the Soviet colours, she was renamed *Soyus* in 1980 and was scrapped a year later, after a 58-year career.

MALOJA (20,837 grt; 1923 - 1954)

She was one of the four 'M-Ships' of P&O, built for their London – Melbourne – Sydney route via Suez. The first two vessels, the English-built *Moldavia* and *Mongolia*, were of 16,000 grt and were turbine-driven, while the *Maloja* and her sister *Mooltan*, were of almost 21,000 grt but still had old fashioned quadruple expansion engines.

They were the largest liners in The Peninsular & Oriental Steam Navigation Co.'s fleet. Like many P&O liners of the time, they carried comparatively few passengers for their size – 327 in first class and 329 in second, making 656 in all.

Both came safely through the Second World War and then resumed their Australian service until displaced by new passenger tonnage in 1954. In both cases, they were scrapped in Scotland.

Certainly one of the World's largest combination passenger-cargo ships, the Atlantic Transport Line's 21,000-ton Minnewaska was also one of the least fortunate. During the Depression, it proved difficult to fill her huge cargo holds and she had an active career of only ten years. *(Laurence Dunn Collection)*

MINNEWASKA (21,716 grt; 1923 - 1934)

Built for the American-owned but British flag ATL, Atlantic Transport Line, and used on their London – New York run, the Minnewaska and her sister vessel Minnetonka were large combination passenger-cargo ships (carrying only 369 all-first class passengers, but with big holds for freight) and, like all their predecessors in the company, they had a name starting with 'M'. Unfortunately, the historic American company, founded back in 1882, was among the saddest victims of the Depression and by 1936 they ceased to exist.

The Minnewaska and Minnetonka, which together with their fleet mate Minnekahda were known as the 'Minnies', had the sad task of making the last commercial voyages ever of their owners in Spring 1932, when all their other fleet-mates had already been sold or were in lay up. While the Minnekahda had been mothballed since 1931 and did not find any employment until sold for scrap in 1936, the other two 'Minnies' were chartered in May 1932 for the Red Star Line tourist trade between Antwerp, Southampton and New York.

By October 1933, however, they went into lay up and one year later, when not much more than ten years old, they were sold for scrap, as even secondhand buyers could not be found in those hard times.

MINNEWASKA and DE GRASSE

Repainted in gray, with blacked-out windows and with a gun (under wraps) at her stern, the French Line's cabin-class ship *De Grasse* continued to cross the Atlantic in the early days of the War. This photograph was taken in New York on November 20th, 1939. (CA/ME)

DE GRASSE (17,707 grt; 1924 - 1962)

The French Line originally intended calling this ship *Suffren*. She represented the more moderate thinking of most Atlantic passenger ship owners in the early 'Twenties and was an intermediate liner, with a basic profile and unpretentious quarters for 399 in cabin class and 1,712 in a spartan third class.

Built by a British yard, Cammell Laird at Birkenhead, she was eventually completed in France, at St. Nazaire, owing to a strike of shipyard workers. Although intended for the North Atlantic route, she also ran to the West Indies and was considered, in the late 'Thirties, for a new French Line service in the South Pacific, which, however, never materialized. Laid-up at Bordeaux with the fall of France in 1940, she was deliberately sunk by the retreating Germans in the summer of 1944. She was salvaged a year later and restored, now with a single broad stack. Almost single-handedly, she reopened French Line service to New York in 1947.

In 1953, she became the *Empress of Australia* for Canadian Pacific, running Liverpool – Montreal sailings; and then the Italian *Venezuela* in 1956, trading between Europe and the Caribbean. She might have continued even longer, but she stranded near Cannes on March 17th, 1962, and was so badly damaged that she had to be scrapped.

AORANGI (17,491 grt; 1924 - 1953)

Something of an odd ship, she was the largest passenger vessel of her day to sail from the South Pacific, trading between Australia, New Zealand and Vancouver.

Although a notable early motorliner, she had tall, steamship-like stacks. She was built at Glasgow, originally for the Union Steamship Co. of New Zealand but was soon transferred to a joint subsidiary of that company and Canadian Pacific, known as the Canadian Australasian Line. She flew the British flag. She was used as a trooper during the War.

"Afterwards, the Australian government rebuilt her and she became known around Sydney and Melbourne as the 'iron lung' for keeping local shipyards alive with her frequent repairs," remembered Frank Andrews. She resumed her Pacific sailings in 1948 but in 1953 she returned to Scotland to be scrapped. (*Photograph CA/ME*)

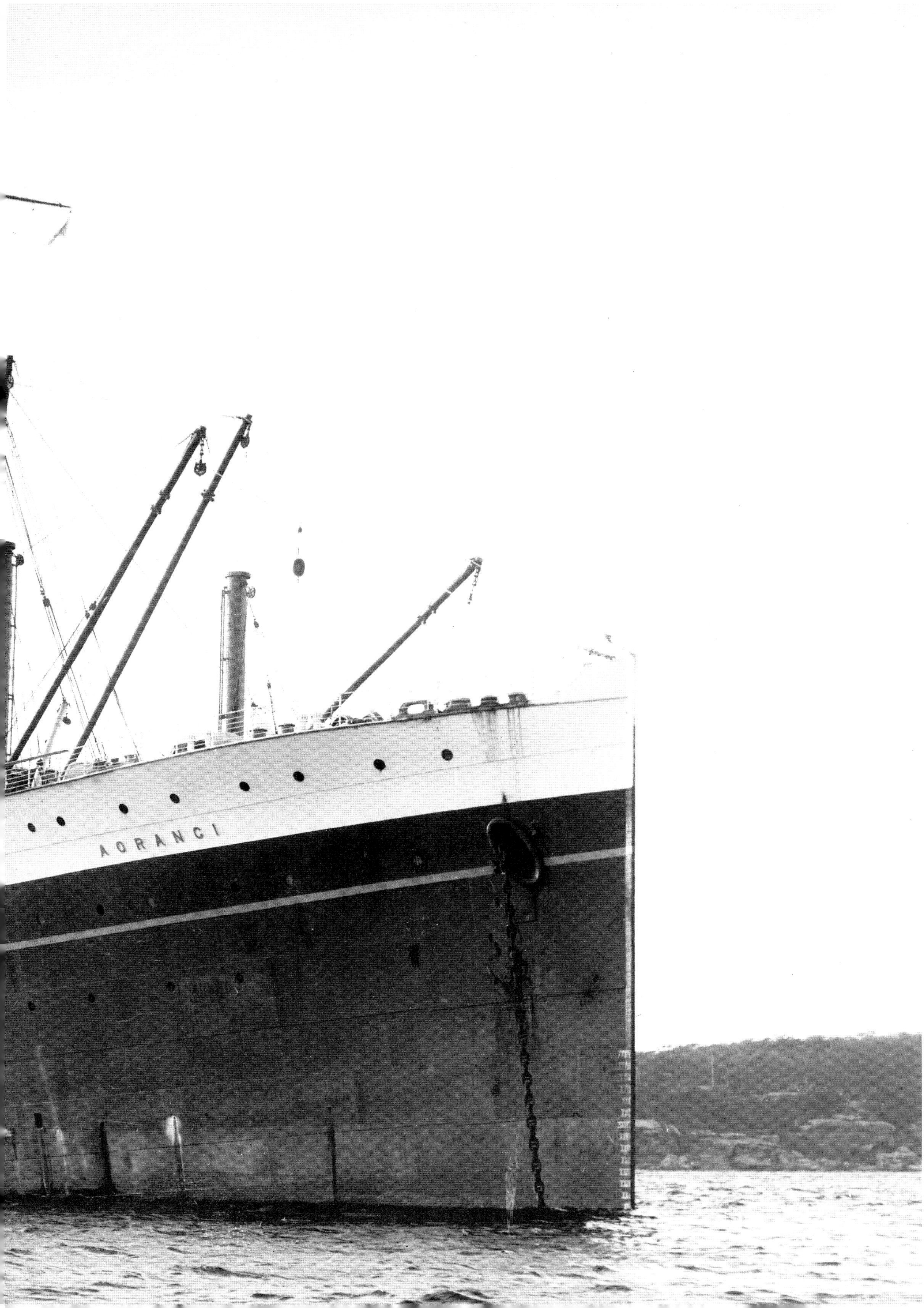
AORANGI

The First Post-War Liners

The *Columbus* is here seen after she had been refitted to make her more compatible with her new running-mates *Bremen* and *Europa* in North German Lloyd's service to New York. She was given new, more powerful engines and her funnels were shortened. (CA/ME)

A skylight provides natural illumination in the tourist class Smoking Room on the *Columbus*. Although much less imposing than the equivalent room in first class, this is still a very masculine space. (CA/ME)

Stateliness at sea: the first class Smoking Room aboard the *Columbus*. Although in some ways outclassed by her new fleetmates *Bremen* and *Europa*, the *Columbus* continued to be popular both as a trans-Atlantic liner and as a cruise ship. (CA/ME)

COLUMBUS (32,354 grt; 1924 - 1939)

When the First World War erupted in that dramatic summer of 1914, the North German Lloyd had two 32,000-ton liners under construction – the *Columbus* and the *Hindenburg*. Both sat on the stocks during the war years and, afterward, the intended *Columbus* was ceded to Britain as reparations and became White Star's *Homeric*. In a stroke of Allied generosity, however, the proposed *Hindenburg* was left to the Germans. She now took her sister's name *Columbus* but her construction and completion were sluggish. Launched in 1922, she was not completed until spring 1924. Having been laid down in 1914, her total time at the Schichau yard at Danzig had been ten years.

Until the arrival of the mighty *Bremen* in 1929, the *Columbus* was Germany's largest, fastest and most luxurious liner. In August, 1927, however, one of her engines was ruined. The starboard shaft broke, causing the engine to race wildly. Temporarily, a substitute was taken from the freighter *Schwaben* and installed in the injured liner, reducing her service speed to 17 knots. But in 1929, with the imminent introduction of the record-breaking *Bremen* and *Europa*, plans were made to take the *Columbus* in hand and install new steam turbines. This raised her service speed to 22 knots, still far short of the new ships' 27 knots, but sufficient to make her more of a running-mate for them. She was also restyled with twin squat funnels so as to make her more closely resemble the larger pair.

"The *Columbus* was very beautiful, actually my favorite North German Lloyd ship," said Everett Viez. "She was the proper size and was top-notch in every way. For some years, she was also very popular as a cruise ship, always full in wintertime. But later in the decade, she had decreasing loads on her New York cruises. There were mostly Jewish passengers going to the Caribbean during the cold season and the *Columbus* suffered increasingly from her Nazi tone and attachment."

Caught on a Caribbean cruise when the War started in September, 1939, she fled to Mexico. Then, while attempting to return to German waters, she was approached by a British warship off the coast of Virginia. In order to prevent her being captured, her crew set her on fire and sank her on December 19th.

The second of the handsome *Monte Sarmiento* class, the *Monte Olivia* is seen being shifted from the Hamburg-South America Line's cargo sheds in Hamburg harbor to the Overseas Landing Stage to take on passengers. The Japanese *Terukuni Maru* is in the background.   *(Richard Faber Collection)*

MONTE SARMIENTO (13,625 grt; 1924 - 1942)

Blohm & Voss, the illustrious Hamburg shipbuilders, produced a set of five moderately-sized twin-stackers for the local Hamburg-South America Line, better known as Hamburg-Sud. With their large passenger capacity, they were especially suited for the migrant trade and for economy cruising. The first of the series, the *Monte Sarmiento* of 1924, carried 1,328 passengers in third class and 1,142 in even less expensive steerage. The *Monte Olivia* followed in 1925; the *Monte Cervantes* in 1928; and then a final pair, the *Monte Pascoal* and *Monte Rosa*, in 1931. They became well-known in Germany. "Third class aboard these *Monte* ships had cabins with 3, 4 or 6 berths," according to Arnold Kludas. "Steerage was all dormitories and was for Spanish and Portuguese seasonal workers going to and from South America and boarding at Vigo and Lisbon. There were also some migrants in steerage. On cruises, when the total capacities were reduced to about

MONTE OLIVIA and MONTE PASCOAL

while on a South American cruise around Tierra del Fuego in January, 1930. (Her remains were not salvaged until the early 1950s but then her hulk sank while being towed to Ushuaia in October, 1954.) With their capacity for large numbers of passengers, the remaining members of the class were deemed suitable to be used as accommodation ships during the Second World War. The Monte Sarmiento was sunk during an Allied air attack on Kiel in Febraury, 1942 and the Monte Olivia was also bombed and sunk in the same port, but at the very end of the War, in April, 1945. The Monte Pascoal was loaded with chemical weapons and deliberately sunk by the British on New Year's Eve, 1946. Finally, the Monte Rosa was also taken by the British, but refitted as the Ministry of Transport trooper Empire Windrush in 1945-46. Notoriously, she caught fire in the western Mediterranean on March 28th, 1954, had to be abandoned and then sank while under tow for Gibraltar.

1,500, the steerage quarters were not used. The Monte Pascoal and Monte Rosa were the two superior ships. They not only made cruises from Germany, but also from Holland – to the Norwegian fjords, the Baltic cities, Spitsbergen, the British Isles and down to the Mediterranean, West Africa and the Canaries. After 1934, these two ships were chartered to the KdF (Kraft durch Freude - the Nazi government's bid to attract party members by offering ocean voyages), but retained their Hamburg-Sud colours. Now, they mostly sailed on cruises to Norway." The Monte Cervantes, which had nearly sunk during an Arctic Sea cruise in 1928, was wrecked

The ships of the Monte Sarmiento class were popular for their low-fare cruises in the 'Thirties. Some of them were used in the Nazi Party's Kraft durch Freude (KdF) program. Here we see the Monte Olivia in Norwegian coastal waters. (Richard Faber Collection)

THE FIRST POST-WAR LINERS

Four well-known liners crowd into Tilbury Docks on January 9th, 1934. The three-funnel *Belgenland* of the Red Star Line is in the middle distance to the left, with the Orient Line's *Oronsay* behind her. To the right are two other Orient Line ships, the *Orontes* (front) and the *Otranto* (behind). *(CA/ME)*

ORAMA (19,777 grt; 1924 - 1940)

The *Orama* was one of five twin-stack sisters built for the Orient Line's service between London and Australia via Suez. They were among the premier ships sailing out of Melbourne and Sydney in their day. They were also among the largest. "They had a lighter look on the inside than earlier Orient Line ships and especially when compared to the rival P&O liners. They had the flavour of Robert Adam. They also seemed brighter because of their many open decks. They were all similar, but not exactly the same," remembered Frank Andrews. He saw them during their visits in the 'Thirties and then saw the *Orontes* again in the early 'Sixties, in the twilight of her career. "By now, she seemed far less bright. We were comparing her by then with a new generation of P&O-Orient liners such as the *Orsova*, *Arcadia* and *Iberia* and then, of course, the *Oriana* and *Canberra*."

The five sisters were built at staggered paces in the 'Twenties: *Orama* (originally to be called *Oriana*) came first, in 1924; *Oronsay* and *Otranto* in 1925; then they were joined by the *Orford* in 1928 and the *Orontes* in 1929. As built, the *Orama* could carry 592 first class passengers and 1,244 in third class. Like the *Oronsay* and the *Orford*, she was lost in the Second World War.

The *Otranto*, used as a one-class migrant ship in later years, was scrapped in 1957, while the *Orontes* was the lone survivor of the quintet when she went to the breakers in 1962.

In the late 'Thirties, the black hulls of the Orient Line ships were repainted in an attractive corn-colored shade. Here, the *Orama* lies at her berth in Tilbury docks, downriver from London. Note her rim-topped funnels, typical of the Orient liners. *(Laurence Dunn Collection)*

THE FIRST POST-WAR LINERS

TRANSYLVANIA (16,923 grt; 1925 - 1940)
CALEDONIA (17,046 grt; 1925 - 1940)

The Anchor Line, for a time a Cunard subsidiary, ran a series of medium-sized passenger ships on the North Atlantic in the 'Twenties and 'Thirties. Sailing to New York from their home port of Glasgow, they included this pair of three-stackers, as well as several single-stackers such as the *Cameronia*.

"Anchor Line ships were known for their solid comfort," recalled Everett Viez. "They were economical and well-run, but they were actually quite slow." The *Transylvania* was built by Fairfield Shipbuilding & Engineering at Glasgow, while the *Caledonia* came from the Alexander Stephen yard, also at Glasgow. In an attempt to look like some of the larger Atlantic liners, they were given dummy first and third stacks. They had comfortable first and second class accommodations, but they relied heavily on third class traffic going westbound to America from Scotland and Ireland. Unfortunately, this declined sharply as a result of the restrictions on immigration into the United States and the Anchor Line was also hit by Prohibition, since whisky had figured largely in their westbound cargo trade.

The ships were also used for cruising, especially in the hard-pressed Depression years.

Both the *Transylvania* and the *Caledonia* were converted to armed merchant cruisers soon after the War was declared in September, 1939. Unfortunately, they were early casualties, sinking just two months apart in the summer of 1940. The *Caledonia*, which had been renamed *Scotstoun*, was torpedoed by a Nazi U-boat on June 13th; the *Transylvania* was hit on August 10th and later sank. Six perished on the former *Caledonia* and 48 on her sister.

The Anchor Line did not resume passenger service on the North Atlantic after the War, although they still ran cargo vessels. "They lost interest," according to Viez. "Many of their liners had been sunk and the third class migrant trade was gone. They did resume their other service, between Liverpool, Karachi and Bombay, though, with three passenger ships – the *Cilicia*, *Circassia* and a new *Caledonia* which came out in 1948."

The inbound *Transylvania* is seen in New York's Lower Bay on October 10th, 1938. Although very similar to the other Anchor trans-Atlantic liners built in the Twenties, the *Transylvania* and *Caledonia* were given a more imposing appearance, thanks to dummy funnels on either side of the single working stack. (CA/ME)

TRANSYLVANIA, CALEDONIA, CHITRAL and CATHAY

In addition to its North Atlantic and Indian services, the Glasgow-based Anchor Line, for some years a Cunard subsidiary, was well-known for its cruises out of New York, especially in the 'Thirties.. Here we see the *Caledonia* anchored in Havana harbor.

CATHAY (15,104 grt; 1925 - 1942)
CHITRAL (15,248 grt; 1925 - 1953)

The *Chitral* and her sister *Cathay* came from famous yards (Alexander Stephen and Barclay, Curle, respectively) but, recalled Frank Andrews, "They were not as fancy as the 1931-built *Carthage* and *Corfu*. They worked the U.K. - Australia trade but had originally been intended for P&O's Indian service.

In the 'Thirties, the Aussie trade was rather more demanding, whereas the P&O Indian sailings were mostly for army personnel and civil servants – a secure market, British government-sponsored. The Australia passenger trade was more competitive. Ships built specially for that run tended to have better décor as well as better food and service."

The *Cathay*, which carried a mere 306 passengers (203 first class and 103 second) plus cargo, was a victim of the Second World War. She was bombed and sunk by German aircraft off the coast of Algeria in November, 1942. The *Chitral* survived but was revived only as a migrant ship, still on the Australian run. She went to breakers in Scotland in 1953.

In a busy scene at Gibraltar, the *Chitral* is still wearing the original P&O livery with 'stone'-colored upperworks. Later, they were lightened and, eventually, painted white.
(*Laurence Dunn Collection*)

The First Post-War Liners

BERLIN (15,286 grt; 1925 - 1986)

The *Berlin* was one of the smaller, more intermediate German passenger ships built after the devastating First World War. She represented the more moderate pace of her owners, the North German Lloyd, as they re-emerged as an Atlantic passenger liner operator. Copied, to some extent, from the earlier but larger *Columbus*, she was followed within four years by two very different ships, the giant speed-sisters *Bremen* and *Europa*. Sadly, the *Berlin* would have a very tragic end – not for the Germans, but for the Soviets.

Before that, however, in October, 1937, she made interesting and mysterious headlines at New York when she was loaded with 6,000 tons of scrap metal, obviously sold to the Nazi government – but through intermediaries. She sailed from Pier 86 without even a single passenger. Just two weeks earlier, another Nazi-German liner, Hamburg America's *St. Louis*, had loaded 3,000 tons of scrap and she too had sailed eastbound without passengers. *Berlin* sailed for another year and then, in October, 1938, she was laid up in Bremerhaven, where she remained idle until the War, except for two cruises for the Nazis' 'Kraft durch Freude' organization in May, 1939. During the conflict, the *Berlin* was used as a hospital ship, but then struck a mine and sank off Swinemünde on February 1st, 1945. She was underwater for nearly four years before the Soviets, claiming the wreckage, successfully salvaged her and began an eight-year restoration and refit. She re-emerged in 1957 as the all-white, squat-stacked *Admiral Nakhimov*, trading mostly on the local Black Sea routes out of Odessa, with an occasional crossing to Havana in later years.

It was during a mini-cruise on September 15th, 1986, that the by now 61-year old liner met her end. Forty-five minutes after leaving the port of Novorossisk, she was rammed by another Soviet ship, the 41,000-ton bulk carrier *Pyotr Vasev*. The *Admiral Nakhimov* sank within 8 minutes and nearly 400 passengers and crew drowned in what was called one of the worst peacetime shipping disasters in Soviet history. The masters of both ships were later found to have been at fault and were given prison sentences.

Berthed on the north side of Pier 86 and with the Empire State Building on the horizon, the North German Lloyd *Berlin* loads scrap metal on October 14th, 1937. Sailing without passengers, she delivered her cargo for use in Nazi munitions factories. Note the "goose neck" cranes. (CA/ME)

THE FIRST POST-WAR LINERS

Wearing Swedish neutrality markings, the *Gripsholm* was used for diplomatic exchange service during the Second World War. She is seen here arriving in New York harbor on December 1st, 1943, bound for Pier F in Jersey City where she was to land exchange prisoners and some refugees. (CA/ME)

GRIPSHOLM (17,993 grt; 1925 - 1966)

Built by a British yard, Armstrong, Whitworth at Newcastle upon Tyne, the *Gripsholm* looked like a conventional steamship but was actually the North Atlantic's first large motorliner. (She had Danish-built Burmeister & Wain diesels). She ran in Swedish American Line's Gothenburg – New York service, but also made frequent cruises. Repainted white overall in 1932, she developed an impeccable reputation for superb service and splendid cuisine. "She was a beautiful ship on the inside," noted Everett Viez. "She had Old World charm, classic decorative styles – very traditional. She was, of course, spotless and after becoming all-white she looked like a big yacht. I much preferred her to the slightly larger *Kungsholm* that

arrived three years later, in 1928." The *Gripsholm* served as an International Red Cross exchange ship during the War, carrying prisoners, the wounded, evacuees and diplomatic personnel. As a consequence, she was able to resume service quickly, in 1946, but then had a major refit in 1949-50, emerging with two new, wider funnels which were more pleasing.

In February, 1954, she became West Germany's first full-scale post-War passenger liner when, still as the *Gripsholm*, she began sailing for the new Bremen-America Line (owned 50% by Swedish American and 50% by the slowly reviving North German Lloyd). The following year, she passed into full Lloyd ownership as the *Berlin*. She was not retired for another eleven years, being demolished in Italy in the winter of 1966-67.

The Scottish-built *Conte Biancamano*, here seen in 1932 in the Italian Line livery, was an enlarged and improved version of her forerunners and fleetmates *Conte Rosso* and *Conte Verde*. The three vessels were products of the Dalmuir-based shipyard of William Beardmore, thanks to his friendship with Guglielmo Marconi, president of the shipowning company Lloyd Sabaudo.

CONTE BIANCAMANO (24,416 grt; 1925 - 1960)
CONTE GRANDE (25,661 grt; 1928 - 1961)

Built for the Lloyd Sabaudo's Genoa – New York service, these near-sisters were integrated into the combined fleet of the new Italian Line in 1932. For some years, Lloyd Sabaudo had a close connection with the William Beardmore company of Glasgow and it was from their shipyard that the *Conte Biancamano* came in 1925. The later *Conte Grande* was Italian-built, however, by the Trieste-based Stabilimento Tecnico. Both passed into American hands during the War, serving as the troopships *Hermitage* and *Monticello*, respectively. They were returned to the Italians in 1947 and were extensively rebuilt for use mainly on the Genoa – South America route, although they did also see service on the New York run. Everett Viez remembered, "Before the War, these nice-looking liners were typically Italian baroque on the inside. They were very ornate and very beautiful, like castles. But after being gutted and refitted by the Americans and then refurbished by the Italians, they lost their great charms. They were no longer Italian baroque, but Italian modern."

They became, in fact, the forerunners of the long series of stylish, modern liners which the Italians introduced in the post-War years. Both went to the breakers in the early 'Sixties, although a portion of the forward superstructure of the *Conte Biancamano*, including the bridge and the first class ball room, was carefully disassembled and rebuilt at the "Leonardo da Vinci" science museum in Milan, where it can still be admired.

Although very similar to the *Conte Biancamano*, the *Conte Grande* was built in Trieste. Like many Italian liners of the period, both were notable for their rich interiors. Much remodelled, the two ships went on to give good service after the Second World War.

The First Class dining room of the *Conte Grande*. She was one of the most hyper-decorated liners ever.

The *Conte Biancamano* interiors were less elaborate, more conservative than those of her sistership *Conte Grande*.

A product of the Barclay, Curle yard, like many British India Line vessels, the classic-looking *Rajula* was an unglamorous but much-loved ship which carried enormous numbers of Indian and Malayan passengers during a career which lasted nearly fifty years. *(Alex Duncan)*

RAJULA (8,704 grt; 1926 - 1976)

In years past, in the days of British and European colonialism, and long before to-day's era of sleek, hotel-like cruiseships, Singapore was a very busy passenger port, a great crossroads. Mostly, the passenger vessels that called there were not fancy, pleasure-filled luxury liners, but hardworking and often quite austere steamers. Despite her old-fashioned machinery and modest speed, one of the very best-known was the evocatively named *Rajula*.

In 1988, when I was sailing along Alaska's Inside Passage aboard Princess Cruises' *Royal Princess*, I reminisced about ships like the old *Rajula* with Ian Tompkins, then a Deputy Captain onboard. He had served in her. Compared with the contemporary age of bow thrusters and satellite navigation, computer technology and in-cabin television, the era of the 1926-built *Rajula* seemed like centuries rather than decades ago. Built by Barclay, Curle on the Clyde for the British India Steam Navigation Company, part of the huge P&O group, she was designed as a "workhorse" for a then busy route of that long-vanished British Empire. She sailed across the Bay of Bengal, from Madras in India to Penang in Malaya and to Singapore. In fact, after leaving the ship-yard, *Rajula* never saw British waters again. Her work, and that of her sister *Rohna*, was strictly in the East. With British officers but a mainly Goanese and Indian crew, and fitted with very basic quarters, the *Rajula* had in those pre-War years, the highest peacetime capacity ever to put to sea – over 5,000 passengers in all. Considering her rather small size, this was even more extraordinary. The biggest liner in the World in the mid-'twenties, the 56,000-ton *Majestic* carried 3,000 passengers – 2,000 less than the 8,700-ton *Rajula*. This British India ship, and others like her, had been built for a booming trade, certainly one that was guaranteed and where fares were low and passengers expected little in the way of amenity or comfort.

During the Second World War, she served as a trooper and also as a hospital ship. Afterward, she returned to her original trade but, in view of Indian independence as well as new regulations, she became somewhat more comfortable, somewhat less crowded. Her capacity was cut drastically – to 1,750 or so, with a mere 37 in first class and 133 in second. The remainder were in so-called "deck class", travelling without cabins or even bunks.

Ian Tompkins remembered: "We carried Indian businessmen and traders in the cabin quarters, in first and second class. But our biggest trade was with Indian workers in deck class – there was a steady relay of them to and from the big Malaysian rubber plantations. For her small size, she seemed to have enormous deck spaces, which we used to the fullest for these deck passengers. It was "rough accommodations", of course. They lived on the open decks under awnings, between and around the cargo hatches, and they brought their own bedding and utensils. There were public toilets and general cooking facilities."

Housekeeping on a forty-year old, crowded ship was evidently quite a chore. According to Captain Tompkins, "In the first and second class quarters, there was lots of brass and woodwork, but to the very end she was always a ship of 'spit and polish'. Especially on the return runs to Madras, when we had less passengers, every part of the *Rajula* was scrubbed and cleaned. And she had fantastic stability. Of course, there weren't any stabilizers but she was just an amazingly solid old ship."

She was finally retired by British India in 1974, from a by then largely shrunken British worldwide passenger fleet, but there were some loyalists – mostly former crewmembers – who wanted to save her. She might have been a wonderful reminder of that vanished era of British colonial passenger steamers. In fact, the Indians bought her and renamed her *Rangat*, using her for a couple more years before handing her over to Bombay scrappers. She was in service just short of 50 years. Indeed, the *Rajula* was an amazing old ship!

ROMA and AUGUSTUS

ROMA (32,583 grt; 1926 - 1946)
AUGUSTUS (32,650 grt; 1927 - 1945)

These fine ships, built for NGI, Navigazione Generale Italiana, were Italy's largest and grandest liners prior to the *Rex* and *Conte di Savoia* of 1932. The *Roma* was given conventional steam turbines, whereas the *Augustus* had diesels and ranked as the largest motorliner in the World. Integrated into the fleet of the new Italian Line in 1932, they sailed both on the North Atlantic route from Genoa to New York, sometimes teamed with the larger *Rex* and *Conte di Savoia* in the express service, and across the South Atlantic to the East Coast of South America. They also made cruises. It was planned to rebuild them in 1939 with more powerful machinery as well as modernized exteriors, but this never came to pass. Instead, after the start of the War, they were selected for conversion to become the Italian Navy's largest aircraft carriers. Work on the *Roma* started first, in October, 1940, but by the time she was nearly complete and renamed *Aquila* in the summer of 1943, she was taken over by the Nazi occupation forces. In 1945, both the Italian partisans and the Germans tried to sink her. After the War, plans to rebuild her as a passenger ship proved unfeasible and she was scrapped. The *Augustus* was still being transformed into the carrier *Sparviero* when she fell into German hands. In their retreat, the Nazis sank her so as to block the harbor entrance at Genoa. Her remains were later broken up on the spot.

The *Roma*, here seen in her cruising white livery, was a steamer, while the otherwise similar *Augustus* was the World's largest motor-driven passenger ship when completed in 1927. They were the pride of the Italian merchant fleet until the debut of the superliners *Rex* and *Conte di Savoia* in 1932.

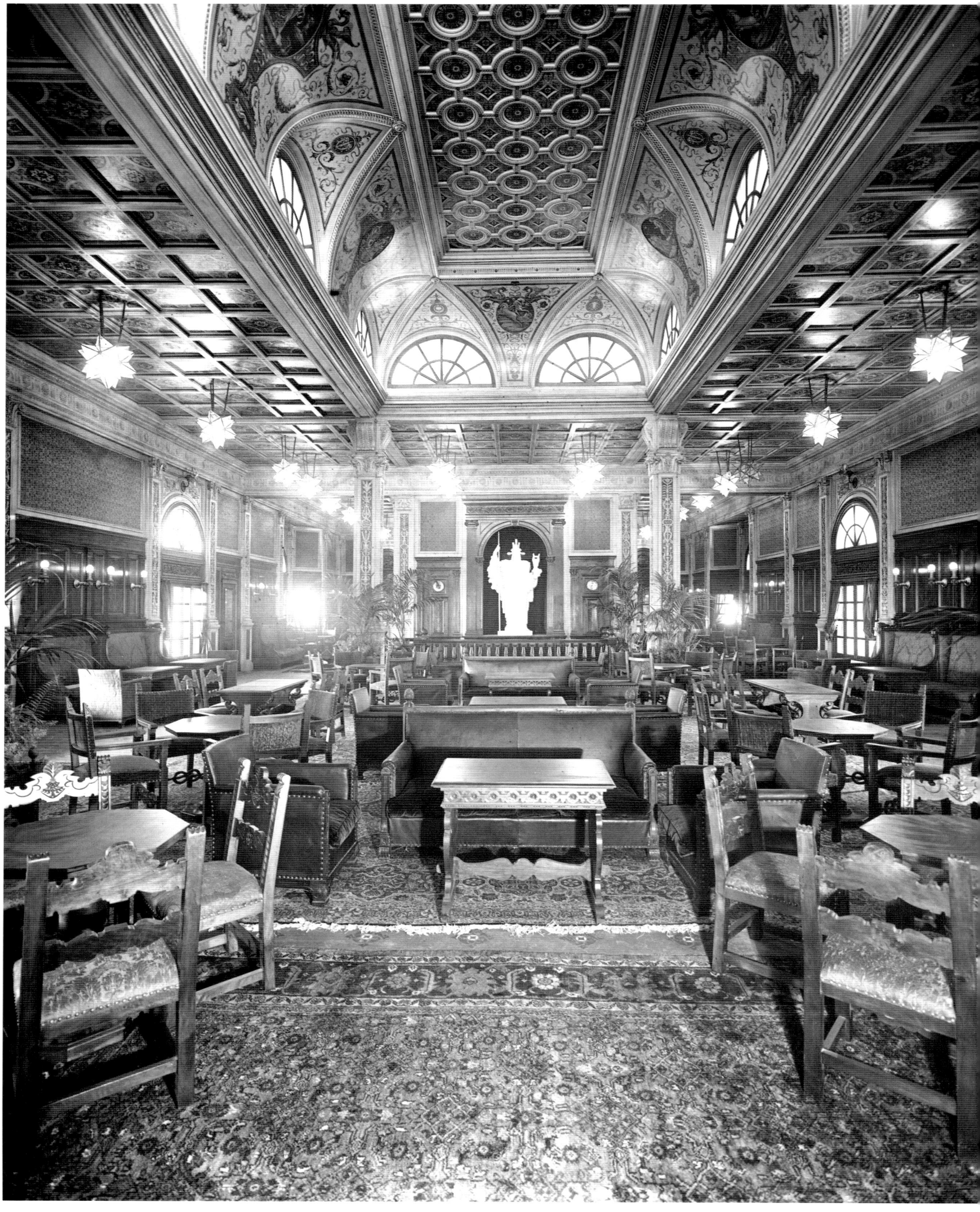

In brisk North Atlantic weather, a wave breaks over the foredeck of the *Augustus*, the largest motor ship of her time. (*Frank Pichardo Collection*)

Originally built for the Navigazione Generale Italiana, the *Augustus* and *Roma* were transferred to the new Italian Line in 1932. The *Augustus*, here seen leaving Genoa, was the largest Italian ship until the advent of the *Rex*, which is visible on the right, being fitted out.

Previous page: the highly baroque Ceremonial Lounge of the *Roma* was dominated by a statue of the Goddess after whom the vessel was named and which is now preserved in the maritime station at Genoa.

The First Post-War Liners

Despite her staid appearance, the German-built Athos II was one of the most popular and long-lasting of the passenger-cargo liners belonging to the Messageries Maritimes. She was one of the mainstays of their Marseilles - Far East service. (Richard Faber Collection)

ATHOS II (15,275 grt; 1927 - 1959)

France's colonial links out to Indo-China supported a busy passenger service run by the Marseilles-based Messageries Maritimes. One of their largest ships on this Far Eastern route, which ran via Port Said, Suez and Djibouti to Colombo, Madras, Rangoon, Singapore, Bangkok, Saigon, Haiphong, Hong Kong, Manila, Shanghai, Kobe and Yokohama, was the staid-looking, German-built *Athos II*, with that suffix indicating that she was the company's second ship of that name, the first one having being sunk during the First World War.

She had a near-sister, *D'Artagnan*, built in France and their accommodations reflected their trade – a large cargo capacity and berths for 420 passengers (165 in first class, 155 second and 100 third). The voyage from Marseilles to Yokohama took some 42 days in the 'Thirties. First class fares started at $420, second class at $330 and third at $190.

In late 1937 she underwent a long refitting at La Ciotat; in the process her passenger accommodation was improved and two additional turbines were installed, increasing her maximum speed by 2.5 knots, up to 18.5. In this way she could match the speed of the motorhips *Félix Roussel* and *Aramis*, her running mates, which had also undergone improvements in the same yard earlier. At the beginning of the War, the French goverment requisitioned twelve passenger ships to transform them into auxiliary cruisers. They were allocated, two by two, to six divisions. The sixth one was composed of the *Mexique* and, as an alternative option, the *Athos II* or the *Aramis* of Messageries Maritimes.

The *Athos II*, however, remained idle at Algiers at the start of the War, until July, 1940, when she made a repatriation voyage carrying French soldiers from Alexandria to Marseilles. From December, 1942, she served as an Allied trooper before resuming peacetime Far Eastern sailings in 1946. She was broken-up in Italy in 1959. While lacking the trans-Atlantic prestige and style of the French Line ships, she was nevertheless one of France's more interesting liners.

ATHOS II and ALCANTARA

Taken up for war service in 1939, the *Alcantara* had her forward funnel, a dummy, removed. She survived the War and afterwards, still with only one funnel, she gave her owners a further ten years of service on the South American route. *(Roger Sherlock Collection)*

ALCANTARA (22,181 grt; 1927 - 1958)

Among the finest liners ever to sail the South American run, the *Alcantara* and her sister, the *Asturias* (1926), were the pride of Britain's Royal Mail Lines. They sailed from Southampton via Lisbon and Las Palmas and then across the South Atlantic to Rio de Janeiro, Santos, Montevideo and Buenos Aires; and also in the 1930s they ran cruises. Built by the illustrious Harland & Wolff yard at Belfast, they were trendy-looking ships with long, low superstructures and twin squat, motor ship stacks. At first, they were powered by Burmeister & Wain-type diesels but both sisters underwent extensive rebuilding in 1934, when their diesel engines were replaced by steam turbines, which increased their service speed by a full 2 knots, up to 19. They now had two large funnels, which gave them a different, more powerful appearance.

Although the *Asturias* was torpedoed in 1943, she remained afloat and was later repaired. She became a fulltime trooper and then a migrant ship. She went to shipbreakers at Faslane in Scotland in 1957 but before being scrapped she served as a set for the movie *A Night To Remember*, the story of the *Titanic*. The *Alcantara*, on the other hand, was transformed into an auxiliary merchant cruiser, and at over 21,000 grt was the largest ever to serve as such for the Royal Navy, together with the *Queen of Bermuda*. Her forward, dummy stack was removed.

Critically damaged off Rio de Janeiro in July, 1940 during a gun battle, she was later refitted at Birkenhead as a troop transport. She returned to the South American run after her war service in October, 1948, following a lenghty refit by her builders. She was now partnered with the splendid *Andes* of 1939. She was sold to Japanese breakers in May, 1958. For the voyage out to the East, she was specially renamed *Kaisho Maru*. Her end came at Osaka, in a location where another pre-War liner, the famous *Ile de France*, would be finished off the following year.

The First Post-War Liners

ARANDORA and BERMUDA

Arandora Star, originally *Arandora*, underwent several refits which transformed her from a passenger and cargo liner in the South American trade into one of the best British cruise ships of the 'Thirties.
Here we see her in September, 1938 alongside the jetty at Palmers Hebburn Co. On the other bank of the Tyne, the *Dominion Monarch*, the largest liner ever built for Shaw, Savill & Albion, is being fitted out at the yard of Swan, Hunter & Wigham Richardson.

(*Laurence Dunn Collection*)

ARANDORA (12,847 grt; 1927 - 1940)

The *Arandora* began life in May, 1927 as a combination passenger-cargo ship on the London – East Coast of South America run; she was the last of five sisters built almost simultaneously for Britain's Blue Star Line, the others being the *Almeda*, *Andalucia*, *Avila* and *Avelona*. Their Spanish names caused confusion with the similar names used by Royal Mail liners, and, in May, 1929, the word 'Star' was added to them. The *Almeda*-class were Blue Star's first passenger vessels. The company had been built up in the early 1900s to participate on the frozen meat trade.

When renamed *Arandora Star*, the ship was at the Fairfield yard for the first of many refits that made her one of Britain's finest and most popular cruise ships in the 'Thirties. She re-emerged with a white hull and minus her funnel-cowls and now had superb accommodations for 354 first class-only passengers. She underwent further alterations in 1934 and again two years later, when her main mast was removed, in an effort to overcome her tendency to excessive rolling.

She sailed to the Mediterranean, West Africa, Scandinavia, the Baltic capitals, around the British Isles and crossed to the Caribbean in the winter. She was one of the earliest ships to call at Miami, then an infant Florida port but today the cruiseship capital. Unfortunately, the *Arandora Star* was an early wartime loss. While sailing off Ireland on July 2nd, 1940, carrying German and Italian prisoners of war, she was torpedoed by a German submarine with the tragic loss of 761 souls.

BERMUDA (19,086 grt; 1927 - 1932)

The vacation run between New York and Bermuda, a mere two-night trip of some 600 miles, became increasingly popular during the 'Twenties and with the adoption of the Eighteenth Amendment to the American constitution and the start of Prohibition, the attractions of the sub-tropical Bermudas were further enhanced. The Furness-Bermuda Line, an offshoot of the British shipping giant Furness Withy, dominated this trade and, after using second hand tonnage for some years, they saw fit to order a luxury liner for the route. She was built at the Workman, Clark yard at Belfast and carried 616 first class passengers and a token 75 in second class.

"She was probably the prettiest Furness liner of them all," said Everett Viez. "Although a little stubby (and nearly 40 feet shorter than the subsequent *Monarch of Bermuda* and

The First Post-War Liners

Hugely successful but sadly short-lived, the elegant, British-owned *Bermuda* was the first large luxury liner to run continuous New York - Bermuda passenger and cruise service. She is seen here in the Hudson River, having just left Pier 95, Manhattan. (CA/ME)

Tragedy: watched by curious onlookers, fire rages aboard the *Bermuda* as she lies at her Front Street berth at Hamilton, Bermuda in the morning of June 16th, 1931. The blaze was eventually brought under control but virtually the whole superstructure had been destroyed. (CA/ME)

More tragedy: five months later, after being towed to the Workman, Clark yard at Belfast to be rebuilt, the *Bermuda* suffered a further fire. This time, she was completely burned out. Nearby, at Harland & Wolff, the White Star *Georgic* was being fitted out. As yet, she had only one of her two funnels. (CA/ME)

Queen of Bermuda) she had classic lines. She had the most attractive public rooms. And she cost only $10 - $12,000,000 to build."

Unfortunately, she had a very short life, and then further tragedies even in the end.

While docked at Hamilton in the early morning of June 16th, 1931, she caught fire and was heavily damaged. "When the *Bermuda* burned, there were still horse-drawn fire-fighting wagons on Bermuda," added Viez. "This tragic fire led to the introduction of motorized fire trucks on the island. It was a sad accident to a fine ship."

Towed back to Belfast a month later for repairs, she burned again that November and sank at the outfitting quay of her original builders. She was refloated on Christmas eve but, by now declared a total loss and abandoned to the insurers, the hulk was bought by the yard. They gutted her upperworks and then could remove and salvage her four precious Doxford oil engines, still intact.

What remained of the former handsome liner was sold to scrappers at Rosyth. But while being towed there in June, 1932, she went aground along the Scottish coast and was eventually destroyed by the sea.

Such had been the success of the *Bermuda*, Funess Bermuda Line had ordered a running mate, *Monarch of Bermuda*. Now she was urgently needed as a replacement but was not yet ready. Several transatlantic liners had to be chartered - not difficult to find in those years - including *Veendam*, the *Franconia*, the *Carinthia* and the *Duchess of Bedford*.

THE FIRST POST-WAR LINERS

A time of crisis: the *New York* was the last German ship to leave an American port with commercial passengers before the start of the Second World War. The date is August 28th, 1939 and this view is taken from the inbound *Normandie*. (CA/ME)

NEW YORK (21,455 grt; 1927 - 1949)

The *New York* and her sister *Hamburg* were built as follow-ups to the earlier *Albert Ballin* and *Deutschland* and were very similar to that pair – not express liners but solid, very comfortable ships. The *New York* was given more powerful engines in 1930 and was lengthened in 1934. She ran in the weekly Hamburg - Channel ports - New York service until the start of the Second World War. In the spring of 1945, she was used in the German evacuation of the Eastern territories and was then bombed and set afire while lying at Kiel in April. Her wreck was raised and towed to Britain for scrapping in 1949. The *Hamburg*, too, was involved in the evacuation from the East but hit two mines while at Sassnitz in March, 1945. In 1950, she was raised by the Soviets for restoration as a passenger ship, the *Yuri Dolgoruki*. The process was almost complete when Soviet officials changed their minds and, instead, had her further reworked as a whaling fleet mother ship. She finally entered service in 1960 after a refit which had taken ten years. She was scrapped in 1977.

A corner of the first class Social Hall on the *New York* of the Hamburg America Line. She and her three running mates were well-known for their midnight sailings from New York. (CA/ME)

The great *Cap Arcona* at her homeport of Hamburg in 1939. She is flying the swastika and ahead of her lies the Nazi cruise ship *Wilhelm Gustloff*. Both were sunk with horrific loss of life at the end of the Second World War, in 1945. *(Richard Faber Collection)*

CAP ARCONA (27,560 grt; 1927 - 1945)

"She was a very special ship, the finest of her day on the Europe – South America run. She was also very modern for her time," according to Arnold Kludas. "And she was popular. Every year, for example, usually in July, she made a luxury cruise from Buenos Aires to Montevideo, Santos and Rio de Janeiro, limited to 500 rich South American passengers."

Built by Blohm & Voss at Hamburg, she was the best ship of the Hamburg – South America Line (known in Germany as Hamburg-Sud). Based on the earlier *Cap Polonio*, she was a grand three-stacker and could make the run from Hamburg to Buenos Aires in just over two weeks. She had fine quarters for 1,315 passengers in three classes. Expectedly, first class was the most notable – all cabins in this class had private bathrooms as well as lots of daylight. The dining room, with no less than 20 panoramic windows, was placed above the Promenade Deck, then a very unusual feature, and other amenities included a heatable saltwater swimming pool with an air-bubbling plant, a large gymnasium and an extensive sports deck that included a full tennis court. Beloved at her homeport of Hamburg, she was claimed to be "the most wonderful ship in the German merchant navy."

Unfortunately, she met with a horrific end. Used as an accommodation ship at Gdynia during the War, she was pressed into service in the winter and spring of 1945 as an evacuation ship from the Nazi-occupied Eastern territories. In all, she carried 26,000 people to 'safety' in the West. But on May 3rd, 1945, just days before the official end of the War, the *Cap Arcona* was attacked by British bombers and set afire off Neustadt, in the Bay of Lübeck. She was loaded with over 6,000 souls, guards, crew but mostly inmates from the

The First Post-War Liners

Neuengamme Concentration Camp. Despite being relatively close to the shore, the vessel soon rolled over and the majority of those on board remained trapped: the disaster claimed over 5,000 (some estimates say over 5,200) lives.

Dr. Horst Uppenburg, then a young naval cadet in the faltering German Navy, recalled seeing the *Cap Arcona* at that time: "The ship's officers had refused to take command and so the SS forced a freighter captain to take over. The British forces were very, very close and the War was just about over. RAF 'planes bombed the ship in error. They did not know she was carrying camp inmates. Using the *Cap Arcona* in the first place was a Nazi party decision and not a military one. The plan was to kill the prisoners and sink the ship. No matter, there would have been further atrocity."

Kludas concludes, "After the War, in 1950, Hamburg-Sud actually thought of entering the Hamburg-New York run with a new 40.000-ton *Cap Arcona*, but the plan never developed. They also hoped to build big new ships for the Hamburg – Rio de Janeiro – Buenos Aires service but there was a lack of encouragement by the South American countries. They supported the Argentinian lines instead and Hamburg-Sud contented themselves with some combo ships carrying a limited number of passengers."

Aglow with lights, the *Cap Arcona* prepares for another midnight sailing from the Overseas Landing Stage at Hamburg. The pride of the Hamburg-South America Line, she was one of the very finest liners on the route between Europe and the East Coast of South America.

(Richard Faber Collection)

The *Malolo* was an innovative ship, the first of four superb liners which secured the Matson Line's position in the services from the West Coast of America to Honolulu and to Australia. Here she is seen as the renamed *Matsonia* after being modernized in 1938. (CA/ME)

MALOLO (17,232 grt; 1927 - 1978)

Built at the famous William Cramp yard at Philadelphia, the *Malolo* was the first true luxury liner for the then infant California – Hawaii tourist trade. Splendidly appointed, she carried only 693 all-first class passengers. She had been designed by William Francis Gibbs, who went on to create the *America* (1940) and the speed champion, *United States* (1952), among others. She was nearly lost in a collision while on her trials in May, 1927 but, such was the attention to safety that Gibbs had lavished on her, she remained afloat and could be repaired. "She was the prettiest of the Matson liners of the 'Thirties but not the best 'sea boat'," according to Everett Viez. "She was dubbed 'the holy roller of the Pacific'. But she had great interiors, high standards and brought the Matson company to luxury levels."

She was refitted and modernized in 1937 and became the *Matsonia*, still on the Hawaiian run. She trooped during the War and then briefly returned to Matson Line service, but was sold to one of the Home Lines companies in 1948. At first, she sailed as the *Atlantic* under the Panamanian flag and then, after 1954, as the Greek-registered *Queen Frederica*.

Very long-lived, she was last used as a Mediterranean cruise ship in the early 'Seventies. She was then idle from 1973 to 1977 before catching fire while being broken up in 1978. The hull was later scrapped.

Long and low, the Italian *Saturnia* (seen here) and *Vulcania* were examples of "motorliner style" in the late 'Twenties and early 'Thirties. Although very modern externally, they were among the last liners to have ornate, traditional interiors. Both ships were immensely popular and had long and successful careers.

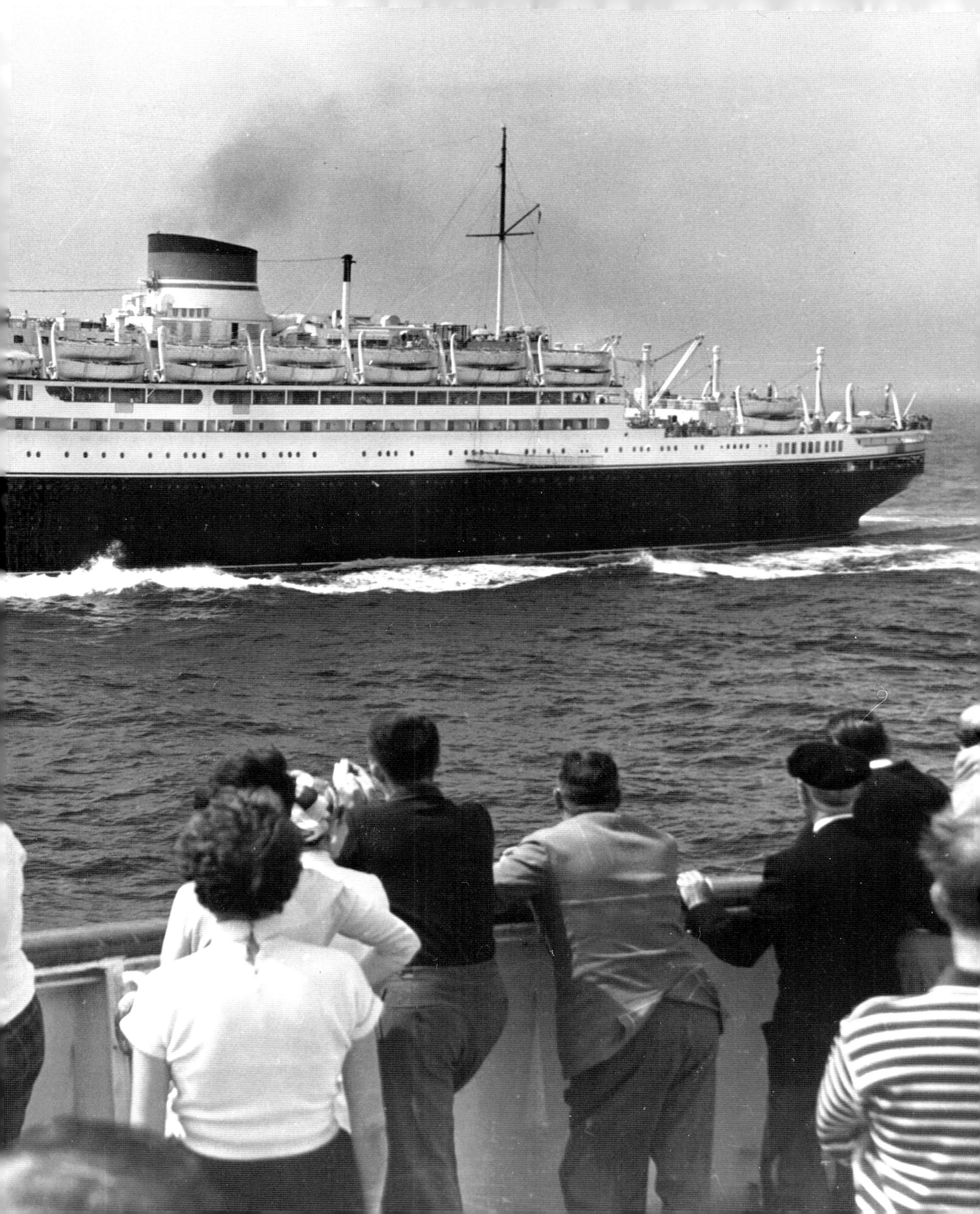

THE FIRST POST-WAR LINERS

The First Class writing gallery on board the Vulcania. She and her sister ship Saturnia gained a well-deserved reputation for their luxurious interiors. They remained virtually unaltered after the War, offering a voyage into the past to their post-war passengers.

SATURNIA (23,940 grt; 1927 - 1965)
VULCANIA (23,970 grt; 1928 - 1974)

"These ships were very charming. We tended to discount them in the 'Thirties because of their flat profiles and stump funnels," said Everett Viez. "But, on the inside, they were Italian baroque to the hilt. They were like cathedrals gone to sea. They were also novel - they introduced the private verandah to ocean liner travel. There was an entire deck of first class cabins with verandahs. It was the first time ever and not just for a few, but for many. Those cabins were top drawer and very much in demand, especially on the warm weather Mediterranean run. The two ships were also favored for their fine Italian cuisine and service. The Cosulich Line of Trieste, their original owners, had an excellent reputation and maintained the highest onboard standards."

In 1932, the Cosulich Line fleet was included in the amalgamation which created the new Italian Line, although the name Cosulich persisted for a few more years. Used on the Trieste - New York run, the *Saturnia* and *Vulcania* were among the largest and finest motorliners of their time. After Mussolini entered the War in 1940, however, they were rarely used. Then, after the Italian surrender in the fall of 1943, both liners fled to Allied waters. Two years later, the *Saturnia* became the American hospital ship *Frances Y. Slanger* before reverting to her original Italian name. Both ships resumed sailing for the Italian Line in 1947 and remained in service until 1965. The *Saturnia* then went to the breakers, while the *Vulcania* found further service with another Italian shipowner, the Siosa Line, who renamed her *Caribia*. She sailed in Europe - Caribbean service and later exclusively on cruises. However, she grounded off Cannes in September, 1972 and was considered too old for costly repairs. She went to Spanish shipbreakers the following year, but they resold her to Taiwanese scrappers. She sank in Kaohsiung harbor on July 20th, 1974 but was later pumped out and broken-up.

A NEW GENERATION, A NEW STYLE

Hitherto, most ocean liners had been given traditional interiors, their first class public rooms often imitating the fashions of previous ages. But times were changing: a new, less ornate but more startling, more modern style was emerging which in later years would be given the name 'Art Déco'. An exhibition staged in Paris in 1925, L'Exposition des Arts Décoratifs et Industriels Modernes, attracted huge attention. It was only a matter of time before the new style went to sea. The *Ile de France* of 1927 marked its entry into the world of the ocean liner. She was a sensation. While some ships were still being built with the old-fashioned interiors which many passengers found most comfortable, things would never be the same again.

The Germans pushed this re-thinking of the ocean liner style even further, with their greyhounds *Bremen* and *Europa*. While the *Ile de France* still had a traditional exterior, with three tall cylindrical stacks and a flat fronted superstructure, the North German Lloyd sisters sported racy, streamlined profiles, with two low funnels placed further forward than usual, enhancing the impression of speed. A few years later, in 1932, the two legendary Italian superliners *Rex* and *Conte di Savoia* clearly expressed the paradox between the old and new schools.

While the owners of the *Rex* decided to re-design the profile of their vessel while she was still on the drawing board, her interiors remained faithful to the old classic style, although less baroque than those of previous members of the fleet. The *Conte di Savoia* interiors, on the other hand, reflected the changing tastes of the 'Thirties. She was one of the best example of modernism at sea, but not quite everywhere. When the board of directors saw the mock ups for the First Class lounges, some of them were shocked by the plain design and the ample use of modern materials such as polished stainless steel. They rejected the design for the main lounge and commissioned another architect to create the most classic design possible, to compensate for the 'avant garde' of the other rooms. Ironically, this spectacular ballroom, called the 'Colonna Hall', became the best known feature of the ship and the *Conte di Savoia* has often been erroneously considered one of the several 'old fashioned' Italian vessels of the time.

The *Ile de France* at speed. Despite her traditional-looking external profile, her 'Art Déco' interiors were new and sensational, when she debuted on the Atlantic in 1927. She made an extraordinary and unexpected contrast with her French fleetmates, which had often been referred to as 'castles at sea' because of their elaborate interiors. (CA/ME)

A New Generation, A New Style

Off to war: with her superstructure now painted gray, the *Ile de France* is seen departing from her lay-up at Staten Island. The date is May 1st, 1940 and, loaded with war materials, the great liner is bound for the Far East. (CA/ME)

ILE DE FRANCE (43,153 grt; 1927 - 1958)

Built as a follow-up to the highly successful *Paris* of 1921, the *Ile*, as she was widely known, was added to the French Line fleet in 1927. Although she continued with the basic three-funnel design of the earlier ship, her interiors were nothing short of revolutionary. Previous passenger ships, especially the larger Atlantic liners, had for years tended to copy land-based styles – imitating palaces, mansions, country houses, hunting lodges and sometimes adopting exotic Arabian, Egyptian or Moorish themes. Now, the *Ile* introduced the new style to the high seas. She epitomised the "Roaring Twenties".

This was an age of streamlined design, white pianos, glossy floors and geometric-patterned upholsteries. "Not to copy, but to create" was the motto.

She was a raving success and many liners followed her example. Some of the more daring designers of shoreside structures and décor took up the ocean liner theme. "She had stunning public rooms," said Frank Braynard, "but they were rather oddly contained in a ship of quite conservative exterior design. Actually, she was quite ordinary as a three-stacker. I think she looked better after the Second World War when the original three funnels were replaced by two of wider, more proportioned design." She was, of course, a predecessor to the magnificent, even more impressive *Normandie*, which first appeared on the Le Havre – New York run eight years later.

The *Ile* had a heroic war, sailing as a trooper for the Allies, at first under P&O management and then Cunard-White Star. She was the only survivor of the larger French Line ships and when she returned to the Atlantic route, she was paired with the refurbished *Liberté* which had been the *Europa* of the North German Lloyd.

Sold to Japanese breakers at the end of 1958, the *Ile* appeared in the film *The Last Voyage*, playing the rôle of the fictional *Claridon*, a doomed trans-Pacific liner, before meeting the wreckers at Osaka.

ILE DE FRANCE

'The patron has to know how to handle thin stemmed glassware and shall take the necessary time to properly choose its contents'; with such an admonition in her brochure, 'limiting the entry' of her guests to the smoking room (or cocktail lounge), the *Ile the France* was an oasis where Americans could quench their thirsts during the years of Prohibition.

A corner of the 'Salon Mixte' on board the *Ile the France*. The uplit sconces in Sèvres porcelain were the work of Ruhemann, while the large oil on canvas on the wall was by Jean Dupas.
(Paolo Piccione Collection)

A New Generation, A New Style

The luxurious Swedish-American motorliner *Kungsholm*, completed in 1928, had noticeably more modern interiors than her consort, the *Gripsholm* of 1925. In the winter of 1940, with Europe at war, she ran cruises from New York to the Caribbean and is here seen making a call at the Port of Miami. *(CA/ME)*

KUNGSHOLM (20,233 grt; 1928 - 1965)

"She was quite different from the *Gripsholm* of just three years earlier. The *Kungsholm* came from German builders, Blohm & Voss of Hamburg, and not only had a nicer appearance but broke the decorative trend of the early Swedish American Line ships," noted Everett Viez. "She started Scandinavian modern, a sort of Viking contemporary with Art Deco touches. I actually preferred *Gripsholm* but there was no denying that *Kungsholm* was a very nice ship. She had the same top-notch service and cooking. She was always full, especially on cruises."

In 1942, she was sold to the US Government and refitted as the trooper *USS John Ericsson*. Damaged by fire while at New York in 1947, she was then resold to the Swedish American Line. They in turn passed her to one of the component companies of the newly-formed Home Lines, in which they had a financial interest.

Based in Genoa, she flew the Panamanian flag. Renamed *Italia*, she went on the Italy - South America service and later on the North Atlantic run to New York and to Canada.

She was made over to a fulltime cruiseship in late 1960 and established Home Lines' very successful New York – Nassau cruise service. Sold in 1964 to Bahamian interests, she became the short-lived *Imperial Bahama Hotel* moored at Freeport before slipping into bankruptcy. She was auctioned-off to Spanish scrappers in 1965.

The *Nieuw Zeeland* manoeuvring in the Bay of Sydney in a photograph dated July 21st, 1930, with the famous bridge in the background still under construction. At a service speed of 15 knots, she and her sister ship *Nieuw Holland* took almost four months to complete a round trip. *(Laurence Dunn Collection)*

NIEUW HOLLAND (10,903 grt; 1928 - 1959)
NIEUW ZEELAND (10,906 grt; 1928 - 1942)

These Dutch liners, belonging to KPM (the Koninklijke Paketvaart Maatschappij), worked in Eastern waters, linking the Dutch East Indies and Australia. They were regular visitors to Melbourne and were well remembered by Frank Andrews, who saw them in the 'Thirties. "They were absolutely gorgeous ships! Like the German liners, the Dutch ships had attractive winter gardens. They made good use of potted plants and this left a nice impression on a visitor such as myself. These sisters were also two of the best-looking ships ever. They had perfect balance and shapely counter sterns. They were like two beautiful yachts."
During the War they were taken over by the British and used mainly for the Mediterranena campaign.
The *Nieuw Zeeland* was torpedoed in the Mediterranean in November, 1942 but the *Nieuw Holland* survived the War and went back to her original route in 1947 for the new concern Koninklijke Java China Paketvaart Linjen. She was sold for scrap in Hong Kong in February, 1959.

On board the the *Nieuw Holland* (pictured) and the *Nieuw Zeeland*, the 63 First Class cabins were large and commmfortable, with many of them having an old fashioned entrance from the exterior promenade to cope with the hot climates of the long journey 'down under'. *(Laurence Dunn Collection)*

A New Generation, A New Style

The *Duchess of Atholl* was one of a class of four Clyde-built liners which, until the coming of the fabulous *Empress of Britain*, were the mainstays of Canadian Pacific's service between Liverpool and the St. Lawrence. The *Duchess of Atholl* was lost during the Second World War but two of her sisters re-emerged as 'Empresses'. *(Richard Faber Collection)*

DUCHESS OF ATHOLL (20,119 grt; 1928 - 1943)

Canadian Pacific ordered four fine sisters for their Liverpool – Montreal service, as well as cruising, in the late-'Twenties. The *Duchess of Atholl* was the first, being completed at the William Beardmore yard at Glasgow in the summer of 1928. She was unfortunately sunk in the South Atlantic in October, 1942. Of her sisters, the *Duchess of Bedford* had the longest career: after war service, she was briefly renamed *Empress of India*, and then *Empress of France*, and sailed the North Atlantic until 1960, when she was broken-up in Wales. The *Duchess of Richmond* was also revived after the War, as the *Empress of Canada*, but then burned and capsized at her Liverpool berth in January, 1953. Although later righted, she was sold to Italian breakers in the fall of 1954. The fourth sister had originally been intended as the *Duchess of Cornwall* but she was, in fact, named *Duchess of York* for the lady who later became Queen Elizabeth and then Queen Elizabeth, the Queen Mother. This ship, too, was a war casualty, being bombed off the coast of Portugal in July, 1943. Her burning wreckage was later sunk by an Allied warship.

VIRGINIA (20,773 grt; 1928 - 1964)
PENNSYLVANIA (20,526 grt; 1929 - 1964)

The *Pennsylvania* and her sister ships *Virginia* and *California* were built by the Newport News shipyard for the Panama Pacific Line's New York – San Francisco service through the Panama Canal. They were the largest passenger vessels ever built for the US intercoastal trade and they were the first in the World fitted with turbo-electric propulsion: they had two 8,500 HP electric motors manufactured by General Electric, giving them a speed of up to 18.5 knots. They could carry about 750 passengers, half in First Class and half in Tourist Class, plus considerable cargo and had been ordered as replacements for the company's elderly *Finland*, *Manchuria* and *Mongolia*.

Intended to be single-stackers, they were completed instead with two funnels.

Everett Viez opined, "They were lovely ships. In fact, the *Virginia* was slightly less interesting – the other two were better, with dome-covered main lounges. All three had the best promenade decks at sea in the early 'Thirties,

DUCHESS OF ATHOLL, VIRGINIA and PENNSYLVANIA

When this photograph was taken on October 18th, 1929, the *Virginia* (left) was the biggest liner yet to come from an American yard. She and her two sisters, the newly-built *Pennsylvania* (right) and the *California*, maintained the Panama Pacific Line service between New York and California via the Caribbean and the Panama Canal. (CA/ME)

very wide and spacious. But the Depression years were troublesome, especially for expensive American-flag passenger ships, and a lack of cargo was also a big problem." In 1938, they were sold to the U.S. Maritime Commision and, after an extensive refit, went onto the New York – Buenos Aires run for the American Republics Line, a subsidiary of Moore-McCormack Lines, maintaining a 38-day round trip itinerary.

The *California* became the *Uruguay*, while the *Virginia* and the *Pennsylvania* were re-christened *Brazil* and *Argentina*, respectively.

"They looked their best after 1938," according to Everett Viez. "The original two stacks came off and one larger, wider one went in their place. This looked much better, gave them a more impressive appearance. They were also much more successful in this phase – they gave their best performances and were popular and profitable."

Running in an area of the World untouched by the atrocities of the War, they continued their service until 1942. That year, they were transferred to the U.S. War Shipping Administration and served as valiant troopers until 1946. The following year they re-entered they pre-War passenger service, now for Moore-McCormack itself. They were scrapped in 1964.

A poignant view of the classic-looking *Statendam*, with neutrality markings painted on her sides, making her final departure from the Holland America Line's Hoboken terminal in New York harbor on December 12th, 1939. This ill-fated ship was the line's only three-stacker. (CA/ME)

STATENDAM (29,511 grt; 1929 - 1940)

The design for this ship was very much based on that of the previous *Statendam*, which saw not much more than a year of service before being torpedoed and sunk in 1918. The replacement *Statendam* had a complicated first decade. She was ordered in 1919 and laid down in 1920, but her launching at Harland & Wolff's' Belfast yard was delayed until 1924. The collapse of the migrant trade to America caused further postponement but eventually the incomplete ship was towed to a Dutch yard, finally emerging in the spring of 1929.

By then, the *Statendam*'s interiors were considered by some to be rather old-fashioned. Others liked her, including Everett Viez. "She was the best of all the Holland America liners, even better than the superb Art Deco *Nieuw Amsterdam* of 1938. She had the most beautiful public rooms. They were in the best Dutch decoration and style. And, although not a very streamlined-looking ship, she was noted as an excellent 'sea boat'. I saw her in 1929 after her maiden voyage and the great impression she made on me has never changed."

In addition to her Atlantic crossings, the *Statendam* was a popular cruise ship in the 'Thirties. Laid-up in Rotterdam, she was trapped by the invading Nazi armies in May, 1940. Set afire, she burned for four days and her remains had to be scrapped. She had a tragically brief career, actually sailing for only ten years.

STATENDAM and HIGHLAND BRIGADE

HIGHLAND BRIGADE (14,131 grt; 1929 - 1965)

Owned by the British-flag Nelson Line, this squat-stacked motorship was one of a class of six built by Harland & Wolff for the London – East Coast of South America run. The first in the series, the *Highland Monarch*, was delivered on September 24th, 1928, the last one, *Highland Patriot*, on May 14th, 1932. In this space of time, the other four were named *Highland Chieftain*, *Highland Brigade*, *Highland Hope* and *Highland Princess*. Unfortunately, the *Highland Hope* despite her name, was lost when only ten months old: on November 19th, 1930, she ran onto the Farilhoes rocks becoming a total loss.

The Highland-class vessels carried about 700 passengers as well as freight, especially large consignments of Argentine beef. In 1932, after the collapse of the parent Kylsant Group, they were all transferred to Royal Mail Lines. and subsequently had varied careers.

When the conflict broke out, the five sisters were taken over by the British Ministry of War Transport and converted into supply and troop tranports. The *Highland Patriot* was the only one which did not survive the War; she was torpedoed on October 1st, 1940 off Bishop Rock by the German submarine *U 38* while en route to Glasgow from Buenos Aires with a vital cargo of meat.

The others survived and resumed South American service until 1959. The *Highland Monarch* was then scrapped. *Highland Chieftain* became the Antarctic supply ship *Calpean Star* but very soon, in June, 1960, sank following an engine-room explosion off the coast of Uruguay. The *Highland Brigade* became the Greek pilgrim ship *Henrietta* (later *Marianna*) but was scrapped on Taiwan in 1965. Finally, the *Highland Princess* was the longest survivor by far. She too was sold to the Greeks, becoming the *Marianna*, but was quickly resold to Czechoslovakian interests as the *Slapy* before going to the People's Republic of China as *Guanghua*. She sailed for another twenty-five years before being scrapped.

The *Highland Brigade*, one of a class of sisters built for the Nelson Line but soon incorporated into the Royal Mail Lines fleet, was a typical Harland & Wolff motorliner. A big carrier of refrigerated meat from Argentina to Britain, she had a split superstructure to give access to one of her holds.
(Royal Mail Lines)

A New Generation, A New Style

ASAMA MARU (16,975 grt; 1929 - 1944)

One of Japan's finest and largest pre-Second World War liners, the *Asama Maru* was built by Mitsubishi at their Nagasaki yard. Carrying up to 822 passengers in three classes, she was used on the trans-Pacific run between Hong Kong, Shanghai, Kobe, Yokohama, Honolulu, San Francisco and Los Angeles. In the mid-'Thirties, fares for the 23-day voyage from San Francisco to Shanghai started at $325 in first class and $260 in cabin class. Third class seems not to have been generally offered going westbound, but only to migrants coming eastwards.

In September, 1937, the *Asama Maru* was blown ashore by a hurricane at Hong Kong. Her salvage, was one of the most difficult and extraordinary in history. In order to lighten her so that she could be refloated, part of the hull and of the upperworks had to be cut away in order to have two of her four diesel engines removed. It was a whole year before she could re-enter service. Used as a troopship during the War, she was, like almost all Japanese passenger ships, a casualty. She was sunk by an American submarine on November 1st, 1944.

MILWAUKEE (16,699 grt; 1929 - 1946)

Built for Hamburg America Line's trans-Atlantic service to New York, the comfortable, medium-sized *Milwaukee* and her twin *St. Louis* were often used for cruising.

Indeed, the *Milwaukee* became a fulltime luxury cruiseship after a refit in 1935. The *St. Louis* is perhaps best remembered for her May, 1939 voyage to Cuba carrying 900 Jewish refugees, who were refused permission to land there and in the United States. In the end, they had to sail back to Europe (in fact, to Antwerp). It was an attempt by Nazi ministers to stress that it was not only in Germany that Jews were thought undesirable, but also in other countries. Although damaged by bombing at Kiel in 1944, the *St. Louis* survived the War, but only to become an accommodation ship at Hamburg until scrapped in 1952. The *Milwaukee* also survived. She was seized by the invading British forces in May, 1945 and was intended to become the troopship *Empire Waveney*, under management of the Cunard-White Star Line. However, while being refitted at Liverpool in March, 1946, she caught fire and sank. Her remains were cut-up in Scotland a year later.

NYK Line's splendid *Asama Maru* was one of the largest and finest trans-Pacific liners of the 'Thirties. She and her sister offered formidable competition to the American-flag ships of the Dollar Line, later American President Line, but, like so many Japanese vessels, were sunk during the Pacific war.

(Gillespie-Faber Collection)

Asama Maru and Milwaukee

The German cruise ship *Milwaukee* visiting Barcelona in 1939. In the foreground is the wreck of the British steamer *Stancroft*, which had been bombed after running the Nationalist blockade of Republican ports during the Spanish Civil War. *(Richard Faber Collection)*

A view of the Boat Deck on the Hamburg America Line motor ship *Milwaukee*. After the First World War, the company maintained its North Atlantic passenger service with moderately sized but very comfortable liners. In 1935, the *Milwaukee* was refitted as a white-hulled cruise ship, in which rôle she became very popular. *(Richard Faber Collection)*

A New Generation, A New Style

No less than five New York tugs are at the *Bremen*'s bow as she berths on the south side of pier 86. It is the late 'Thirties and her funnels have been heightened to stop soot falling on her after decks. She is flying the swastika from her mainmast. (CA/ME)

BREMEN (51,656 grt; 1929 - 1941)

During a visit to Bremerhaven in August, 1982, I was taken round the busy harbor by Arnold Kludas. As Germany's finest and most exacting shipping historian and author, he knew that port better than almost anyone else. He knew the history of every location, dock area, backwater. At one point, we peered along the River Weser, then at low water, and saw a small section of rusted steel protruding above the water. "That is the last remnant of the double bottom of the pre-War *Bremen*," he said. "After her fatal fire in 1941, and then the scrapping, these last remains were towed down river and deliberately sunk."

It was quite extraordinary how the Germans had regained trans-Atlantic supremacy. They had some of the World's largest and fastest ships in the glorious fifteen-year period prior to the outbreak of the First Great War in the summer of 1914. But they had lost just about everything by 1918-19. In the 'Twenties, Britain still held the Blue Riband with Cunard's exceptional *Mauretania* as well as the prized title for the World's largest ship, White Star's 56,000-ton *Majestic*, which had, of course, been Germany's *Bismarck*. But by 1927-28, German shipyards were busily creating what would become the nation's mightiest liners yet, the twin-funnel speed champions *Bremen* and *Europa* of the North German Lloyd Line.

"They had initially been intended to be 40,000-ton ships, slightly enlarged versions of the *Columbus* (34,000-tons). But early in 1927, in the very earliest stages of construction, plans

The quadruple-screw record-breaker *Bremen* on the ways just prior to her launching in August, 1928. Her hull was of a very advanced design, intended to enable her to cut more efficiently through the water. She was, for instance, the first vessel fitted with a bulbous bow. On her maiden voyage, she took the record for the fastest North Atlantic crossing from the *Mauretania*. (*Arnold Kludas Collection*)

A New Generation, A New Style

The Bremen *was a symbol of the nation's recovery after the humiliation of defeat in the First World War and 1920s German modernity is clearly evident in this view of her imposing first class Main Lounge. Appropriately, she had been built in Bremen.* (CA/ME)

were changed," according to Arnold Kludas. "They were now to be two superliners, prompted by the huge successes of the late 'Twenties. There was a great, pre-Depression optimism. And at first it was justified, especially as both sisters successively won the Blue Riband for the fastest North Atlantic crossing. But as the economic situation worsened in the 'Thirties, they were operating at only 50% of capacity. Neither ship was a huge commercial success. But they did well enough, especially compared to the struggling White Star Line."

"I saw the *Bremen* in the early 'Thirties, docked at the Brooklyn Army Terminal because no New York City pier was available to handle her," remembered Everett Viez. "She was immaculate – all spit and polish. Her teak decks were like freshly fallen snow. She and the *Europa* were superb pieces of marine architecture. They were typically modern German with very contemporary, very nice interiors. But they suffered from anti-German feelings – left over from the First World War and then because of the Nazi regime. The important American-Jewish trade avoided them completely. Other passengers resented the cold, aloof attitude of the Teutonic crews." Used on the express run (with the *Columbus* as the third ship in a weekly pattern), the two sisters took 6 days to sail between New York and Bremerhaven with quick stops en route at Cherbourg and Southampton.

Like her sister, the *Bremen* also did occasional cruises. "But she was actually too big for cruising," according to Viez. "Her 1938 cruise around South America was really a test by the Nazi government to see if she could go through the Panama Canal. She was chartered for this luxury voyage by Raymond Whitcomb, the big New York travel company. But she almost ruined them. She attracted only 200 passengers and lost $1,000,000, a sizeable amount in the late 'Thirties. Fortunately, that same year Raymond Whitcomb also chartered the *Normandie* for a Carnival-in-Rio cruise. It was a complete 'sell out' and earned $2,000,000. That money saved Raymond Whitcomb."

The *Bremen* and *Europa* were laid-up at Bremerhaven during the War. "Doors had actually been cut in the sides," according to Arnold Kludas. "It was planned that they would carry tanks on the intended invasion of England, but the tanks proved too heavy. Blohm & Voss also made drawings of them as aircraft carriers. But the *Bremen* was ruined in a fire and capsized in March, 1941."

"It is interesting to note," concluded Kludas, "that the North German Lloyd and their great rival, the Hamburg America Line (Hapag), were 90% owned by the German Reich by 1934. The government sold their shares in 1941, however, to a Mr. Reemtsma, a Hamburg cigarette tycoon. He wanted post-War control, forseeing victory and two huge fleets. Instead, by 1946 he lost interest and sold North German Lloyd to Bremen investors and Hapag to Hamburg investors."

The mighty *Europa* is ready for launching at the Blohm & Voss yard at Hamburg in August, 1928. With the introduction of the *Europa* and her sister *Bremen*, North German Lloyd challenged Cunard's supremacy on the North Atlantic. (CA/ME)

EUROPA (49,746 grt; 1930 - 1961)

She and her sister *Bremen* were among the largest and most powerful liners of the time. They were intended to be 40,000-tonners, styled after the earlier *Columbus* of 1924. The *Europa*, built at Hamburg by Blohm & Voss, was to have come into service between Bremerhaven and New York about two weeks before the Bremen-built *Bremen*. By then, of course, plans had been changed and enlarged to make the ships 50,000-tonners with far more powerful propulsion. "There was great envy by the North German Lloyd over the Hamburg America Line at that time," noted Arnold Kludas, "and so these giant ships were intended to secure the top position for the Lloyd on the North Atlantic. The *Europa* was meant to capture the Blue Riband from the British."

But on March 26th, 1929, she was almost destroyed by a huge fire while lying at her fitting out berth. She nearly had to be scrapped. In the end, repairs and completion took another ten months, postponing her inaugural until March, 1930. By then, the *Bremen* had taken the Blue Riband from the *Mauretania* in the previous July, but the *Europa* snatched the honors on her maiden run at a record speed of 27.91 knots. The Germans held this prized distinction until it passed to Italy's *Rex* in August, 1933.

The *Europa* spent the war years in Germany, largely ignored and forgotten. "Doors had been cut into the sides for her use as a landing ship, but the idea of carrying tanks onboard proved too heavy. It was all impractical," added Kludas. There were plans to convert the two ships into aircraft carriers, but nothing came of that either.

"By 1945, as the War was nearing its end, the *Europa* was neglected and rusting. All of her lifeboats were gone and were serving as tenders, some as far away as Gdynia. She was a sorry sight when the Allied forces took Bremerhaven in May, 1945."

For a short time, the former Lloyd record-breaker sailed as the *U.S.S Europa*, an American trooper, but she was plagued with fires and other problems. She was given to the French in 1946 as a replacement for the *Normandie* and, after a long refit, she was resurrected in 1950 as the *Liberté*.

In all, she had a career of 31 years, being retired from the North Atlantic run in November, 1961 and then cut up for scrap at La Spezia in Italy. By then, of course, she was the last of the former German speed champions.

A New Generation, A New Style

While she was fitting out, on March 26th, 1929, the *Europa* caught fire and could well have been totally destroyed. In fact, her fore section was totally burnt out and had to be rebuilt. Her maiden voyage to New York was delayed by ten months. (CA/ME)

Used by the Americans for a short time after the collapse of Nazi Germany in May, 1945, the *Europa* is here seen arriving in New York as the US Navy transport USS *Europa* on November 25th, 1945. She was carrying 6,200 returning servicemen. (CA/ME)

The Nederland liner *Johan van Oldenbarnevelt* leaving Genoa during an unusual call while en route from Amsterdam to the Dutch East Indies via the Suez Canal. She and her sister ship *Marnix van St. Aldegonde* entered service in 1930.

JOHAN VAN OLDENBARNEVELT (19,040 grt; 1930-1963)

They belonged to the Nederland Line and had two of the longest names ever to put to sea: *Johan van Oldenbarnevelt* and *Marnix van St. Aldegonde*.

These two Dutch sisters sailed on the lengthy route to the East Indies and were their owners' largest and finest liners until the introduction of the *Oranje* in 1939. *Johan van Oldenbarnevelt*, often conveniently referred to as the *JVO*, survived the Second World War but the *Marnix* was sunk by German aircraft off the Algerian coast on November 6th, 1943. The *JVO* sailed on for the Dutch until late 1962 when she was sold to the Greek Line, who renamed her *Lakonia* for cruising. She was refitted in Genoa in early 1963 and in April made her first cruise from Southampton to the Canary Islands. She was disastrously destroyed by fire on the 22nd December, 1963, while she was on a Christmas cruise out of Southampton to the Atlantic islands. 128 perished. The still burning ship sank seven days later while she was being towed towards Gibraltar by the Norwegian salvage tug *Herkules*.

The *Johan van Oldenbarnevelt* was extensively refitted at Amsterdam in 1959 as a one-class ship for 1,414 passengers before starting a new career as a round-the-World liner on the Amsterdam-Sydney-New York-Amsterdam service, which she maintained until the end of 1962.

A New Generation, A New Style

Although influenced by the new style, as shown by the modern chairs and chandeliers, the first class interiors of the *Johan van Oldenbarnevelt* still had a great deal of dark, typically Dutch panelling. *(Laurence Dunn Collection)*

Speed Queen of the Pacific: Canadian Pacific's splendid 26,000-ton *Empress of Japan* was the fastest liner in trans-Pacific service in the 'Thirties. After Japan entered the War on the Axis side, she was renamed *Empress of Scotland*. *(CA/ME)*

After the War, the *Empress of Scotland* was transferred to her owners' North Atlantic service. Here, she arrives in New York on December 19th, 1950 after crossing from Liverpool. Her funnels are now adorned by the company's checkered logo. She was about to begin a series of wintertime cruises to the Caribbean. (CA/ME)

EMPRESS OF JAPAN (26,032 grt; 1930 - 1966)

A somewhat smaller version of the 1931 *Empress of Britain*, the *Empress of Japan* was the finest and fastest liner on the trans-Pacific run in the 'Thirties. Her record for passages between Vancouver, Victoria and the Far East remained intact until as late as the 1960s. Built by Fairfield Shipbuilding & Engineering at Glasgow, she entered service in June, 1930. She had accommodations for 1,173 passengers: 399 first class, 164 second class, 100 third class and 510 steerage. But she too became a trooper soon after the War started in September, 1939. She was renamed *Empress of Scotland* in 1942, following the Japanese attack on Pearl Harbor. Not returned to her owners until 1948, she underwent a two-year restoration, but now for Liverpool – Quebec City sailings and for winter cruising from New York. Sold to the West German-flag Hamburg-Atlantic Line in 1958, she was rebuilt at Hamburg (with two funnels replacing the original three) and ran to New York as the very popular *Hanseatic*. Her career ended prematurely, however, when she caught fire on September 7th, 1966 while she lay at Manhattan's Pier 84. Severely damaged and pervaded by the smell of smoke onboard, she was sold to Hamburg shipbreakers soon afterward.

Although hardly recognisible as the former three-stacker *Empress of Scotland*, the *Hanseatic* remained a beautiful vessel, with a distinctive and well proportioned profile.

Although less famous than the *Empress of Britain*, Canadian Pacific's *Empress of Japan* had equally magnificent first class rooms. She was one of the finest liners on the highly competitive pre-War trans-Pacific routes.   (*Laurence Dunn Collection*)

BRITANNIC

In this view from the early 'Thirties, the ultra-modern *Britannic*, has just sailed from Pier 61 in New York. The *Britannic* and the *Georgic* were the last attempt by the ailing White Star Line to update its North Atlantic fleet. Although not express liners, they were very sturdy, very seaworthy ships. *(Everett Viez Collection)*

BRITANNIC (23,943 grt; 1930 - 1960)

In the late 'Twenties, the already struggling White Star Line had hoped to build a 60,000-ton superliner, the *Oceanic*, to rival the proposed new Cunard giant, the 80,000-tonner that was rumored to be named *Victoria* but which became the illustrious *Queen Mary*.

Early work on the *Oceanic* at Harland & Wolff's yard at Belfast was soon abandoned and, in view of the onset of the Great Depression, White Star turned more sensibly to a pair of 27,000-ton motorliners, the *Britannic* and a close sister, the *Georgic*. Low and sleek, with twin stump funnels (the forward one was in fact a dummy), these ships later became part of the merged Cunard-White Star Line in 1934. They were sturdy, steady ships and beautifully furnished.

The *Britannic* survived the War and, when sold for scrapping in late 1960, was the last of the remaining White Star passenger liners.

On a rare occasion, the near-sisters *Britannic* (right) and *Georgic* (left) are resting together between voyages at Cunard-White Star's New York pier 54. Note the extension which was added to the pier in earlier days for the likes of the *Aquitania*. *(CA/ME)*

A New Generation, A New Style

Like several Messageries Maritimes motorliners of this period, the *Félix Roussel* and *Georges Philippar* had extraordinary square funnels. They were built for the company's service to French Indo-China and beyond, but the *Georges Philippar* was lost on her return maiden voyage. *(Laurence Dunn Collection)*

FÉLIX ROUSSEL (16,753 grt; 1930-1974)

"During the War, I returned home on the troopship *Félix Roussel*. Being temporarily under American control, she was 'dry'. I played bridge all the way home to Liverpool from Bombay via Suez and Cyprus," recalled Colonel Norman Dodd. "Even in those war years, the food that came out of her kitchens was quite good. The French cooks were still on duty. It was a particularly good voyage considering it was wartime. All the people onboard were quite wonderful to one another – the Americans, the British, the French, the Indians and others – which was not always the case on troopships, even in War." Together with several other ships belonging to Messageries Maritimes, she had a design unique to the French and to these owners. It was quite eccentric, with two square, very flat funnels. It suited the "motorship moderne" of the time. Used on the Marseilles – Far East route via Suez, the *Félix Roussel* was in most ways a typical colonial passenger ship of her day. Along with her freight spaces, she had comparatively limited passenger quarters, for 398 in all and divided into three classes. In 1935 she was lengthened and re-engined. After the War, she was rebuilt with a single large, more conventional stack and resumed eastern sailings. She was sold in 1955 to the Arosa Line, Swiss-based but using a Panamanian flag, and became the trans-Atlantic *Arosa Sun*. After the line went bankrupt, she was auctioned off in 1960 to Dutch interests, who used her as a workers' accommodation ship at Ijmuiden. She endured until 1974, when she was towed off to Spain and scrapped.

She had had a much longer life than her similar running-mate in the Messageries Maritimes fleet, the *Georges Philippar*, which was destroyed by fire in May, 1932 when making her maiden return voyage from the Far East.

The *Félix Roussel*, just renamed *Arosa Sun*, waiting to be refurbished in 1955 at Lloyd Werft of Bremerhaven for her new Swiss owners.

The *Cabo San Augustin*, at anchor in Genoa in the early 'Thirties, was a lesser liner on the emigrant run to South America, but another fine example of modern design at a time when builders and owners of motorliners wished to distinguish them from the traditional steamships.

CABO SAN AUGUSTIN (11,868 grt; 1931 - 1941)

Specifically built for their emigrant and mail service to South America, the *Cabo San Augustin* and her sister ship *Cabo Santo Tomé* bore charactersitic Ybarra Line names. The Spanish company Ybarra & Cia of Seville, dated back to the middle of the previous century, and so far had almost always given their ships names of Spanish capes.

The Spanish emigrant trade to South America, revitalized after the First War War by the restriction imposed by the U.S. government on new entries into their country, boomed after the Wall Street crash and the start of the Great Depression.

For this reason, the company, which in 1927 had started a passenger service from Barcelona to the River Plate, placed the order in 1929 with the Cia Española de Construcción Naval of Bilbao for three emigrant and mail motorliners (by far the largest built in Spain, despite their modest 12,000 gross tons) challenging the Italian supremacy on the route.

Indeed, their new ships started their long voyages from Genoa, calling en route at Barcelona.

The single-funnel *Cabo San Antonio* came first, in April 1930, while *Cabo San Augustin* and *Cabo Santo Tomé* followed one year later. They had limited, low superstructures, as they did not have any first class accommodations (only 12 second class passengers and 500 third) and thus no space was required for large lounges on the upper decks. Also, they sported a second dummy funnel, which balanced their sleek profile, giving them a racy appearance, despite their mere 15 knots of service speed. Both vessels were used as troop transports for the Republicans during the Spanish Civil War. The *Cabo Santo Tomé* was attacked and sunk on October 10th, 1937 by the Nationalist gun boats *Dato* and *Canovas*, while the *Cabo San Augustin* was seized by the Russians while lying at Feodosia at the end of the Civil War, and was reactivated as their troop ship *Dnepr*. In this guise, she would meet her end in October 1941, when torpedoed off Anapa by a German aircraft.

A New Generation, A New Style

The *Morro Castle*, the new flagship of the Ward Line, goes down the ways at Newport News on March 5th, 1930. She was one of the finest American liners of her day and also one of the fastest turbo-electric passenger ships. Note that, like the *Bremen* and *Europa*, she had a bulbous bow. (CA/ME)

MORRO CASTLE (11,520 grt; 1930 - 1934)

Another liner which famously became a victim of fire was the *Morro Castle*. "She was the very best 'little' American liner of the early 'Thirties, lovely looking and quite beautiful on the inside," according to Everett Viez. Her owners, the New York-based Ward Line, ordered her (and a twin sister, the *Oriente*, scrapped in 1957) for their New York – Havana trade.

She had space for 530 passengers, 430 of them in high standard first class and 100 in second class.

"The two ships ran 6-day roundtrip cruises and had 80% load factors on almost every sailing," continued Viez. "They were very, very popular ships with fine public rooms, excellent service and about 75% of their cabins had private facilities." Unfortunately, on September 8th, 1934, while off Asbury Park, New Jersey, during a return voyage to New York, the *Morro Castle* caught fire and had to be abandoned. In all, 133 people perished in the headline-making tragedy. Later beached, the ship smouldered for days afterward.

The burned-out hull was scrapped the following year. The event prompted extensive investigations and led to improved safety standards on all future American-flag passenger ships.

"The Ward Line had labor problems and there were suggestions that the *Morro Castle* was sabotaged. There were also political problems with the Cubans. It seemed unlikely that two fires could have started at once onboard such a high-standard, advanced ship," Viez opined.

MORRO CASTLE

The *Morro Castle* and her sister ship *Oriente* were the finest liners on the higly popular New York - Havana route. Thanks to their service speed of 20 knots, they took six days to cover the journey in either direction.
(Laurence Dunn Collection)

Following her tragic fire on September 8th, 1934, the *Morro Castle* drifted into the beach resort of Asbury Park, New Jersey. Thousands came just to see the smouldering, gutted ship. She continued to burn for several days.

TATSUTA MARU (16,975 grt; 1930 - 1943)

Built by Mitsubishi at their Nagasaki yard, the *Tatsuta Maru* was a twin sister to the aforementioned *Asama Maru*. Both sailed for Nippon Yusen Kaisha (the NYK Line) in their trans-Pacific service to and from San Francisco and Los Angeles. The photograph shows a festive occasion, when she arrived at San Pedro in the port of Los Angeles on July 10th, 1932. Among her passengers were the Japanese Olympic team. In 1938, the name of the *Tatsuta Maru* was modified to *Tatuta Maru*. Used as a troopship after 1941, she, like most Japanese liners, was a war casualty. She was torpedoed by an American submarine off the Japanese coast in 1943. (CA/ME)

TATSUTA MARU and LAFAYETTE

Dressed in flags, the new motorship *Lafayette* is anchored in Lower Bay, New York at the end of her maiden voyage from Le Havre in May, 1930. She was one of two intermediate liners ordered by the French Line in which first class was replaced by a cheaper, but still magnificent, cabin class. The other was the turbine-powered *Champlain* of 1932. (CA/ME)

LAFAYETTE (25,178 grt; 1930 - 1938)

She was an intermediate liner for the Le Havre - New York service of the French Line and was built in 1929-30 by the famous yard of Penhoët in Saint Nazaire, on the Loire river.

"This ship, with her squat single stack and mast above the wheelhouse, marked the adoption of unconventional profiles by CGT, the French Line, when she first appeared in 1930," said Everett Viez. "She also continued the trend toward more modern interiors in their ships, which had started three years earlier with the *Ile de France*. This led, of course, to the *Champlain* and then the sensational *Normandie*.

But *Lafayette*, a motorship driven by two 9,000 hp MAN oil engines, failed operationally, owing to her limited service speed of just 17 knots. Immediately, the French Line returned to steam turbines for the *Champlain* which appeared two years later. And then, in 1935, they went to steam turbo-electric propulsion for the *Normandie*."

Lafayette fell victim to the fate of many French passenger ships. On May 4th, 1938, while idle in the big graving dock at Le Havre during a French seamen's strike, she was swept by fire. It was thought that flames from an engineer's blow torch ignited the ship's fuel tanks. The ship, covered by a $5 million insurance, was declared a complete loss. Her charred, twisted remains were towed to Rotterdam afterward and scrapped.

A New Generation, A New Style

The stylish two deck-high cabin class Dining Room on the *Lafayette*. Surrounded by Art Deco splendor is a tapestry depicting Robert Lafayette, the Frenchman who was a hero of the American Revolution. *(CA/ME)*

Lafayette burned out on May 4th, 1938 while docked at Le Havre. The fire broke out in the lower fuel tanks of the vessel and, despite prompt action by the port fire brigade, it spread quickly to the upper decks. *(CA/ME)*

The Rotterdam Lloyd built a number of fine motorships for their service to the Dutch East Indies. The *Dempo*, pictured, and her sister *Baloeran* were distinctively modern-looking liners, although their interiors had a dark, typically Dutch atmosphere. *(Richard Faber Collection)*

DEMPO (16,979 grt; 1931 - 1944)

Two of The Netherlands' finest pre-War liners for the colonial service to the East Indies were the *Baloeran* and the *Dempo*; Dutch companies always showed a preference for oil engines compared to other nations and indeed these two Rotterdam Lloyd vessels were fitted with Sulzer diesel engines. The *Baloeran* came first, in March 1930, a product of the Fijenoord NV yard of Rotterdam, while her twin *Dempo* entered service one year later, her builders being the De Schelde yard of Vlissingen.

They carried considerable freight, like most colonial liners of the day, plus three classes of passengers (236 first, 70 third and 48 fourth class.) With their hulls painted a cooling dove gray and capped by single all-black funnels, they were rivals to the ships of the Nederland Line-Royal Dutch Mail. Indeed they were ordered simultaneously to their rivals *Johan van Oldenbarnevelt* and *Marnix van St. Aldegonde*, which were covering the same route at the same time (all four motorships had identical engines) but using Amsterdam as terminus port instead of Rotterdam.

Calling at Southampton and passing through the Suez Canal, they would take about 30 days from Rotterdam to Batavia. The twins were separated by the conflict: one was seized by the Germans, the other went to the Allies. Sadly, both ships were war losses. The *Baloeran* was taken over by the Nazis when they invaded Holland and became their hospital ship *Strassburg* in 1941. She struck a mine near Ijmuiden in September, 1943; she was beached to prevent her sinking but was bombed and set afire by British planes before any salvaging operation could be attempted.

The *Dempo*, on the other hand, became an Allied trooper but was torpedoed by a German submarine off the Algerian coast in March, 1944 while sailing in convoy from Naples. After the War, Rotterdam Lloyd became Royal Rotterdam Lloyd in honor of the company's courageous efforts during the conflict.

VICTORIA (13,062 grt; 1931 - 1942)

A very fine Italian liner was Lloyd Triestino's *Victoria*. Unquestionably, she was that company's best passenger ship, although not the largest, but certainly one of the finest motor-liners of the time. She was noted for her sumptuous first class quarters, her powerful diesel engines and her speed. Painted all-white, she ranked as the fastest motorliner afloat at that time, capable of a maximum speed of over 23 knots. She had been intended for Mediterranean service but was soon put to work on the Genoa – Suez – Bombay service, later going still further, to Shanghai and Hong Kong. She became so popular on the Far Eastern run that she was often preferred to the well-known P&O liners that sailed to the same destinations. Even British travellers went by train to Italy just to sail in her. Like so many other Italian liners, she was a casualty of the Second World War, being sunk off the Libyan coast on January 24th, 1942 after being attacked by British aircraft.

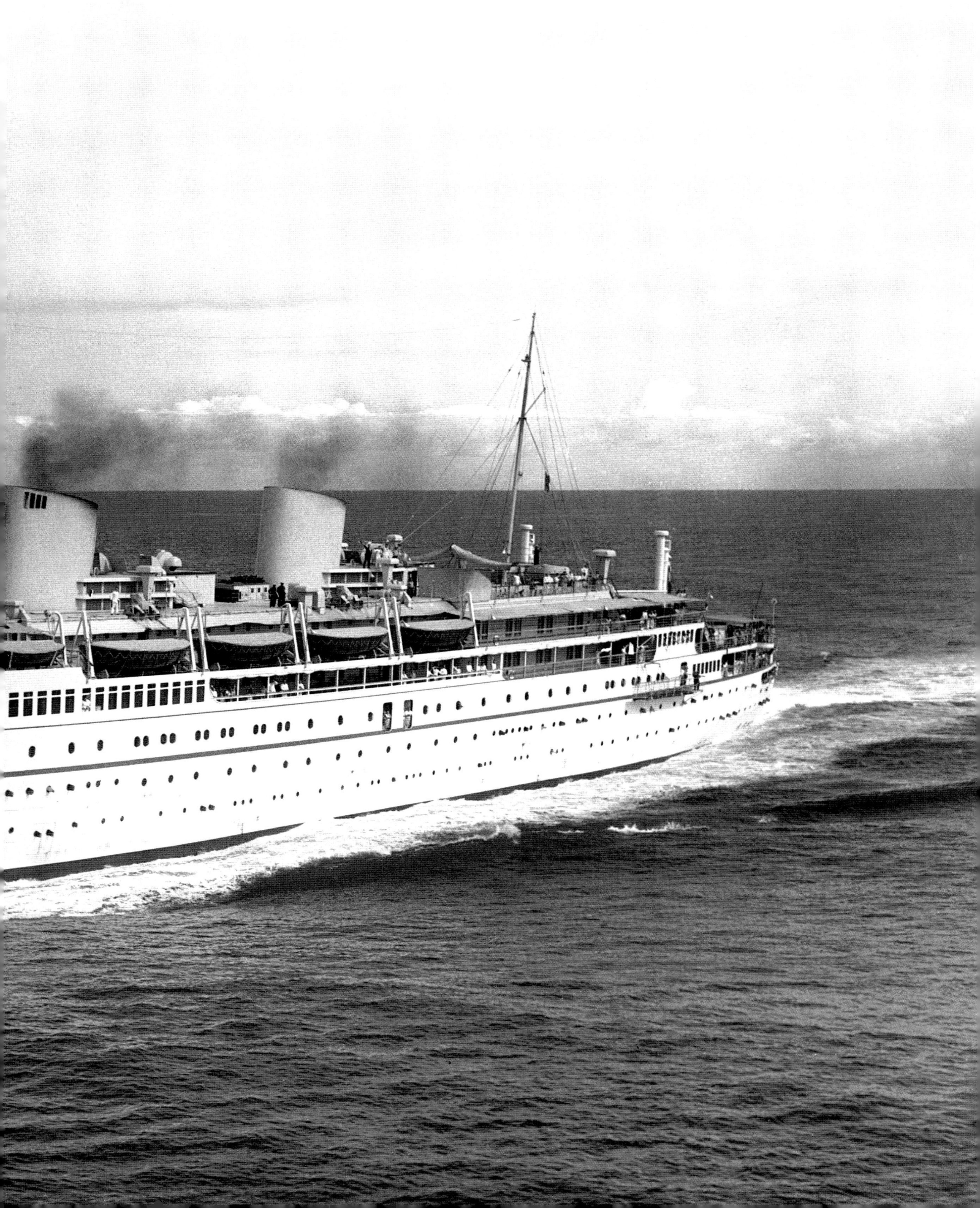

A New Generation, A New Style

The French Line's *Colombie*, was smaller than the liners used on the New York run, but was nevertheless a fine ship. Built for the service to the Antilles, she did make a cruise to New York in August, 1939 for the World's Fair. Here, she is berthed at Pier 88. (CA/ME)

COLOMBIE (13,391 grt; 1931 - 1970)

Built at Dunkerque for CGT, the French Line, this intermediate-sized liner sailed not on the prestigious northern route to New York, but from Le Havre to the Caribbean, primarily French colonial Guadeloupe and Martinique. She also made cruises, including a special voyage to New York in August, 1939 for the World's Fair. Although a modest liner, she had fine interiors in the contemporary style. She was used by the Americans during the War, serving as a trooper and then as the hospital ship *Aleda E.Lutz*. Restored and now with a single tapered stack instead of her original two, she sailed for the French until sold to Greek owners, Typaldos Lines, in 1964. They sailed her, mainly in the Mediterranean, as the *Atlantica*. Laid-up in 1967, she was partly scrapped near Piraeus in 1970 and the task was completed four years later when the remaining hull was towed to Barcelona.

THE GLAMOROUS 'THIRTIES

Virtually all the main shipping companies brought one or more outstanding new vessels into service in the 'Thirties, which often represented a milestone in their existance. There was a sort of domino effect, started a few years earlier by the introduction of great ocean liners such as the *Ile de France* and the *Bremen* and *Europa*, prompting other leading lines to order superlative new tonnage. The period started with the likes of *Empress of Britain*, the largest liner to bear the colours of Canadian Pacific, and *L'Atlantique*, the biggest and, possibly, best-appointed liner ever to run from Europe to South America. It was also a time of great rivalry for the Blue Riband and the epoch of the giant passenger ships: despite the grim Depression, the 80,000 tonners *Normandie*, *Queen Mary* and *Queen Elizabeth* were all built in this era, and they remained the largest transatlantic liners ever built until 2004, when their record size was eclipsed by the *Queen Mary 2* of 148,000 gross tons. *Queen Mary* and *Normandie* are still remembered as two of of the greatest ships ever. Their rivalry made headlines in the press and they were national champions challenging for the title of the biggest and fastest vessel on the Atlantic. The *Normandie* is considered by many to have been the most beautiful and glamorous liner of all times, while the beloved *Queen Mary*, preserved as a floating hotel and museum in Long Beach, California, is now all that remains to us of those glorious days. The 'Thirties also saw the boom of cruising: travel at sea became a popular vacation and the modern cruise industry began to take shape, encouraged by the need to find work for under-employed ocean liners in those difficult times. Marine technology rose to new heights: modern oil engines started to rival the traditional steam plant, while electric motors for propulsion and air-conditioning brought new standards of modernity and comfort, typical of the cruise ships of our own day.

The Prince of Wales, later King Edward VIII, went to Southampton specially to witness the maiden departure of the mighty *Empress of Britain* on May 27th, 1931. It was hoped that her voyages to and from the St. Lawrence would not only carry passengers from Canada but would also attract traffic from the United States. (CA/ME)

The Glamorous 'Thirties

In November, 1931, the *Empress of Britain* is being overhauled in the big floating dock at Southampton in preparation for her winter World Cruise from New York. Unlike some companies, Canadian Pacific still opted for huge funnels. Here they are being scraped and repainted. (CA/ME)

EMPRESS OF BRITAIN (42,348 grt; 1931 - 1940)

London-based Canadian Pacific Steamships were very busy in the late 'Twenties and early 'Thirties. Simultaneously, they were creating the largest, fastest and finest liners for both their Atlantic and Pacific passenger services. The 26,000-ton *Empress of Japan* was to be the new flagship of the Vancouver – Far East service; even larger at 42,000 tons, the *Empress of Britain* was intended as one of the ultimate North Atlantic luxury liners, in fact the very finest sailing to Canada, between Southampton and Quebec City. She was launched in June, 1930 by the Prince of Wales (later King Edward VIII and then the Duke of Windsor) at the John Brown yard at Clydebank. "I remember seeing the *Empress of Britain* docked at Pier 60, at the foot of West 20th Street in Manhattan," recalled John Gillespie, who as a boy lived just a few blocks away. "My first view was on a winter's night and those three funnels were floodlit. They looked like gas tanks. They were overwhelmingly big, but they worked on the *Empress*. They added to her great appeal as a true luxury liner. In every way, she was one of the greatest ships of her day."

She entered service in May, 1931, unique for that time in being specially designed for a dual purpose: crossings for about eight months of the year and then, when the St. Lawrence was frozen, for cruises, usually a four-month trip around the World. On the Atlantic run, she could carry 1,195 travellers in three classes (which made her very spacious for a liner of this size) but then a club-like 700 for those wintertime circumnavigations. The cost of these sailings started at about $2,000. But despite her popularity, her size and her luxury and grandeur, she was a great money-loser both on the Atlantic and when cruising. Any thought of a sister was soon forgotten by her disappointed owners in those hard-pressed times. Even after the War, in 1946, when a replacement was suggested by the British government, it was politely declined by the Canadian Pacific directors. "She was the most gorgeous

The Cathay Lounge, done in Oriental Deco, was one of the *Empress of Britain*'s most magnificent public rooms. Canadian Pacific were determined that their new flagship should rival the grandeur of the great liners on the more prestigious New York run. (CA/ME)

ship, probably the most luxurious world cruiseship of all time," according to Everett Viez. "Her Mayfair Lounge was extremely beautiful and the Cocktail Lounge was delightful. She had more cabins with private facilities than any other ship doing long cruises. Actually, I think she was better known for her cruises than her crossings. Externally, of course, she did have a top-heavy look – those stacks were too large. But it all worked. And she was so symmetrical. Her cruiser stern was another attractive feature."

In June, 1939, she carried Their Majesties King George VI and Queen Elizabeth home from their friendship-building North American tour to Canada and the United States. Queen Mary, Princess Elizabeth (today Her Majesty, the Queen) and Princess Margaret were at Southampton Docks to greet them and the flag-bedecked Canadian Pacific flagship. Months later, in the fall, she was called to war duty, as a trooper. But it was all too brief. While homebound from South Africa, she was attacked by Nazi bombers off the Irish coast on October 26th, 1940. Burning but still afloat, she was then attacked two days later by an enemy submarine. In all, 49 lives were lost.

The Glamorous 'Thirties

The ill-fated *L'Atlantique* at the Pauillac-Trompeloup wharf at Bordeaux, on September 19th, 1931, prepares for her maiden departure to South America. Like several other liners of the time, she had her funnels heightened later in her career because of problems with soot falling on the after decks.   (Philippe Cazade Collection)

L'ATLANTIQUE (42,512 grt; 1931 - 1933)

While the Germans had the *Cap Arcona* and the British had the sisters *Alcantara* and *Asturias*, the French built the largest and grandest liner ever for the Europe – South American trade. Operated by the Compagnie de Navigation Sud-Atlantique, she was claimed to be a "first cousin" to the *Ile de France*. The new ship was launched, appropriately as *L'Atlantique*, in April 1930 and was completed the following year. She too had sumptuous Art Deco interiors, especially for her 414 first class guests (the remaining accommodation was 158 second class and 584 third). She sailed from Bordeaux to Rio de Janeiro, Santos, Montevideo and, finally, a turnround at Buenos Aires.

It would seem that her only shortcomings were in her external appearance and in her arrival in the depths of the Depression. As built, she looked top-heavy, almost clumsy. Even when her three funnels were remodelled, she never looked quite right. And her passenger loads were surely affected by the bleak times, except possibly the third class space on the westbound voyages, when European emigrants were seeking new lives and fresh opportunities in Latin America. Tragically, her career was extraordinarily brief. During a positioning voyage from Bordeaux to Le Havre for overhauling, *L'Atlantique*, then the twelfth largest liner in the World, caught fire in the English Channel on January 4th, 1933.

The blaze, which started in an empty first class cabin, quickly engulfed the entire ship. Nineteen crew members perished. Fortunately, the ship had been sailing without passengers. Abandoned and adrift for a time, *L'Atlantique* was eventually taken in tow by French, Dutch and German tugs and brought into Cherbourg. She was soon abandoned by her owners as a total loss but a financial battle then ensued with the insurance underwriters. In the end, in 1936, the huge liner was sold to Scottish shipbreakers and the underwriters paid the Compagnie de Navigation Sud-Atlantique $6.8 million. There were varied theories about the cause of the blaze and hints of possible sabotage.

The French, always rather prone to fires aboard their passenger ships, lost five liners in the 'Thirties and early 'Forties, including *L'Atlantique*. The *Georges Philippar* of Messageries Maritimes

A corner of the Grand Salon of *L'Atlantique*. Fully equal to the great French liners on the North Atlantic, she was just as luxurious and as splendid. *(Richard Faber Collection)*

burned and then sank on the way back from the Far East on her return maiden voyage, no less, in May, 1932.

Then, the French Line was hard hit. *Lafayette* burned while being overhauled at Le Havre in May, 1938 and was a complete loss. The *Paris* burned in an adjacent berth eleven months later, and capsized as well. And then, of course, the splendid *Normandie* burned out at New York a few years later, in February, 1942.

The Glamorous 'Thirties

The short-lived President Hoover *of the American-flag Dollar Line, loading cargo at Yokohama in the early 'Thirties. One of two notable sisters, she was wrecked in Japanese waters on December 10th, 1937 and the Dollar Line collapsed the following year.* (CA/ME)

PRESIDENT HOOVER (21,936 grt; 1931 - 1937)

The *President Hoover* and the *Presiden Coolidge*, sisterships built at Newport News in Virginia, were two of the finest American passenger liners in Pacific service. Like other American vessels of the time, they were propelled by turbo-electric plants; their 33,000 hp were supplied by a General Electric Co. installation in the *Hoover*, and by one from Westinghouse in the *Coolidge*, permitting a service speed of 20 knots, and a maximum of 22.

They were routed from San Francisco and Los Angeles via Honolulu to Yokohama, Kobe, Shanghai, Hong Kong and Manila. Built for the Dollar Line (which became American President Lines in 1938), they had very short careers. *President Hoover* stranded on a reef in Japanese waters on December 10th, 1937 and became a complete loss. She was later scrapped on the spot. The *President Coolidge* became a troopship in 1941 but struck a mine in the South Pacific on October 26th, 1942. Her remains are a lure to divers to this day.

STRATHAIRD (22,544 grt; 1932 - 1961)

Frank Andrews recalled seeing the splendid P&O sisters *Strathaird* and *Strathnaver* at Melbourne in the 'Thirties. "They were quite different from the earlier P&O passenger ships. Their interiors were lighter, far more contemporary. In some areas, they had blonde woods with a mat finish, for example. Elsewhere, though, the decoration was similar to the classic English manor house. They were also unique in being the first P&O liners to appear with all-white hulls, the first ever in Australia. They resembled the big Atlantic liners, with their three funnels, the first and third of which were dummies and put on just for effect. After the War, those extra stacks never reappeared and these sisters looked much more like the subsequent *Strathmore* and *Stratheden*."

Both sisters survived the War and in the 'Fifties were back in passenger service on the London-Sydney route; in 1954 they underwent a more extensive refit becoming one-class ships. Both were broken up in Hong Kong in 1961-62.

The *Strathaird*'s first and third funnels were actually 'dummy stacks', for effect. Here she is seen at Naples on October 5th, 1937. The *Strathaird* and *Strathnaver* introduced many innovations to the hitherto rather conservative P&O company and greatly improved the London - Australia mail service. (CA/ME)

Three P&O liners, all driven by the latest turbo-electric machinery, lie in Tilbury Docks in January, 1932. The *Viceroy of India* of 1929 is in the foreground, while in the distance are the *Strathnaver* and the just completed *Strathaird*. With their white hulls, buff funnels and modern profiles, the 'Strath sisters' transformed the look of the P&O fleet. (Laurence Dunn Collection)

THE GLAMOROUS 'THIRTIES

Shipboard elegance: while still exhibiting touches of the old classically-influenced style, the first class Lounge on the *Strathnaver* nevertheless had a more modern tone, comparable for instance with the lighter décor of the Orient Line's *Orion* of 1935. *(Richard Faber Collection)*

REX (51,062 grt; 1932 - 1944)

Launched on August 1st, 1931 at the Ansaldo yard, near Genoa, the *Rex* was Italy's largest and fastest superliner of the 'Thirties. Initially ordered by Navigazione Generale Italiana, she was transferred to the newly created Italian Line early in 1932. She entered service in the September of that year and between 1933 and 1935 held the Blue Riband for the fastest crossing of the North Atlantic. Her interiors were expectedly sumptuous, though not modern in style like those of the *Conte di Savoia* with which she ran on the Genoa – New York express route. Some people preferred her. Everett Viez said, "The *Rex* had great interiors. She was one of my favorites in the 'Thirties. She was very spacious and had an especially fine main stairwell. In all ways, she was magnificent."

She was laid-up in the summer of 1940, when Italy entered the War, eventually being sent to Trieste for safety. In fact, she was never to sail again. After Italy's armistice of September 8th, 1943, she was seized by the Nazis and all her furnishing and hotel equipments were disembarked, and treated as war prizes; some of the valuable things on board were sent to Germany, others were sold on the black market and scattered all over the area.

After the Trieste port was bombed twice by Allied planes, on September 5th, 1944 she was towed a few miles South towards the Istrian coast to prevent her destruction, but three days later she was attacked by British and South African bombers and set afire, later capsizing in shallow water.

Her remains were scrapped mostly in 1947-48, but the final pieces were not removed until 1958.

The *Rex* was destroyed also for political reasons. The Allies wanted Italy to be dependent on them once the War was over, rather than on the nearby Soviet block nations. Trieste might have become Jugoslavian and only in 1954 was it assigned to Italy. There was a serious threat that the ships close to the Istrian coast would have been seized by the Soviet countries, so the Allies destroyed the *Rex* and other passenger ships, such as the *Sabaudia* (ex-*Stockholm*), *Duilio* and *Giulio Cesare*.

The *Rex* running at full speed in the Gulf of Genoa during her trials in September 1932. The photograph clearly shows the well balanced, racy profile of the vessel, with her classic counter stern perfectly matching the modern design of her hull and upperworks.

THE GLAMOROUS 'THIRTIES

Another goddess in ruins: the *Rex* lies on her side following attacks by British and South African aircraft in September, 1944. The fires onboard have subsided but inspection teams later find that she is damaged beyond any reasonable hope of repair. (CA/ME)

The large swimming pool which in better days had been a focus of la dolce vita onboard the *Rex*, has been ruined by the fires that engulfed the ship. The lifeboats had been removed before the attacks - hence the empty davits. (CA/ME)

In a grand gathering of Italian liners at Genoa, we see, from left to right in the foreground, the *Roma*, *Giulio Cesare*, *Rex*, *Atlanta* and then the *Conte di Savoia*. In the distance, undergoing repairs, are the three-funnelled *Lombardia* (ex-*Resolute*) and, behind her, the *Augustus*.

CONTE DI SAVOIA (48,502grt; 1932 - 1943)

Originally ordered by the Lloyd Sabaudo company and possibly to have been called *Conte Azzurro*, this great liner entered service for the new Italian Line when Mussolini reorganized the country's main shipping companies in 1932, in the depths of the Depression. Her running-mate was the 51,000-ton *Rex*, which had been laid down for the rival NGI company. Together, they had triumphant years on the Genoa - New York run, "the sunny southern route", as it was called.

The *Conte di Savoia* was indeed one of the greatest liners of the 'Thirties, especially known for her external good looks, her broad outer lido decks (with a pool between the two funnels) and her ornate Colonna Lounge ("like the Sistine Chapel gone to sea", according to one writer of the day). In fact, that lounge was an exception, since all the rest of her public rooms were in a much simpler, more contemporary and very beautiful style.

When Italy went to War in 1940, the *Conte di Savoia* was laid-up at a secluded anchorage at Malamocco, near Venice. Fifty crew looked after the otherwise silent, darkened supership. Her active days had spanned less than eight years. She was destroyed by mistake when the war in Italy was over.

On September 8th, 1943, Italy joined the Allies. By the next morning, the Germans turned on their former friends and they began shooting at each other in mass confusion. That same day, there was news on the Italian radio that 'Savoia' was trying to escape to the south of the country. Actually, the broadcast referred to a member of the Savoy family, the Royal House of Italy, but the Nazis misunderstood and thought of the ship. They sent five bombers to attack her. Just before the broadcast, the German High Command had given orders to move her to the canal at Piazza San Marco in Venice for closer control. But in reality, she would have been far too deep in draft to berth there. After the bombing started, the Germans

The Glamorous 'Thirties

The 48,500-ton *Conte di Savoia* was assuredly one of Italy's finest liners. Big, fast and elegant, she sailed in partnership with the record-breaking *Rex*. She is here seen arriving at the Italian Line pier in New York on October 19th, 1938. (CA/ME)

realized their mistake and orders were given to stop, but by then at least four bombs had hit the giant liner. The crew then tried to sink her to contain the fire, but it was too shallow at Malamocco. The *Conte di Savoia* burned two days, down to the main deck. A few days later the Italian Line sent their technicians to make a first inspection.

Much of the upperworks were destroyed, but they found that her hull was still in sound condition. That blistered hulk was refloated in 1946 but then remained at Malamocco for another two years.

There were encouraging reports on the state of her once-powerful steam turbine machinery and, briefly, some form of rebuilding seemed a possibility.

Drawings were made at the Italian Line's Genoa headquarters. She would have had one funnel in a center position. The original three-class quarters would have been changed to take 3,000 in third class, even 3,500, all migrants bound for South America. Two of the original turbine sets and propeller shafts would have been removed and she would have been a slower, twin-screw ship, similarly to what happened to the post-War *France* when she became the *Norway*. And her famous gyro stabilizers, which received so much publicity in the early 'Thirties, but which were really not quite effective, would have been removed to create more storage space. Unfortunately, there was no money in Italy for such a rebuilding at that time and there were problems with her overall size and her deep draft: the drawings went into the Italian line's basement files and were forgotten. There were further reports that either the Holland America Line or the French Line might buy her and rebuild her for their North Atlantic service. But nothing came of it. The remains of the *Conte di Savoia* were towed to the Monfalcone shipyard and were docked at the fitting-out berth. They were still being scrapped in 1950 when the brand new 27,000-ton *Giulio Cesare*, Italy's first major post-War liner, was being constructed. Together, the two ships represented two great generations of Italian liners.

The richly furnished first class Grand Salon aboard the *Rex* (above), and the same space on board the *Conte di Savoia* (below). The conservative décor of the *Rex* was in evident contrast with the modernism of her running-mate. *(Above: Sal Scannella Collection)*

The Glamorous 'Thirties

April 24th, 1950: after a study to transform her into an Italian emigrant liner and negotiations with the French Line to rebuild her as a consort to their *Liberté* were dropped, the hulk of the *Conte di Savoia* arrives in Monfalcone, just a few miles from her birthplace, to be broken up.

The crowd gathered at the Monfalcone yard to witness the launching of the first post-war Italian liner, the *Giulio Cesare*, on May 18th, 1950 (whose stern is visible on the left) pays a last homage to the remains of the giant *Conte di Savoia*, which is waiting to be dismantled. *(Laurence Dunn Collection)*

SANTA PAULA

Modestly sized but stately, the inbound Santa Paula passes the Lower Manhattan skyline. Two of her sisters were lost during the War but Santa Paula and Santa Rosa resumed Grace Line's prestigious New York-Caribbean service to great acclaim. (Alex Duncan Collection)

SANTA PAULA (9135 grt; 1932 - 1972)

The Santa Paula was one of an exceptional quartet of mini-liners, very advanced in design. Created by William Francis Gibbs and built at the Federal Shipbuilding and Dry Dock yard at Kearny in New Jersey, they were predecessors to the America of 1940 and then the record-breaking United States of 1952. The Santa Paula and her sisters, Santa Rosa, Santa Lucia and Santa Elena, belonged to the New York-based Grace Line. They ran a Caribbean-intercoastal service from New York to the West Indies, then through the Panama Canal to Los Angeles, San Francisco and Seattle. While the Santa Lucia and Santa Elena were lost in the War, the Santa Paula and the Santa Rosa returned to Grace Line service in 1947 on a 12-day New York – Caribbean run.

Laid-up in 1958, they were sold to Greek buyers, the Typaldos Lines, two years later and were renamed Acropolis and Athinai respectively. They sailed mostly in the Mediterranean until laid-up in 1967, when Typaldos went bankrupt. The Acropolis was scrapped in 1972-74, with the final remains being cut-up in 1977. The Athinai, the former Santa Rosa, lasted longer: in 1978-79, she was used as a floating prop in the film Raise the Titanic. Afterward, she returned to lay-up and further decay until she was finally scrapped in Turkey in 1989.

Grace Line's Santa Elena is launched at Kearny, New Jersey in October, 1932. The Santa Paula is at the fitting-out berth and a third sister, Santa Lucia, is still under construction. In the background is Pulaski Skyway, one of the biggest bridge-highway systems in the World when completed in 1926. (CA/ME)

The Glamorous 'Thirties

On July 18th, 1931, *Mariposa* has just gone down the ways at Bethlehem Steel's yard at Quincy, Massachusetts. Fittingly, being intended for the Australian route, she was launched by the wife of the vice-president of the Matson Line with a bottle filled with water from Sydney harbor. (CA/ME)

MARIPOSA (18,017 grt; 1932 - 1974)

The *Mariposa* was one of three sisters built for the Matson Line. "They were among the most beautiful liners of the 'Thirties," in the opinion of Frank Andrews. "They were so difficult to visit in Melbourne in those days, but I somehow managed. They would arrive at Station Pier on a Thursday and then sail at mid-day on Saturday. Internally, they were very modern, very American. They were just exquisite. They were not true Art Deco but they had some influences and touches."

"I was onboard the *Lurline* during her maiden call at New York. Bethlehem Steel, the builders, were still in charge and remained so all the way out to San Francisco, her homeport," remembered Everett Viez. "And so, Beth Steel ran a trans-Canal cruise, her maiden commercial voyage. She was an absolutely gorgeous ship, both inside and out. She had a very Hawaiian style to her décor, a Pacific island theme, blended with American modern. She proved to be a long-lasting ship as well. She and her sisters were very solid, very strong." The *Lurline* joined the *Malolo* on Matson's Hawaiian route, while the *Mariposa* and the *Monterey* maintained the longer service to Australia.

The *Mariposa*, used as a trooper during the War and then laid-up, was sold to Home Lines in 1953 and became their very successful *Homeric* under the Panama flag. After a fire off the New Jersey coast in July, 1973, she was sold to Taiwanese scrappers. The *Monterey* also saw service as a trooper and was then laid-up, but she was re-activated as the *Matsonia* in 1957. She took over the name *Lurline* in 1963 and continued Matson's Hawaiian sailings until 1970, when she was sold to the Chandris Lines of Greece.

The *Mariposa* was the first of three sisters built for the Matson Line services from San Francisco to Honolulu and to Sydney. She entered service in February 1932 and was followed two months later by the *Monterey*, while the *Lurline* left on her maiden voyage in January 1933. *(Laurence Dunn Collection)*

They refitted her as their *Britanis* and she survived as a popular cruise ship until she was laid-up in 1996, by then 64 years old. She was sold to intermediary buyers, renamed *Belofin I* and sold for scrapping. The *Lurline* had gone to the same Greek buyers, Chandris, in 1963 and was restyled as the *Ellinis*. She was broken-up in Taiwan in 1987.

Left: the main lounge of the *Lurline* in her pre-War days was furnished in a semi-classic style, but with Hawaiian touches.
Above: the *Mariposa* was sold in 1953 to Home Lines, becoming their popular *Homeric*.

The Glamorous 'Thirties

The *Champlain*, with her distinctive slope-topped funnel, is here seen on June 25th, 1932, making her maiden arrival in New York. Unlike *Lafayette*, her running-mate in French Line's Cabin Class intermediate service on the North Atlantic, she was a steamship. (CA/ME)

CHAMPLAIN (28,124 grt; 1932 - 1940)

CGT, the Compagnie Générale Transatlantique – the French Line to North Americans – had an enviable reputation on the Atlantic run for their décor, their service and, expectedly, their food. Following in the wake of the superb *France* of 1912, CGT began a building program of four liners: the *Paris*, intended for 1916 but delayed until 1921 by the First World War; the sensational *Ile de France* of 1927; the motorship *Lafayette* of 1930; and, finally, the *Champlain* of 1932.

Built at the famous St. Nazaire shipyard, the *Champlain* made her début on the Le Havre run in June, 1932. She looked modern, even different. "Although not intended to be an express liner, she was a test ship for the forthcoming *Normandie*," claimed Everett Viez. "She had the same uncluttered decks, the modern funnel, the mast above the wheelhouse. She was typically French moderne for the 'Thirties. But later, when that funnel was raised and given a curious lip at the top, her good looks were spoiled somewhat. She was also a follow-up to the diesel-driven *Lafayette* but that ship had operational problems and so the French Line reverted to steam turbines for the *Champlain*."

"I always felt that, internally, she was too severe, too modern," Viez attested. "The ceilings were boxed, very cubist. But she was very popular, offering top-drawer CGT service and cuisine. She was intended to be a first class liner but because the United States were introducing their *Manhattan* and *Washington* as cabin class ships, the French followed suit with the *Champlain* (and the *Lafayette*). Berthing on the *Champlain* was 623 cabin class, 308 tourist class and 122 third.

Unfortunately, she was an early war casualty. She struck a mine and sank off western France on June 17th, 1940. 330 were lost. Rather amazingly, it took eighteen years, from 1946 to 1964, to salvage her and scrap her remains.

The Cabin Class 'Salon Mixte', or main lounge, on board the French *Champlain*. Although a three-class intermediate liner of less than 30,000 tons, she carried mostly cabin class passengers and her lounges were extremely large and as well appointed as those of her larger fleet-mates. (CA/ME)

A profile photograph of the *Champlain* after her 1936 refit, when the funnel was heightened; owing to the curious top which was added to her stack, she was nicknamed 'Caplain' by New York port workers.

MANHATTAN (24,289 grt; 1932 - 1964)

"The *Manhattan* and *Washington* were probably the very nicest American liners of all," in the opinion of Everett Viez. "They had beautiful, conservatively-styled interiors that were, in fact, the same aboard both. I went to Europe on one and returned on the other, but couldn't feel the difference. The first class dining room had the novelty for the early 'Thirties of air-conditioning. The Carrier Corporation made the system. Before hot, very humid summertime sailings from New York, when I was seeing clients off to Europe and was dressed in a collared shirt and tie, I always went to the dining room to cool off."

Built at the New York Shipbuilding Company's yard at Camden, New Jersey, which was located just across from Philadelphia, these fine sisters were designed for the United States Lines' North Atlantic service (New York to Plymouth, Cherbourg or Le Havre and Hamburg). As built, they had very small, paint can-style stacks but these proved to be impractical and so they were raised, which altogether improved the ships' appearances. They were the original cabin class liners of the early 'Thirties, a move which prompted other companies, at least temporarily, to rename first class as cabin class so that they could lure more passengers with lower fares. Consequently, there was no first class on these ships and the *Washington* listed her passenger capacity as 582 cabin class, 461 tourist class and 196 third class. The two sisters were very successful and they soon prompted the United States Lines to think of a larger variation of their design, a ship which was launched as the *America* in 1939. Both the *Manhattan* and the *Washington* were among the small fleet of US-flag liners that evacuated stranded tourists and others out of Europe in the fall of 1939 when many foreign-flag passenger ship sailings ceased abruptly.

In 1941, both sisters were extensively converted for wartime trooping. The *Manhattan* changed to *USS Wakefield*, while the *Washington* became the *USS Mount Vernon*. *(Photograph: CA/ME)*

THE GLAMOROUS 'THIRTIES

In 1940, with her regular service to Europe suspended, a flag-bedecked *Manhattan* departs from New York on a cruise to the Caribbean. Later she served as a troopship but was badly damaged by fire in 1942. She never returned to civilian service. (CA/ME)

The former *Washington* continued unscathed and, after the War, was revived by the United States Lines, but for all-tourist class sailings between 1948 and 1951. She then went into lay-up along the upper Hudson River, preserved under the watchful eyes of US Government engineers and their crews. The ex-*Manhattan* was less fortunate. She caught fire and was abandoned for a time in western Atlantic waters in September, 1942. Heavily damaged, she was towed to port and was later repaired and rebuilt at considerable expense, resuming military sailings in April, 1944. However, she was laid-up soon after the War ended and never returned to service. She was moored alongside her sister in later years but both ships were declared surplus in 1964 and the following year were towed downriver to the former Federal shipyard at Kearney, New Jersey and quickly dismantled. There had been some talk that Greeks, namely the Chandris Lines, were interested in buying them for Europe – Australia service but, after so many years in mothballs, the cost of restoration would perhaps have been prohibitive.

QUEEN OF BERMUDA (22,575 grt; 1933 - 1966)

"There were few ships better than the *Queen of Bermuda*. She was a true favorite," said Everett Viez. "She had more luxury about her than many trans-Atlantic liners. The service was impeccable and the food top-notch. She was an immaculate ship, first class in every way, and very, very popular on the 6-day roundtrip run between New York and Bermuda. In fact, the Bermuda service was a veritable gold mine for her British owners."

The *Queen of Bermuda* was indeed one of the great liners of the 'Thirties. She was completed in February, 1933 by the Vickers-Armstrongs yard at Barrow-in-Furness and, together with her near-sister, the *Monarch of Bermuda* (1931), she brought great luxury to the Bermuda cruise trade. Along with splendid public rooms, a large main restaurant, an indoor pool and spacious sports and sunning decks, she had an added novelty for her time: every cabin had a private bathroom.

One of New York's favorite and most familiar liners, *Queen of Bermuda* makes a Saturday afternoon departure for her namesake island. In this 1949 photograph, the Lower Manhattan skyline is to the left, with Brooklyn Heights in the background to the right. (CA/ME)

The roundtrip fares in the 'Thirties began at $50, making this the ideal honeymoon cruise. Indeed, the Furness-Bermuda Line dubbed their two liners "the honeymoon ships". They sailed in regular tandem up to that fateful late summer of 1939 when war started in Europe and they were called to more urgent, far less glamorous duties.

"It was the end of August in 1939 and we came home from Bermuda 'blacked out'," recalled Viez. "We were re-routed a few hundred miles during the normal 600-mile passage but actually arrived in New York two hours early. The ship had already been requisitioned by the British government and so every wartime precaution was being taken but, at night, the full moon shone on her snow white upperworks and her silver gray hull, making us all the more vulnerable. There were no lights or even cigarettes allowed on deck. Stewards jumped out of nowhere when a passenger forgot and lit up in an open area.

The lights were dimmed in the outside cabins and the thick drapes in the public rooms were kept closed. There was a tense mood onboard."

The *Queen of Bermuda* put into her West 55th Street pier along Manhattan's West Side early on Saturday morning, September 1st. Other liners such as the *Queen Mary* and the *Normandie* were already laid-up for safety but the *Queen of Bermuda* would go into immediate war service. The disembarkation of over 700 passengers was especially hurried. "A fuel barge arrived almost immediately," added Viez, "and by 11am the ship had gone off to war. There would be no 3 o'clock sailing that afternoon – nor until well after the War, in the late 'Forties. There were reports that enemy U-Boats were everywhere, even in the western Atlantic off the coast of the United States. Another British liner, the *Athenia*, was sunk two days later."

The *Queen of Bermuda* survived the War, returned to the Bermuda run in February, 1949 and sailed in that service until, by now well into maritime old age, she was sold to scrappers in Scotland in late 1966.

"She was a wonderful, very reliable ship and a great fixture at New York harbor for decades," remembered Frank Braynard. "She does have a special distinction: built with three funnels, she was cut down to two during the War and then modernized with one in 1961-62. She therefore sailed as a three-stacker, a two-stacker and a one-stacker!"

The Glamorous 'Thirties

A 1930s view of the First Class Smoking Room on the illustrious *Queen of Bermuda*. Sometimes known as "the honeymoon ship", this fine liner was immensely popular with passengers seeking a luxurious but not necessarily expensive sea trip to the sun. *(Everett Viez Collection)*

OCEANIA (19,507 grt; 1933 - 1941)

According to her designers, the *Oceania* and her sister ship *Neptunia* were intended as "the reaction against the excessive baroque mannerism, with a profusion of rooms furnished in modern style with good taste and simplicity. Aesthetically, their appearance is characterised by a majestic set of central superstructures, surmounted by a sole, imposing funnel. The sharply raked bow and the cruiser stern confer sleek lines upon the profile, while the funnel and the masts ensure vertical continuity and add further grandeur to the overall effect, without creating any imbalance or angles of incidence that disturb the line of vision. The distinguishing feature of the interior of the ship is the ease of access, on and between the decks".

In order to make the passenger spaces even roomier, the uptake from the diesel engines was led up to the funnel via two side casings, leaving an uninterrupted space on the decks amidships. This system had been used for the first time in 1914 on the German steamship *Vaterland*. These liners "à la mode", as they were dubbed, were built in the Monfalcone shipyard for the Cosulich Line and intended for the express service between Trieste and South America. The *Neptunia* came first; she was launched on December 27th, 1931 and 10 days later the keel of her twin, *Eridania*, was laid on the same slipway. She was eventually launched at the end of the following September with the new name of *Oceania*.

Both vessels were propelled by four diesel engines, each one coupled to a three-bladed propeller. They enabled a service speed of 19 knots and top speed of over 22 knots; the diesels on the *Oceania* were manufactured by Fiat Grandi Motori of Turin, while those on the *Neptunia* were supplied by Fabbrica Macchine Sant'Andrea of Trieste.

The *Oceania*, prior to making her first crossing in September 1933, went on a series of Mediterranean cruises, the first of which left Trieste on July 8th, 1933. After that, except for one voyage to the Italian colonies in Africa, the vessel would spend all her brief service life on the route to South America; as it happened, both sister ships were fated to sink on the same day - war victims laden with soldiers. On September 18th, 1941, while in convoy from Naples to North Africa, they were attacked by the British submarine *Upholder*. Three torpedoes struck the *Oceania*, one the *Neptunia*.

Fortunately, they sank slowly, permitting the majority of the troops on board to be saved. The last Italian liners to be built before the War, they are remembered as one of the best examples of Italian nautical architecture and industrial design in the 1930s.

When delivered to her owners, Cosulich Line of Trieste, in July 1933, the *Oceania* undertook a series of Mediterranean cruises before entering the Trieste-La Plata service the following September.

The *Oceania* and her sister *Neptunia* were advertised as 'ships à la mode', thanks to their modern interiors.

The *Oceania*, originally laid down as *Eridania*, was succesfully launched on September 29th, 1932.

Normandie arrives for the first time at the still incomplete Pier 88, at West 48th Street, Manhattan on June 3rd, 1935. Nearby, work is underway on the adjacent Pier 90, which will be completed in time for the arrival of the *Queen Mary* some twelve months later. (CA/ME)

NORMANDIE (79,280 grt; 1935 - 1942)

"In 1939, when I was thirteen, my father sometimes gave me twenty-five cents and a nickel for each way on the subway to go Downtown and see the liners," remembered Jacob Goldstein. "There were lots of daytime sailings from New York back then, many of them on Saturdays. I remember seeing the *Queen Mary*, *Ile de France*, *Champlain*, *Rex* and many others. Earlier, in 1937, I saw Sara Delano Roosevelt, the President's mother, sailing off on the *Conte di Savoia*. There were lots of security men about that day. But in 1939, I especially remember wanting to see the most fabulous liner of them all, the French Line's *Normandie*."

The 79,000-ton (later 82,799 gross tons), 1,000-foot long *Normandie* was not only the World's largest passenger ship at that time, she was certainly the most luxurious, most extravagant, perhaps the most fanciful. She was a stunning creation of artistry, design and decoration. The first class restaurant, for example, was done in bronze, hammered glass and Lalique and could seat 1,000 guests at 400 tables. The Winter Garden included fountains, greenery and exotic birds in large cages. There was a lavish indoor pool, a children's playland, chocolate and flower shops and even a men's tailor where they could produce a suit within the 5 days it took to cross the Atlantic. Every first class suite and stateroom was done in a different décor, first-run movies

The Glamorous 'Thirties

The magnificent *Normandie* on the ways at St. Nazaire, just prior to launching in October, 1932. Her hull, designed by the Russian émigré Vladimir Yourkevitch, was so efficient that she was able to match the speed of her great rival *Queen Mary* despite having less powerful engines. *(CA/ME)*

NORMANDIE

Photographed in May 1935, just a few days before *Normandie*'s maiden voyage, her vast wheelhouse is on the same grand scale as everything else on this incredible liner. The bridge was simply furnished but extremely well designed, with large windows on the curved front and uninterrupted view from one end to the other. (CA/ME)

were shown in the theater and the cooking was said to be the finest afloat.

Everett Viez was once a passenger aboard the *Normandie*, sailing from New York's Pier 88 for Le Havre on June 30th, 1937. "She was totally luxurious. A one-word description would be 'incredible'! There was no ship like her before or after. She was also well ahead of her time. Her great beauty was in her open spaces, that great sense of flow in the passenger areas. Of course, this eventually led to her demise. The fire in 1942 spread far too quickly. On our crossing, we had superb service and food, even better than anything experienced in the 'Fifties and 'Sixties. But, although the French Line had said that the troublesome vibration was gone, we were in a first class cabin two-thirds to the stern and we could still feel it. Cabin class was uncomfortable and third class was unliveable. On every sailing, it was said that third class was like sailing in the roar of the Niagara Falls!"

"On our voyage, the Atlantic was like glass and the ship was at full throttle most of the way. They were making an attempt to regain the Blue Riband which the *Queen Mary* had snatched from her. But on the fourth day, it was rough and speed had to be reduced. She won the record back on a later voyage but then lost it again. Even in a calm sea, the *Normandie* was like a dying duck. If she'd actually entered service as a trooper during the War, as intended, one torpedo would have done her in. The center of gravity was too high."

Normandie's First Class public rooms were among the most magnificent ever to put to sea. Here is the temple-like Grand Foyer to the Dining Room, one of the most imposing areas on this incredible ship.

But despite his reservations, Viez was favourably impressed. "The Winter Garden was my favourite public space. It was all greenery and marble floors and had a great view over the bow. It was a very restful place but it was barely used. The French were planning to replace it with extra cabins for the 1939 season but, because of the threat of war, it never happened. I wasn't really that impressed with the famous first class Dining Room. It was located inside and was actually quite narrow."

Jacob Goldstein recalled one of her 1939 departures, "I remember the great activity of those big yellow Checker-style taxi cabs as they came and went in front of the French Line pier at 48th Street. It was all very exciting. The *Normandie* was my favourite ship and everything about her was special, including the passengers going aboard. And she was so huge, so gigantic that her bow hung over the street edge."

Young Goldstein paid all of ten cents to board the *Normandie* that afternoon. "I even remember the peculiar smell of the Hudson River on that day," he added. "And I saw the specially posted passenger list. There was Baroness Eugenie de Rothschild with the number of her suite against her name – one of the biggest suites onboard. I went up and saw 25 or 30 steamer trunks stacked about. An older man with a French accent intercepted me and barked that I go away. But the Baroness evidently overheard, came out of the suite and agreed to give me an autograph. I was thrilled! My visit to the *Normandie* was now even more special. The next day, an article in the old *New York Sun* said that the Baroness was returning to her castle in Austria, the same one where the Duke and Duchess of Windsor had been entertained."

Goldstein's ship-visiting was abruptly curtailed that fall when the Second World War erupted in Europe and almost all foreign-flag passenger ships ceased their commercial sailings. The great *Normandie* was laid up at the same slip at Pier 88, but then only to burn tragically and capsize three years later, on February 9th-10th, 1942, while being converted to the troopship *USS Lafayette*. She was later salvaged with immense difficulty, laid-up for a time and then broken-up at nearby Port Newark, New Jersey in 1946-47. "I used to feel a little depressed when I came ashore from my visits to those great liners, wishing that I could sail on them," he concluded. "But I was saddest of all when I saw my favorite ship, that most fantastic liner of all, half-sunk and ruined in 1942."

Sweeping staircases, grandes descentes, were much favored by the designers of the great French liners. Here is the one which led to the *Normandie*'s Grand Salon.

One of the most extravagant rooms on *Normandie* was the famous Winter Garden. Much publicised were its cages of exotic live birds. In fact, this was a feature which the French Line had copied from the Italian *Conte Grande* of 1928.

Destruction of a goddess: the once-splendid *Normandie*, burned at her New York pier on the cold afternoon of February 9th, 1942. The great hulk became overloaded with the ceaseless water pumped into her by firefighters attempting to control the rapidly spreading blaze. She began to list and finally capsized, her port side resting in the murky Hudson mud. This is one of the first daytime views on the morning following the fire. It was taken by a US Air Force plane especially sent from Mitchell Field on Long Island. Thick clusters of ice cling to the piers along 'Luxury Liner Row'. (CA/ME)

The sad progress of the demolition of the great ship was well-documented. Above, workmen are chipping away at the 80-foot long tile covered indoor swimming pool in May, 1947. By end of August (below), only a few sections of the double bottom remain: it is a matter of weeks before they too will be transformed into scrap metal. *(CA/ME)*

THE GLAMOROUS 'THIRTIES

Seen here in 1935, her maiden year, *Orion* was one of the most innovative British passenger liners of her day. Although still recognisably an Orient Line ship, she had a modern single-masted profile and her interiors were the height of Art Déco. *(CA/ME)*

ORION (23,371 grt; 1935 - 1963)

"The *Orion* was done in true Art Deco. Ships such as the *Normandie* were actually beyond Deco," according to Frank Andrews. "On the Australian run in the 'Thirties, the P&O ships had the reputation for the best food but the Orient Line had the better décor. P&O loyalists used to say, 'But you can't eat decoration!' The *Orion* was one of the most distinguished liners ever built. She was to the Australian passenger trade in 1935 what the *Ile de France* had been to the Atlantic eight years before, in 1927. New Zealand architect Brian O'Rorke did the *Orion* and adapted the interiors to what was then the rage, Art Deco, which in those days we called 'contemporary'. He blended all the curves and angles

The fine styling of Orion's public rooms is evident in this view of the First Class Main Lounge. The designer, Brian O'Rorke, achieved a much lighter atmosphere than that on most contemporary British liners. *(Peninsular & Oriental Steam Navigation Co., Ltd.)*

and other marine touches in his design and didn't try to disguise the fact that passengers were actually at sea. The result was beautiful. And she had a great exterior as well. The idea of one funnel and one mast was quite different for 1935. In my view, the only ship calling at Melbourne that came close to her was the *Dominion Monarch*."

The *Orion* was the first Orient Line ship to adopt the corn-coloured hull, after this was tested on the fleet-mate *Orama*. The *Orion* and her sister ship *Orcades* were taken for trooping duties in the Second World War.

The *Orcades* was torpedoed and sunk by a German submarine off Cape Town in October 1942, while the *Orion* survived the hostilities. She resumed service, after a long overhaul at her builders' yard in Barrow, at the end of February 1947 on the London-Sydney route. After the merging of P&O with Orient Line in May 1960, the *Orion* became a one-class ship for 1,691 tourists. She was retired in 1963 but then served briefly as a hotel ship at Hamburg for the International Gardening Exhibition, before being handed over to Belgian scrappers that October.

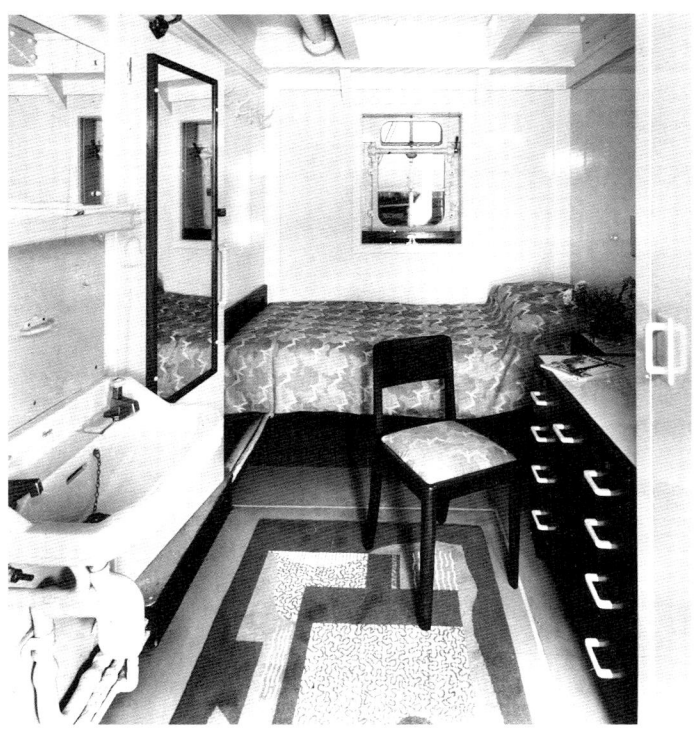

A First Class single-bedded cabin on D Deck aboard the *Orion*. *(Peninsular & Oriental Steam Navigation Co., Ltd.)*

THE GLAMOROUS 'THIRTIES

The *Scharnhorst* and her two near-sisters were actually too large for the Europe - Far East trade but were political gestures by the Nazi government to strengthen German ties with Imperial Japan. In this photograph the light load of the ship clearly shows the shape of her 'Maier-form' bow. (CA/ME)

SCHARNHORST (18,184 grt; 1935 - 1943)

Arnold Kludas notes that "It was not necessary to build these three large combination liners (the others being Hamburg-America Line's *Potsdam* and North German Lloyd's *Gneisenau*). They were never successful. Their construction in the mid-'Thirties was prompted purely by political reasons: the Nazis wanted a link with Japan. Built by Blohm & Voss, the *Potsdam* differed somewhat from her running-mates since she was originally ordered for the Hamburg-America Line but was transferred to the North German Lloyd before completion.

These ships had exceptionally beautiful quarters (149 first class and 144 second class on the *Scharnhorst*). North German Lloyd insisted that they must be the best on the run between Europe and the Far East but, in fact, at 21 knots they were too fast and uneconomical. They did carry many travellers to the Mediterranean but, overall, they never quite fitted." The slightly longer *Scharnhorst* was actually sold to the Japanese in 1942, having been laid up there since 1939. She was converted into the escort aircraft-carrier *Shinyo* but was torpedoed and sunk in the China Sea in November, 1944 by a U.S. submarine.

The *Gneisenau* was also intended to be converted to a carrier, but for the Germans themselves. However, the plan never came about and instead she was sunk by an Allied-laid mine in May, 1943. The *Potsdam* was more fortunate, sitting out the war years as a naval accommodation ship. Seized by the British in 1945, she became a troopship, initially named *Empire Jewel* and then, from 1946 to 1960, *Empire Fowey*.

At first, she proved troublesome but, after being given new boilers and geared turbines, she was very successful. Sold to the Pan-Islamic Steamship Co. of Karachi in 1960, she became the Moslem pilgrim ship *Safina-E-Hujjaj*. She was scrapped locally, at Gadani Beach in 1976.

Unlike many East Asiatic Company motorships, the *Canada* and her sisters were fitted with funnels. Here she is departing from Los Angeles in the fall of 1939 on her last commercial voyage. She was sunk by a mine in November of that year. *(CA/ME)*

CANADA (11,108 grt; 1935 - 1939)

Denmark's East Asiatic Company built three fine combo ships for their service between Northern Europe and the West Coast of North America via the Caribbean and the Panama Canal. The 10,000-ton *Amerika* and *Europa* were built by the Burmeister & Wain yard of Copenhagen and were propelled by a single screw driven by an 8,300 BHP oil engine by the builders. They entered service in 1930-31 on the Copenhagen-Los Angeles-San Francisco route, although the *Amerika*, first of the trio, made her maiden voyage to Siam. The *Canada*, built by Nakskov Skibsvaerft, joined them in the Summer of 1935. Similarly to her sister ships, she carried 55 passengers in all-first class quarters and was driven by the same type of B&W diesel engine, but she differed from them in being fitted with a 'Maier' bow section, with a raked stem instead of a straight one. Therefore she was longer by 9 feet and could manage about one knot more. Unlike most of the other ships in the East Asiatic fleet, which famously lacked funnels, these were twin-stackers.

Sadly, the three sisters were lost during the War; curiously, each of them was sunk by one of the three main threats for a ship during a conflict. The *Europa* was hit by German fire rockets during an air raid, the *Amerika* was torpedoed and the *Canada* struck a mine off Spurn Head in November 1939, becoming one of the first casualties of the Second World War.

The Glamorous 'Thirties

Strathmore, completed in 1935, was alone in the 'Strath' series in not having a sister ship. She was named by the Duchess of York, who was soon to become Queen Elizabeth and still later Queen Elizabeth, the Queen Mother. *(Peninsular & Oriental Steam Navigation Co., Ltd.)*

STRATHMORE (23,428 grt; 1935 - 1969)

Named in April, 1935 by the Duchess of York, later Queen Elizabeth and, still later, Queen Elizabeth, the Queen Mother (her father was Lord Strathmore), this fine liner began her P&O service with a cruise from London to the Canary Islands but then took her place in the regular mail run out to Australia. The lone "Strath" to be built without a sister, she was P&O's first cautious step as the Depression began to ease in the mid-'Thirties and new passenger ship construction could resume.

Used as a trooper during the War, she was out of P&O service for a decade, from September, 1939 until her first post-War sailing on the run to Melbourne and Sydney in October, 1949. In 1963, she was sold to the Greeks, to the Latsis Line and became the *Marianna Latsi* before swapping names with her near-sister, the former *Stratheden*, and becoming the *Henrietta Latsi*. They were both used as Moslem pilgrim ships and the ex-*Strathmore* also served as an accommodation ship at Jeddah. She was scrapped at La Spezia in 1969.

BATORY (14,294 grt; 1936 - 1971)

"*Batory* and her sister *Pilsudski* were what you expected from an eastern European country in the 1930s. They were stark ships on the inside – all vinyl, linoleum and stainless steel. But in their own way, they were quite modern and they were certainly a big improvement on the previous ships in the Gdynia America Line service from the Baltic to New York," noted Everett Viez. "They were the result of a trade agreement between the Poles and the Italians. They were built at Monfalcone by the Cantieri Riuniti dell' Adriatico and the Poles paid for them with consignments of coal."

The two sisters were the largest vessels in the Polish fleet, the flagships of the national merchant marine, and each carried some 750 passengers in two classes. They sailed on the Gdynia – New York run, with occasional cruises. "I attended a travel agents' reception aboard the *Pilsudski* at her Hoboken pier in the late 'Thirties," added Viez. "Whereas we would have multi-course dinners on other liners, the Poles offered a self-service buffet. She was a

Pilsudski and *Batory* came into existence thanks to an agreement between the Italian and the Polish goverments; the latter paid for the building of both sisters with shipments of coal. The Italian shipbuilder CRDA used the plans of their renowned motorship *Victoria* as blueprints. Unusually in the 1930s, both ships were given large bow decorations.

clean, well-served ship but the atmosphere tended to be cold and less than cozy. Later, I saw the *Batory* at St. George's, Bermuda. She was immaculate."

Refitted as a trooper just as the War started in the late summer of 1939, the *Pilsudski* was a very early casualty. While outbound for Australia, she struck a mine off the mouth of the River Humber on November 26th and sank. The *Batory*, however, survived the war years and resumed Atlantic service. However, political problems caused her to be banned from New York in 1951 and she was switched to a North Europe – India service. Later she returned to the North Atlantic, but this time sailing to Montreal. She became a hotel ship at Gdynia in 1969 before going to Hong Kong breakers two years later.

The smart-looking *Batory* which, with her sister *Pilsudski*, represented a big improvement in the Polish service to New York, passes the towering Lower Manhattan skyline on her maiden arrival in May, 1936. (C-A/ME)

(Photograph: CA/ME)

QUEEN MARY (80,774 grt; 1936 -)

"The biggest diamonds were worn on the *Queen Mary*. She had the most elegant first class and carried the most elegant passengers." So remembered Lewis Gordon, although some people might award that accolade to the *Queen Mary*'s great rival, the French *Normandie*. But Mr. Gordon, who crossed the Atlantic on dozens of occasions, had some of his fondest memories of this grand Cunard 'Queen'. She was certainly one of the most beloved liners ever to sail the transocean route between England, France and the USA. Among the superliners of the 'Thirties, those fabulous floating palaces, she was said to be the most profitable. Altogether, she sailed for 31 years, from her triumphant maiden crossing in May, 1936 to her tearful last passage in September, 1967.

This huge ship was built in Scotland, at the John Brown yard at Clydebank. Designed in the late 'Twenties and begun in 1930, she was not completed for five and a half years because of a long delay caused by the Depression. For a time, Cunard directors actually thought of abandoning the project altogether. Fortunately, in the spring of 1934, the British government were persuaded to offer financial assistance – but with provisions. Cunard were forced to merge with their former rivals, the financially-ailing White Star Line. Cunard-White Star Line, Ltd. was formed, with Cunard getting 62% of the stock. In return, the new company was given a three-prong loan: £3 million to complete the new superliner; £5 million for a future sistership or running-mate; and £1 million for emergency working capital. Work on this first ship, Yard Number 534, resumed on April 3rd, 1934 to great rejoicing not only in the shipyard town, which had been badly hit, but throughout Britain. One of the first tasks was to remove 130 tons of accumulated rust from the steel frames of the huge hull.

One of the more charming stories in ocean liner history is the tale concerning the choice of name for this new superliner. Supposedly, the company was overwhelmed with suggestions – everything from *Britannia* and *Galicia* to *Hamptonia* and *Clydania*. There were also some royalist proposals: *Princess Elizabeth*, *Princess Margaret Rose* and even *Marina*, for the popular Duchess of Kent. The most persistent story, though, is that the Cunard directors chose *Victoria*. It was certainly pleasing to the ear and it complied with the company's habitual "......ia" nomenclature. Lord Royden, a Cunard director and a personal friend to King George V, supposedly attempted to gain the monarch's permission to use his late grandmother's name. "Would His Majesty consent to our great new liner being named after the most illustrious and remarkable woman who has ever been Britain's Queen?" The King is supposed to have replied, "This is the greatest compliment that has ever been made to me or my wife. I will ask her permission when I get home."

And so, it is said, Yard Number 534 at John Brown's became the *Queen Mary*. In fact, whatever the truth of that story, the new name was quite fitting. It was a departure in naming policy following the merger of Cunard and White Star. Furthermore, the Government loan prompted consideration for something nationalistic, even inspiring. The monarchy was the perfect vehicle at that time, especially in those bleak days of the lingering Depression. Lastly, and by no means least important, 1935 was to be Silver Jubilee Year in Britain. Old George V and his Queen, by then nearing their seventies, had gained enormous regard: stoic, living icons of a lost age in an ever-changing, often troubled world. Even to little Princess Elizabeth, the future Elizabeth II, her bearded king-grandfather was "Grandpa England". His consort, the bolt upright Mary of Teck, still wearing her Victorian day dresses, choker pearls and toque hats, was equally revered.

Their Majesties, together with the Prince of Wales, entrained from their retreat at Balmoral for Clydebank on Wednesday, September 26th, 1934, for the formal launching of the liner. It was the first time that a reigning Queen of England had named a merchant vessel – an indication of just how important a symbol this great liner was to be. (In due course, the Queen's daughter-in-law and her granddaughter would follow her example.) From behind a glass shield, at just after three in the afternoon, Her Majesty – looking out onto a blanket of some 200,000 umbrellas huddled under a Scottish rain – released a bottle of Australian wine against the freshly painted bow of the liner. In twenty-one words – in fact, her first public speech as Queen Consort – she announced publicly and for the first time the name of the ship. "I am happy to name this ship *Queen Mary*. I wish success to her and to all who sail in her." A hush passed through the crowd – the long secrecy over the naming had ended. Then cheers went up.

Thousands more spectators watched the launch from the opposite shore and still others from the specially moored Anchor Liner *Tuscania*, which had been chartered as a floating grandstand. Within fifty-five seconds, the 30,000-ton shell of the ship was waterborne. Life for "the *Mary*", as she would be affectionately known, had begun. George V called her "the stateliest ship in being". She was also one of the fastest and eventually established her speed supremacy over her great rival, the *Normandie*. With the slightly larger *Queen Elizabeth* not due until 1940, the *Mary* spent the late 'Thirties maintaining the trans-Atlantic express service in company with the veteran *Aquitania* and the ageing *Berengaria*. The Second World War changed all that. The 2,139-passenger *Mary* now became a gray-painted trooper, often carrying over 15,000 men per trip. Her record is still the greatest of all time: 16,683 souls embarked for an Atlantic voyage in July, 1943. Because of her high speed, which enabled her to outpace Hitler's sinister U-Boats, she was known as the "Gray Ghost". Only a collision in October, 1942, when an escorting cruiser, *H.M.S. Curacoa*, sank with the loss of 364 lives, spoiled the *Mary*'s otherwise splendid record.

Leo Reilly sailed aboard her on Christmas Day, 1940. He

was then a very young soldier going off to war. "She was anchored in Sydney Harbor in Athol Bight, just opposite Taronga Park Zoo. It was only her second call at Sydney. She was an extraordinary sight, even in her gray paint. It was a novelty for Australians to see a ship of that size then. We sailed the next day, on the 26th, for Tasmania with the *Aquitania*, *Mauretania*, *Awatea* and *Nieuw Amsterdam* and then made for Trincomalee on Ceylon. I was then transferred to a smaller British troopship, the *Dilwara*. By 1940, the *Queen Mary* had been altered as a full trooper. I was allocated to a crew cabin for 18 that had been changed to berth 84 in sling hammocks. The officers and NCOs were in passenger cabins but all soldiers used hammocks. We were allowed on deck but smoking was banned. It seemed that several thousand personnel all lined up for food at the same time. There was something we called "Bully Beef", corned beef in a tin, and sago pudding. It was Army food, of course. The

Making what must surely have been one of the most exciting maiden arrivals at New York, the *Queen Mary* steams triumphantly into the port on June 1st, 1936. She was regarded as a harbinger of recovery from the devastating Great Depression. (CA/ME)

ventilation was so poor, especially in the Indian Ocean, that we slept on deck. I remember the alarms sounding when a Japanese submarine was thought to have been sighted. Of course, the *Queen Mary* and the *Queen Elizabeth* were sent down to Australia because they were such fast ships. Their safety and security was in their high speed."

Lewis Gordon had rather different memories of the *Mary*. He and his wife crossed in third class in 1938 but by the 'Fifties they were travelling first class.

"There was dancing between courses during dinner in the Verandah Grill. Beef was carved at your table. The Smoking Room had leather chairs and was covered in walnut. We had Leopold Stokowski and Rosalind Russell onboard one sailing. Always very private, Miss Russell used to slip into the ship's theater after the lights went down. But I especially remember that she bid a diamond bracelet as collateral for her bet in the ship's mileage pool."

In the end, by the 'Sixties, the jets had secured most of the Atlantic passenger clientele and great ships like the *Queen Mary* had become huge dinosaurs – old and creaking, out-of-step and money-losing. Retired from Cunard service in the fall of 1967, she found further life, however, as a hotel-museum-restaurant ship at Long Beach, California.

There were many problems in the following years but, under new management, she is now enjoying a noble and assured retirement. She lives on – a sort of permanent shrine, a glorious keepsake in southern California.

QUEEN MARY

British splendor: The First Class Observation Bar and Lounge was and remains to this day a favorite spot aboard Queen Mary.   (CA/ME)

Part of Queen Mary's Gallery. Wood veneers from all over the Empire were used to panel the interiors of this very British ship. (CA/ME)

The famous liner is now in permanent residence as a very popular hotel and museum at Long Beach, California.   (Peter Knego)

169

THE GLAMOROUS 'THIRTIES

The handsome Union-Castle motorliner Stirling Castle leaves Southampton on August 21st, 1936 at the start of her maiden voyage to South Africa. Cunard-White Star's three-funnelled Berengaria and Royal Mail's Atlantis and Alcantara are among the other ships in this view. (CA/ME)

STIRLING CASTLE (25,550 grt; 1936 - 1966)

"She was one of the great pre-War Union-Castle liners," recalled Colonel Norman Dodd. "I remember being aboard her in a wartime convoy, sailing from Freetown in West Africa and then going around the Cape to Bombay. The white stewards were asked to look after some black troops. There was a huge uproar all the way to India."

Completed by Harland & Wolff in early 1936, the *Stirling Castle* and her twin sister *Athlone Castle* were the largest Union-Castle liners built to date. They were long, powerful and had low, motorship funnels. In addition to carrying 297 first class passengers and 492 cabin class, the *Stirling Castle* had enormous cargo capacity for the famed "mail run" between Southampton, Cape Town, Port Elizabeth, East London and Durban.

Both ships were used as Allied troopers during the War and then resumed South African sailings until, in a fleet reduction of older tonnage, they were sold to Far Eastern scrappers in 1966 and 1965 respectively.

KANIMBLA (10,985 grt; 1936 - 1973)

In May, 1995, the 50,000-ton *Crystal Symphony* sailed gloriously into New York harbor at the end of a celebratory maiden crossing from London and from the Finnish shipyard that built her. A stunning, $250,000,000 floating resort with lavish lounges, hot tubs on deck, a Las Vegas-style casino and Asian as well as Italian specialty restaurants, she ranked as the largest and grandest Japanese-owned cruiseship yet. She belongs to Los Angeles-based Crystal Cruises, owned by NYK – or, more fully, Nippon Yusen Kaisha – of Tokyo, then the World's largest shipping company with over 450 vessels. But in 1995, few of those who witnessed her triumphal entry into New York remembered, or had ever known, that years before, Japan's first deep sea cruiseship had been the *Oriental Queen* which sailed in the 'Sixties.

When she was delivered by Harland & Wolff of Belfast in 1936, she was Australia's largest passenger ship. She belonged to the Melbourne firm of McIlwraith, McEachern, who named her *Kanimbla*. Her trade was

STIRLING CASTLE and KANIMBLA

The *Kanimbla* was an outstanding member of the final generation of Australian coastal liners. Here, however, she is seen in later days as the Pacific cruise ship *Oriental Queen*. *(Alex Duncan Collection)*

primarily a coastal one – from Melbourne and Sydney to Brisbane, Townsville and Cairns. She also sometimes sailed on the longer Sydney – Fremantle route. The late Bob Cummins was a steward onboard her in the 'Fifties. "She was the queen of the Australian passenger fleet, unquestionably our very best ship," he remembered. "She was a real beauty, a pocket version of the superb *Nieuw Amsterdam*.

"She had been an armed merchant cruiser and then an assault ship during the Second World War. In addition to our coastal voyages, we used to make two cruises each year from Sydney to Port Moresby, Manila, Yokohama and Kobe. We would spend a full week at Yokohama in those days and the entire cruise took thirty days. These trips were always popular and were booked well in advance."

It was in 1961, that the *Kanimbla* was bought by Japanese owners. According to Hisashi Noma, "she was reconditioned for a new, special cruise service – Japan to Guam and sometimes to Australia, and then back. Renamed *Oriental Queen*, she had a capacity for 364 one-class passengers. There were four suites amongst her accommodations and there was a pool on deck. Toyo Yusen, her new owners, were then big hotel and resort operators in Japan and they hoped this would be a new vacation alternative. But it did not succeed.

"In the 'Sixties and for years thereafter, the Japanese people did not think of cruising for their holidays. The *Oriental Queen* went back to Australia for some charter cruises and then went to Indonesia. She carried Moslem pilgrims between Djakarta and Jeddah, the port for Mecca and, at other times, regular passengers back and forth to Singapore. She was even rumored to have served as a floating brothel, 'a red light ship'."

But with old age setting in, she spent most of her final years at a lonely anchorage.

She went to scrappers in Taiwan in 1973, the end for this first Japanese cruiseship.

AWATEA (13,480 grt; 1936 - 1942)

The 1977-built ro-ro ferry *Rotoiti* is still in service in the Tasman Sea, out of Auckland. She is the last survivor of a once-renowned fleet which ceased activities in 1999. The Union Steam Ship Company of New Zealand, Ltd. was founded in 1875 in Dunedin (the South Island's major port) by James Mills to run coastal freight and passenger services. Its first steamers were the second-hand *Maori*, *Beautiful Star* and *Bruce* and the brand new *Hawea* and *Taupo*. After extending its services to cover the routes between New Zealand and Australia, the Union Company (as it was known) introduced a trans-Pacific service to San Francisco as early as 1885 with modern liners such as the *Mararoa*.

In 1901, the company took a half share in the Canadian-Australian Royal Mail Steamship Company and in a matter of years bought out the other half. Union Steam Ship continued to grow steadily until the outbreak of World War I, which caused it serious financial difficulties: in 1917 the board of directors accepted P&O's proposal to acquire the company, which, however, retained its name and separate headquarters. After the 1924 motorship *Aorangi* and the 1931 turbo-electric driven *Rangatira*, the last outstanding pre-War liner owned by the company was the *Awatea*, which in the Maori language means 'eye of the dawn'. A product of Vickers-Armstrongs of Barrow, this beautiful looking steamer, after a fast delivery passage from England to New Zealand, entered service on the Auckland-Sydney route in September, 1936; she was considered at the time the most luxurious merchant ship in the Southern Hemisphere and also one of the fastest. Her turbines were powerful enough to drive her at over 23 knots.

One of her most exclusive features was her role as an offshore radio station, being fitted with one of the most powerful transmitters of the time. As much of the New Zealand population was scattered in small and distant villages over so vast an area it was not found practical to install shore antennae for transmission and thus the *Awatea* acted as a broadcasting center while cruising the Tasman Sea, obviously becoming very popular with the local communities. The service was inaugurated in September, 1936, when the Hon. Joseph Lyons, Prime Minister of Australia, gave a speech from the vessel's broadcasting center.

In June, 1938, the *Awatea* made headlines when she undocked from Auckland for Sydney at the same time as her rival, the American *Mariposa*. After a few hours side by side, the *Mariposa* overtook the Union Co.'s steamer but at that point the *Awatea*'s master asked for another boiler to be fired (the vessel had six but only four were normally switched on) and thus she entered Sydney first. Accused of having challenged another liner to a race, which was against Union Company rules, the master merely answered that he did not, otherwise he would have switched on two boilers more, instead of one!

After the outbreak of the War, the ship was used also for trans-Pacific crossings to San Francisco and Vancouver. After 54 round voyages, she left Auckland for the last time in August, 1941, when she was transformed into a troop transport and sent to Mediterranean waters. The beloved *Awatea* was one of ten Union Steamship vessels to become a casualty of War. While trooping off North Africa, she was bombed and set afire by German bombers off the Algerian coast during the Allied landing, Operation Torch, in November, 1942 and had to be abandoned. Remaining afloat, she was then sunk by the Italian submarine *Argo*.

(*Photograph: Laurence Dunn Collection*)

THE GLAMOROUS 'THIRTIES

One of several troopships built in the 'Thirties, *Dilwara* belonged to the British India Line, which had a long history of trooping for the British government. Here she is seen arriving at Southampton. (CA/ME)

DILWARA (11,080 grt; 1936 - 1971)

Britain was very much involved in so-called "peacetime trooping", using either chartered liners or purposely-built ships to carry officers, troops and other government personnel to the varied parts of its great but far-flung Empire. Between 1935 and 1939, four 11,000-ton troopers were built by well-known commercial shipping companies for government service.

The first two, *Dilwara* and *Dunera*, belonged to the British India Line. The *Dilwara* was fitted out to carry 104 in first class, 100 in second class and as many as 1,150 troops in dormitory accommodations. The third ship, *Ettrick*, went to P&O and the fourth, the *Devonshire*, belonged to the Bibby Line. All but the *Ettrick* survived the Second World War. The three remaining sisters had interesting second careers after the early 'Sixties. The *Dilwara* became the *Kuala Lumpur* for the China Navigation Co., running Pacific cruises as well as pilgrim voyages from Malaysia to Arabia. She went for scrap in 1971.

The *Dunera* became a schools' educational cruise ship in 1961 and was broken-up in 1967, while the *Devonshire* was sold to British India in 1962 and became their *Devonia*, also serving as a schools' cruise ship and being scrapped in 1967. By then, in the mid-'Sixties, Britain had given up sending troops abroad by sea.

The German East Africa Line's *Pretoria* went aground in Southampton Water on Christmas Day, 1936. An initial attempt to get her off failed but she was finally refloated after thirty six hours.

(CA/ME)

THE GLAMOROUS 'THIRTIES

PRETORIA (16,662 grt; 1936 - 1987)

Built by Blohm & Voss at Hamburg for the German East Africa Line and its associate, the Woermann Line, the handsome twin-stackers *Pretoria* and *Windhuk* were the ultimate German ships in the African trades in the late 'Thirties. They each carried up to 152 in first class and 338 in tourist and became popular on the Hamburg – Cape Town – Durban route.

Both sisters were lost to the Germans during the War years. The *Pretoria* was seized by the invading British in the spring of 1945 and became the troopship *Empire Doon* (1945-49) and then *Empire Orwell* (1949-58). In 1958, she was sold to Britain's Blue Funnel Line, who had her refitted as the Moslem pilgrim ship *Gunung Djati*. Indonesian interests bought her in 1962 but retained her name. In 1979, she was transferred to the Indonesian Navy to become the training ship *Tanjung Pandran*. She finished her days at a Taiwan scrapyard in 1987. The *Windhuk* was caught in African waters as the War started in September, 1939. Two months later, she crossed to neutral Brazil disguised as the Japanese *Santos Maru*. The Brazilian government subsequently seized her and, in May 1942, sold her to the US Navy, who refitted her as the troopship *USS Lejeune*, which entered service in March, 1943. She was idled in 1948 but was not sold to scrappers at Portland, Oregon until 1966.

RUYS (14,155 grt; 1938 - 1968)

The *Ruys* and her two sisters *Boissevain* and *Tegelberg* were the largest and finest built for the Dutch company KPM, Koninklijke Paketvaart Mij, registered in Batavia. They were ordered in 1936 and the *Boissevain* was built by Blohm & Voss at Hamburg, while her two sisters came from Dutch yards: the *Ruys* was launched in Vlissingen by the De Schelde yard and the *Tegelberg* by Nederlandsche SB Mij in Amsterdam.

Originally, the sisters carried just under 700 passengers, including no less than 500 in steerage accommodations, and considerable freight. They were engined with Sulzer diesels and had three propellers driving them to a top speed of 18 knots.

The three ships worked an extensive service, from South Africa to Southeast Asia and the Dutch East Indies and then northwards to Hong Kong and Japan. Used as troopers during the War, all three survived and resumed sailing, but now for the re-styled Java – China – Japan Line, which later became Royal Interocean Lines. By now, the service was even more extended, starting on the East Coast of South America and crossing the South Atlantic to Cape Town before leaving for the Far East.

But by the 1960s, with changes in both passenger ship trading and the shift over to container transport for freight, these liners fell out of step. In 1968, they were sold to scrappers at Kaohsiung on Taiwan.

The *Ruys* is seen here while being fitted out at the De Schelde yard at Vlissingen. She was one of three fine motorships built in the late 'Thirties for the KPM's long route from Japan to South Africa via the Dutch East Indies.

(Richard Faber Collection)

THE GLAMOROUS 'THIRTIES

The *Stratheden* (seen here) and *Strathallan* were last of the five famous 'Strath' liners, which so improved P&O's service from London to the Australian ports via Suez. In addition to First Class passengers, they carried many migrants. *(Alex Duncan Collection)*

A twin-bedded First Class cabin on the *Stratheden*. Many First Class passengers crossed France by train and joined the ship at Marseilles in order to avoid the often stormy passage through the Bay of Biscay. *(Richard Faber Collection)*

STRATHEDEN (23,722 grt; 1937 - 1969)

She and her sister *Strathallan* were the ultimate P&O liners before the Second World War. Their design was an enhancement of the original "Strath" liners, the *Strathaird* and *Strathnaver* of 1931-32. Built by Vickers-Armstrongs at Barrow-in-Furness, they entered the long-haul service between London, Fremantle, Melbourne and Sydney via Suez. They were very handsome ships and, as Frank Andrews said, "about as close as you might get to North Atlantic standards in first class on the Australian run." The *Stratheden* survived the War and sailed for P&O (The Peninsular & Oriental Steam Navigation Co.) until 1964, when she was sold to the Greek-flag Latsis Line for use in the Moslem pilgrim trades, at first as the *Henrietta Latsi* and then, after 1966, as *Marianna Latsi*. When she reached the scrappers at La Spezia in Italy in May, 1969, she was the last survivor of those glorious former P&O "Straths". The *Strathallan* had become a war loss when she was torpedoed off Oran, Algeria in December, 1942.

STRATHEDEN and NIEUW AMSTERDAM

A superbly proportioned liner, the *Nieuw Amsterdam* is here seen while undocking from her berth in Le Havre in 1949; the French Line's *De Grasse* is also visible moored at the same wharf. The hull of the Holland America Line's flagship was later painted in a lighter dove-gray.

NIEUW AMSTERDAM (36,287 grt; 1938 - 1974)

Always one of the North Atlantic's most favoured and popular liners, the *Nieuw Amsterdam* was the largest ship yet built in The Netherlands at the time of her completion in the spring of 1938. Built by the Rotterdam Dry Dock Company for the Holland America Line, she was financed by loans from the Dutch government and was the country's flagship on the route from Rotterdam to New York. Externally, she ranked as one of the most handsome passenger ships of the 'Thirties.

Internally, she was splendidly decorated, an almost peerless example of Art Deco style.

The Dutch handed over the *Nieuw Amsterdam* to the British when Holland was invaded by the Nazis in 1940 and she gave splendid service to the Allies as a troopship. Returned unharmed, she was restored in 1946-47 and resumed sailings on the New York run and on cruises (fulltime after Holland America's final Atlantic crossing in September, 1971) until she was scrapped on Taiwan in 1974.

The *Nieuw Amsterdam* arrives in New York's Upper Bay at the end of her maiden voyage in May, 1938. (CA/ME)

NIEUW
H

The caption for this news photo reads 'Submarines Please Note'. In preparation for her September 5th, 1939 sailing from New York to Rotterdam, workers are painting large letters along the sides of the still-neutral *Nieuw Amsterdam*, with her name and her country. (CA/ME)

THE GLAMOROUS 'THIRTIES

The combination liner Noordam, one of the finest of her type, arrives in New York for the first time on October 7th, 1938, only five months after the maiden arrival of her grander fleetmate Nieuw Amsterdam. The following January, the Noordam was joined by a sister ship, Zaandam. (CA/ME)

NOORDAM (10,704 grt; 1938 - 1967)

The late 'Thirties was a busy period for Dutch shipyards thanks to no less than five new liners ordered by Holland-America Line. The first to be built was the beautiful new Dutch flagship, the Nieuw Amsterdam, which was soon to be followed by four smaller but handsome and innovative combination passenger/cargo ships for the North Europe - USA service: the Noordam, Zaandam, Westerdam and Zuiderdam.

They were intended to introduce club-like, all-one class service. While sold as tourist class, they were in fact first class ships with accommodations patterned after the Nieuw Amsterdam.

The Noordam, first in the series, was the only one to be traditionally launched, by the P. Smit Jr. yard of Rotterdam in April 1938, while the other three sister ships were floated out of the building dock.

Carrying up to 160 passengers, the Noordam was used together with her sister Zaandam on a slower, 9-day service between Rotterdam and New York which appealed to a quieter kind of passenger.

The Zaandam was torpedoed and sunk in November, 1942 while serving as a transport for the Americans. The Westerdam, lying almost completed at the fitting-out quay when the conflict broke out, was sunk and refloated three times; with a six year delay, her maiden voyage Rotterdam-New York started on June 28th, 1946. The Zuiderdam underwent a similar fate during the War years, but, although refloated, she was considered beyond economical repair and thus was scrapped.

The Noordam, however, returned to her owners after the War and sailed on until 1963, when she became the Panamanian Oceanien and was chartered to Messageries Maritimes for Marseilles – South Pacific service, before being scrapped in Split in 1967.

Dressed in flags for a joyous occasion, the German-built *Oslofjord* arrives in New York's Lower Bay for the first time in June, 1938. She had a sadly brief career, being sunk by a mine little more than two years later. (CA/ME)

OSLOFJORD (18,673 grt; 1938 - 1940)

Built at the Weser yard at Bremen, the *Oslofjord* was Norway's finest liner when she was completed in 1938. She was designed for the Oslo – New York service as well as off-season cruises, but her promising commercial career was curtailed by the Second World War. After a period in lay-up in New York, she became a troop transport for the British but she struck a mine off the English east coast on December 1st, 1940 and became a complete loss. A new, Dutch-built *Oslofjord* took her place in the Norwegian America Line fleet in 1949.

WILHELM GUSTLOFF (25,484 grt; 1938 - 1945)

The *Wilhelm Gustloff* belonged to a rather unusual cruise fleet, which has had little documentation outside Germany. The 'Thirties were an age of high spirits as well as upheaval and impending disaster. In Germany, an organization called the KdF (Kraft durch Freude, or Strength through Joy) was created and controlled by the propaganda division of the notorious Third Reich. Adolf Hitler himself took a keen interest in this project, which started in 1934 and was an all-German cruise operation that offered inexpensive holiday voyages to national work-

The Glamorous 'Thirties

The Wilhelm Gustloff lies at the Blohm & Voss yard in Hamburg on March 11th, 1938, being made ready for her maiden voyage. Lavishly furnished and called a 'luxus liner' by the press, she was built to take German workers and their families on cruises under the aegis of Hitler's Propaganda Ministry.   (CA/ME)

ers, and in particular members of the rising Nazi Party and their families. The idea was fuelled by the Depression. It was an alternative use for German liners that might otherwise be out of work and laid-up in those lean years. It became very popular. A German historian, Hans Prager, wrote, "For an enormously large number of 'national comrades', a sea journey in one of those big, white ships was their first encounter with the sea and sea travel altogether; for the great majority of them, it was also an event which a few years earlier could not even have been thought about. Men and women who during their life had scarcely travelled beyond the provincial capital, were now seeing the Norwegian fjords, the Bay of Naples, the Canary Islands and Spitsbergen."

It is generally thought that the onboard entertainment included political lectures and Nazi Party meetings, but evidently this was not the case. Arnold Kludas's researches reveal that "seventy per cent of the passengers on these cruises were ordinary workers and their families. No meetings were held on board. Perhaps the only intention was to have them spread the word of the Nazi movement."

The first ships were recruited from the country's three major passenger fleets: the North German Lloyd, Hamburg America Line and the Hamburg-South America Line. Always decorated with signal flags, KdF pennants and Nazi banners, the fleet included such ships as the *Dresden*, *Monte Olivia*, *Der Deutsche*, *Oceana* and the infamous *St. Louis*, best remembered for her June 1939 voyage to Havana with Jewish refugees, later immortalized in books and in a major film, *The Voyage of the Damned*.

The Third Reich could not have been happier with the response to the KdF project. The ships were filled to capacity. Within three years, by 1937, orders were placed for two specially designed passenger liners. Historically, these rank as the first large, all-cruise vessels ever built. The *Wilhelm Gustloff* came from the Blohm & Voss yard at Hamburg

On a festive day at Hamburg, two grand liners, both dressed in flags, are moored together at the Overseas Landing Stage. The *Wilhelm Gustloff* is in the foreground, with the *Cap Ancona* behind. Crew quarters on the *Wilhelm Gustloff* were said to be equal in style and comfort to those of the passengers. (Richard Faber Collection)

and was commissioned in the spring of 1938. While she was actually owned by the German Workers' Front, her management and staffing were handled by the experienced Hamburg-South America Line.

Both the *Wilhelm Gustloff* and the similar *Robert Ley* were run purely for passengers and carried no cargo at all. Because of their leisure, all-cruise nature, they were comparatively slow ships. But they were fitted with modern accommodations, extremely sophisticated fire safety systems and two very large searchlights, attached to the foremast and mostly used to floodlight coastal areas for the enjoyment of passengers. Hans Prager added, "These ships were, in fact, remarkable vessels in many respects. They became the pacesetters for the construction of specialized cruiseships, even down to the present day. All 1,465 passengers had outside cabins. And the *Wilhelm Gustloff* was the first sea-going ship on which, according to Nazi Party instructions, the crew had to be accommodated in exactly the same manner as the passengers."

Expectedly, the ships and the entire Strength through Joy concept disappeared amidst the ruins of the Second World War. Both the *Gustloff* and the *Ley* were used as hospital ships at first and then as floating barracks in occupied Poland. Later, they were destroyed within two months of each other in the final days of the conflict, in the spring of 1945. Dr Horst Uppenberg was inducted in the German

The lengthy Promenade Deck aboard the *Wilhelm Gustloff*. As with many later cruise ships, she had a very long superstructure and virtually no cargo space. In many ways, she was a very modern ship. *(Richard Faber Collection)*

Navy in August 1944. He recalled those tense times and the massive exodus from the collapsing Eastern Territories, the area round the port of Danzig. "There was very little actual naval warfare going on in the fall of 1944 and the winter of 1945. But we were escorting ships full of Germans fleeing from the Red Army. Anything and everything was used. The Nazi Army held off the Red forces as we loaded ships like the *Robert Ley*, *Wilhelm Gustloff*, *Cap Arcona* and *General von Steuben*. The *Prinz Eugen* and two old cruisers were used to protect them. In all, Admiral Dönitz and his officers brought 2,500,000 back to the west with only a 2% loss of life. By Christmas 1944 everything was being sent to sea for the evacuation. It was a particularly severe winter. Those who fled by land went by sleds, but the Soviet Air Force got them. The Nazis had no air resistance left and no oil. The Soviets planned to kill all the German men and rape all the women. They thought only of complete brutality."

"On January 30th 1945, the fully lighted *Wilhelm Gustloff* was one mile offshore. There were soldiers, WACs and civilians onboard. There were even bunks in the drained swimming pool. A Soviet submarine fired two torpedoes and the ship went down within an hour. The temperature was zero. There were bodies everywhere. In all, only 900 were saved out of approximately 6,000 onboard. We took the living and placed their freezing bodies next to the diesels of our patrol boat for warmth."

The loss of the *Gustloff* ranks as the worst tragedy in maritime history. Some say the actual figure, still vague because of the lack of authentic passenger lists, stands as high as 5,400 lost. This terrible disaster has since been the subject of several German books and films but it has been given surprisingly little attention elsewhere. Many, for example, still think of the loss of the *Titanic* with just over 1,500 casualties as the worst sea disaster ever.

DOMINION MONARCH (27,155 grt; 1939 - 1962)

Classical-looking in the best tradition of sturdy passenger ship design, Shaw, Savill & Albion's *Dominion Monarch* was a product of the famous Tyneside builders, Swan, Hunter & Wigham Richardson. Considered one of the finest passenger firms under the Union Jack, Shaw, Savill ordered her in response to a serious rivalry on the Down Under trade, from England to Australia. Her prime competitors were two sets of brand new sisterships: the *Orion* and *Orcades* of the Orient Line and the *Stratheden* and *Strathallan* of the mighty P&O company. The *Dominion Monarch* was, in fact, a fine passenger-cargo liner with a very large freight capacity. In six holds, there was some 650,000 cubic feet of cargo space. The majority of this was refrigerated, particularly for meats brought homewards from Australia (and New Zealand). Her passenger quarters were of the highest standard and might best be described as club-like. She carried only 508 at full capacity and all of them in first class.

According to Scott Baty, the Sydney-based author of *Ships That Passed*, a commemorative on bygone liners serving the South Pacific, "The *Dominion Monarch* was considered to be the 'Queen Mary of the Clipper Route', the Australian service from Britain that went via the South African Cape

Dominion Monarch, one of the World's largest passenger-cargo liners, is seen off Gravesend on February 16th, 1939, en route from King George V Dock in London, where she has loaded freight, to Southampton to pick up passengers for her maiden voyage to Australia and New Zealand. (CA/ME)

An impressive view looking aft of the hull of the second *Mauretania* under construction at the Cammell Laird's yard at Birkenhead. Her keel was laid on Empire Day, May 24th, 1937.

rather than Suez. Shaw, Savill had a very good reputation at the time and the *Dominion Monarch* was their top ship." Frank Andrews recalled her from visits to Melbourne in 1939. "The *Dominion Monarch* came and went at odd times – she had no strict schedule. She had the loveliest decoration, a position she shared with *Orion*. They were the very best British ships on the Aussie run at the time. The American *Mariposa* and *Monterey* of the Matson Line were also among the most delightful and impressive. The *Dominion Monarch* was done with touches of the Robert Adam style. She wasn't as pleasing on the outside, however. She was nice, but she could have been nicer. The superstructure seemed to come from a White Star liner from thirty years before. She was split just aft of the bridge. The bow was bluff and she lacked an aft mast. She needed more sleekness about her, she was heavy-looking. But, of course, she was possibly the biggest combo ship of her time."

After extensive and heroic wartime service as a troopship (she was nearly captured by the Japanese during the fall of Singapore), the *Dominion Monarch* was restored to her original, luxurious self. In 1962, she was withdrawn but gained a brief reprieve as a floating hotel at Seattle for the World's Fair. Later that year, she was scrapped at Osaka in Japan.

MAURETANIA (35,738 grt; 1939 - 1965)

Cunard-White Star revived the beloved name *Mauretania* for an intermediate ship they added four years after her famous predecessor went off to the breakers. Internally a scaled-down version of the *Queen Mary*, externally she was a smaller version of the huge *Queen Elizabeth*, which was due about ten months later, in April, 1940.

Often incorrectly said to have been built as an occasional substitute for the *Queens* on Cunard's new 5-day express service between Southampton, Cherbourg and New York, the *Mauretania* was best suited to 6- and 7-day passages via Cobh or Le Havre. Transformed into a troop transport in Sydney, in March 1940, she was given back to Cunard Line in September 1946 and sent to her builders in Birkenhead to be refurbished.

Her first post War voyage to New York started in Liverpool on April 26th, 1947, but already in June her British terminus port became Southampton. In her final years, with her hull painted in Cunard's "cruising green" in December 1962, she was used for an experimental Mediterranean – New York service and for cruising, but she was broken-up in Scotland in 1965.

MAURETANIA

With her decks completely plated, giving an idea of her size and of her broad promenades, the *Mauretania* is only a few days away from her launching. She was the largest liner yet built in England (bigger ships had come from yards in Northern Ireland and Scotland).

The Glamorous 'Thirties

Three photographs of the festive launch of the second *Mauretania*, at Cammell Laird's Birkenhead yard on July 28th, 1938. The wife of Cunard Line's chairman, Sir Percy E. Bates, acted as godmother, unveiling her name which had been hidden by British and U.S. flags on the bow.

The *Mauretania* during her last years of service as a cruise ship, with her hull painted in pale green. Somewhat overshadowed by the reputation of the illustrious first *Mauretania* and by the greater speed and size of the *Queen Mary* and *Queen Elizabeth*, she was nevertheless a very fine and popular liner.

Sleek and modern, the *Cristobal* was the third of the George G. Sharp-designed liners of the Panama Line, built to maintain the important link between New York and the Canal Zone. Here she is arriving in the Upper Bay, New York from her builders' yard on August 13th, 1939. (CA/ME)

ANCON (10,021 grt; 1939 - 1973)
CRISTOBAL (10,021 grt; 1939 - 1981)

"The three Panama Railroad Company sisterships *Panama*, *Ancon* and *Cristobal* were ahead of their time," according to Everett Viez. "They were so different, even for 1939. While attractive ships, they were also severe, very modern, extreme in their Art Deco style, with high public rooms and stainless tubular furniture." Built by the Bethlehem Steel Company at their yard at Quincy, Massachusetts, they were created purposely for the New York – Panama Canal Zone service, carrying lots of freight and 216 all-first class passengers. They served heroically as troopships during World War II. "They were quite a contrast to ordinary liners. Although carrying many civilian passengers, they were like the post-War MSTS vessels, the Military Sea Transportation Service – peacetime troopships, but of a higher standard. They were never on my list of interesting passenger ships." My own recollection of these ships is much more favourable. I remember watching their regular departures from New York's Pier 64 and admiring their crisp, modern profile and their immaculate paintwork. The *Panama* had a long career, becoming American President Lines' *President Hoover* in 1957 and Chandris Cruises' *Regina* (and later, *Regina Prima*) in 1965. She survived until 1986. The *Ancon* was scrapped in 1973 and the *Cristobal* in 1981.

The Panama Line's *Ancon* has just come down the ways at Bethlehem Steel's yard at Quincy, Massachusetts on a winter afternoon, February 25th, 1939. Tugs are now shifting her to the fitting-out berth. *(CA/ME)*

The Glamorous 'Thirties

The largest ship built by Royal Mail Lines for their South American service, *Andes* was completed in the fall of 1939, only to be immediately requisitioned for conversion into a troopship in World War II. *(Roger Sherlock)*

In 1959-60, *Andes* was refitted as a single class luxury cruise ship and, repainted all-white, sailed continuously from Southampton. She had already acquired a fine reputation in the British cruise market, perhaps matched only by that of the *Caronia*. *(Alex Duncan)*

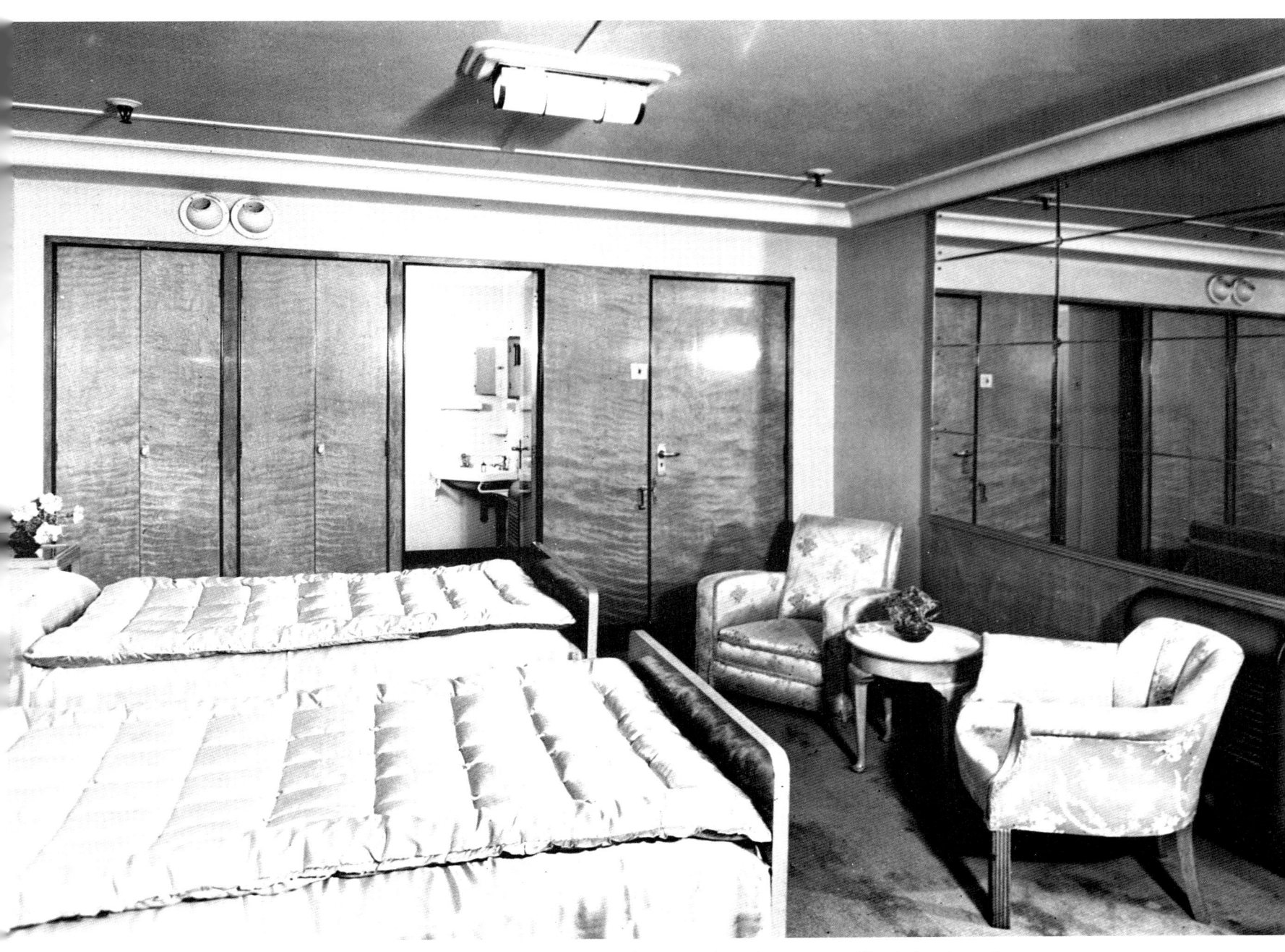

The bedroom of one of the *Andes*' luxury suites. First Class passengers on the services from the east coast of South America to Europe were particularly demanding and expected accommodation of a very high standard. *(Royal Mail Lines)*

ANDES (25,689 grt; 1939 - 1971)

"In the spring of 1945, I returned home as a soldier in the British Army in the *Andes*," said Colonel Norman Dodd. "As troops, we were five bunks high in the former ballroom. We'd climb up to the top bunks on cases. We had all kinds of personnel onboard. There were few diversions during the long voyage up to Liverpool, merely endless days at sea. We'd just sit around being scared. Even though the European peace was declared during the voyage, there were frantic rumours that there were some Nazi subs still about, going mad and sinking carelessly!" The *Andes*, built by Harland & Wolff at Belfast, was intended to be Britain's finest luxury liner on the run to the East Coast of South America. Owned by Royal Mail Lines, she was to have been a competitor to the brand new French *Pasteur*.

But both ships, due in the summer of 1939, were too late to see commercial service and, instead, were pressed into military duties, dressed in gray paint. Her war service finished, the *Andes* was restored by 1948 and sailed her southern water route for about a decade before being converted into an all-first class luxury cruise ship. She built up a following of devoted passengers but was broken up in Belgium in 1971.

The Glamorous 'Thirties

After distinguished service as an Australian hospital ship but maintaining her Dutch crew, the *Oranje* re-entered service on the Amsterdam-Batavia route via the Suez Canal. Here she is seen during a call at Genoa. *(Paolo Piccione Collection)*

ORANJE (20,017 grt; 1939 - 1979)

Built at Amsterdam and completed in the politically charged summer of 1939, this fine liner had barely entered service on the route to the Dutch East Indies before the Second World War erupted in Europe. The flagship of the Nederland Line's service to Batavia via Suez, she was the fastest Dutch colonial liner as well as the most luxurious. "Her décor was in the East Indies style and included priceless woodwork," noted Everett Viez. Controversially, he continued, "She had beautiful interiors, but not a particularly beautiful exterior. This was true of several other large Dutch colonial passenger ships, including the *Johan van Oldenbarnevelt*."

The *Oranje* was used as a Royal Australian Navy hospital ship during the War years. Afterward, she sailed her intended route to the East but later, after the Dutch East Indies had become the independent state of Indonesia, she was switched to a round-the-World service. In 1964, however, she was sold to Italy's Flotta Lauro, who rebuilt her in the modern style as the *Angelina Lauro*. Unfortunately, she burned out at St. Thomas in the US Virgin Islands in the Caribbean in March, 1979. Later that same year, she sank while under tow en route to the breakers on Taiwan.

The royal launch of the *Oranje* by H.M. Wilhelmina, Queen of The Netherlands, took place in Amsterdam on September 8th, 1938.

ORANJE

The brand new Nederland Line flagship *Oranje* is seen leaving her builders' yard to run her sea trials in August 1939. She sailed on her maiden voyage to the Dutch East Indies on September 3rd, 1939, just as the War broke out.

Many of the interiors of the *Oranje* were among the first works by Van Tienhoven, who later became well known for having designed all the major post-War Dutch liners.

The luminous full-width first class restaurant of the *Oranje*, designed in a late Art Déco style by the Dutch architect Lion Cachet.

The Glamorous 'Thirties

The Pasteur, *seen here on the ways at St.Nazaire, ready for launching on February 15th, 1938, was intended to replace* L'Atlantique, *lost by fire, as the French flagship on the route to the east coast of South America.* (Richard Faber Collection)

PASTEUR (29,253 grt; 1939 - 1980)

The French *Pasteur* was intended as a replacement for the luxurious *L'Atlantique*, which had fallen victim to fire in 1933. Delivered just as World War II started in September, 1939, the *Pasteur* was to have taken *L'Atlantique*'s place in the Compagnie de Navigation Sud-Atlantique's service between Bordeaux and the East Coast of South America. In fact, she spent most of the war years as an Allied troopship. Afterward, she was not restored for commercial service but from 1945 to 1956 was used continuously by the French government as a troopship, becoming well-known because of her single huge funnel. She was sold to North German Lloyd in 1957 and rebuilt as the *Bremen*. In 1971, following the recent amalgamation of North German Lloyd with HAPAG, she became surplus and was put on the sale list. In October she was bought by the Greek-owned Chandris Cruises, who renamed her *Regina Magna*. Unsuccessful as a cruise ship because of her high fuel costs, she was laid-up in 1974. Three years later, she was sold to Philippine interests and used as a workers' accommodation ship in Saudi Arabia. She was now called *Saudi Phil 1* and later *Filipinas Saudi 1*. She sank in the Indian Ocean on June 9th, 1980 while en route to Taiwan for scrapping.

After wartime service as a British-flag troopship, *Pasteur* was returned to the Cie. Sud Atlantique. Her huge funnel was painted in their colours even though they chartered her to the French government for full-time trooping duties, mostly to colonial Indo-China. *(Richard Faber Collection)*

With her commercial service cancelled because of the outbreak of the Second World War, *Pasteur* was soon sent to safety on the other side of the Atlantic. Here, she is seen arriving at the French Line's Pier 88 in New York on June 11th, 1940. *(CA/ME)*

On July 9th, 1959, the former *Pasteur* set sail from Bremerhaven for her first voyage to New York as the North German Lloyd flagship *Bremen*. She had been extensively refitted by the Bremer Vulkan yard of Vegesack, including new high pressure boilers, a reshaped funnel and a new fore mast.

CLOUDS OF WAR

When the Second World War broke out in September 1939, besides the *America* and the *Queen Elizabeth* in advanced stage of outfitting, there were three other significant liners on the slipways in Europe and their building would continue slowly during the War: the 29,307 grt *Stockholm*, in Italy, the 41,000 grt *Vaterland*, in Germany and the 17,321 grt *Maréchal Pétain*, in France. The *Stockholm* was one of the most illfated liners ever. Ordered by the Swedish American Line from the Cantieri Riuniti dell'Adriatico yard of Monfalcone in late 1937, she was intended to become an outstanding flagship, extremely modern in her exterior appearance and in her interiors as well. She had been conceived to spend a good part of her life as a one-class cruise ship for 640 guests. Destroyed by a violent fire when almost completed on May 29th, 1938, her hull was cut down to the waterline, re-hauled on the slipway and rebuilt. When she was ready to enter service, in October 1941, her Swedish owners could obviously not take delivery of her, and she remained laid up in Trieste, where she was completely destroyed during a British air raid in July 1944 and later scrapped.

The HAPAG's *Vaterland* could have become a beautiful and distinctive transatlantic liner as well, but launched in an advanced stage of construction by Blohm & Voss in Hamburg on August 24th, 1940, she remained idle at her outfitting quay and, in July 1944, she became a total loss following the heavy air raids which hit the Hanseatic city.

The French vessel, by contrast, would eventually be completed. Laid down at the Constructions Navales yard at La Ciotat in 1939 for the Messageries Maritimes of Marseilles Far East service, her building progressed constantly, although slowly, during the conflict and she was launched on June 10th, 1942 as the *Maréchal Pétain*. Sunk by the Germans while they were retreating from Southern France in August 1944, she entered service five years later on her intended route but now with the name *La Marseillaise*.

A night view of the United Staes Lines' *America* at the fitting-out berth at Newport News, Virginia in the spring of 1940 emphasises what a very streamlined ship she was as originally designed. On the following page, the liner, the new flagship of the entire U.S. merchant marine, goes down the ways on August 31st, 1939. Her importance was underlined by the fact that she was launched by Mrs. Eleanor Roosevelt, the wife of the American President. (CA/ME)

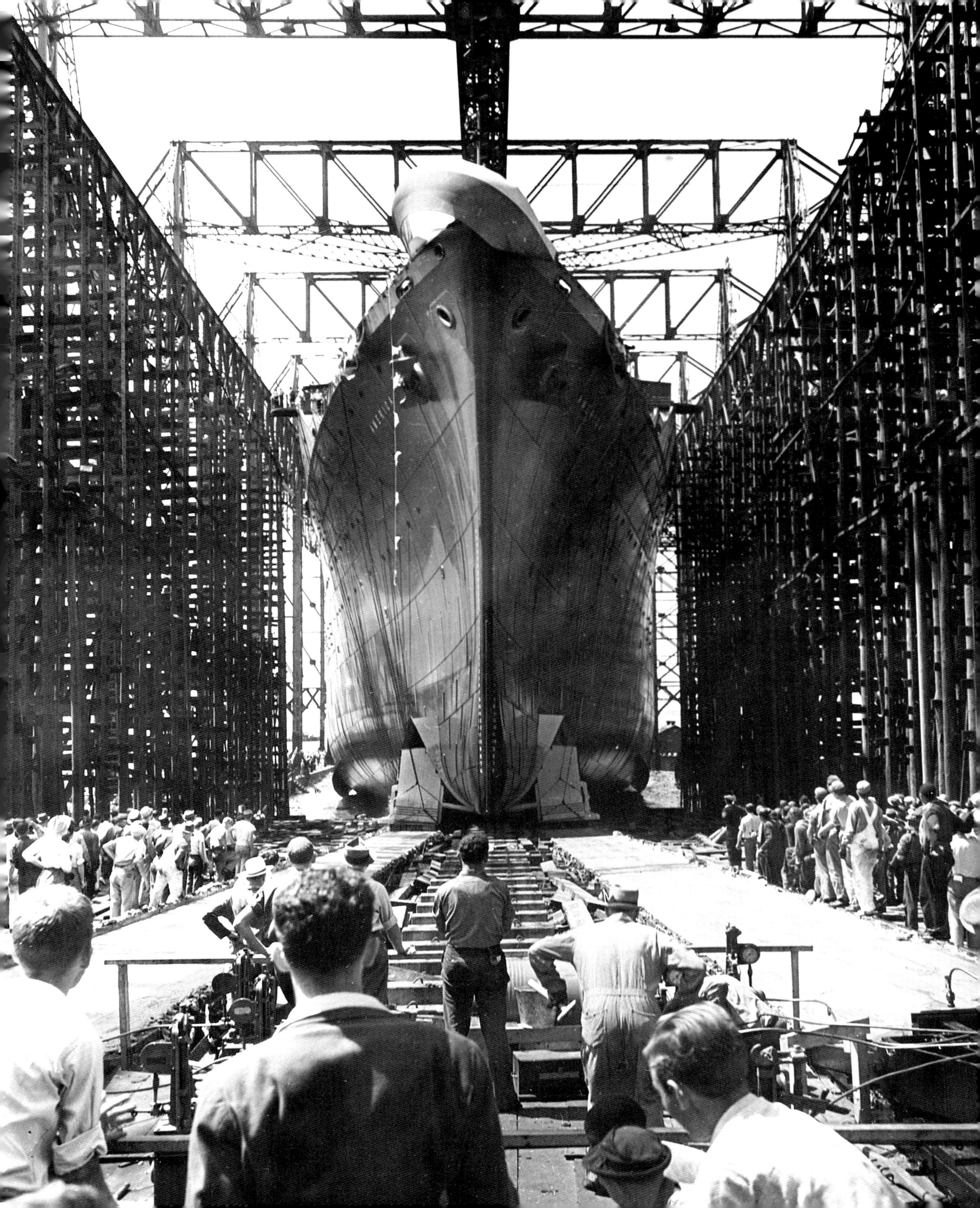

AMERICA (26,454 grt; 1940 - 1994)

By 1936, the U.S. Government decided to encourage the rebuilding of the country's merchant fleet. Washington allocated extensive and liberal loans and operating subsidies to shipowners to renew and strengthen their fleets. Aptly, the first ship in this program was to be the country's largest and finest newly-built passenger liner for the prestigious Atlantic run to Northern Europe. The earlier, German-built *Leviathan* (the former *Vaterland*) was already laid-up, silent and rusting at her Hoboken berth, and only two years away from being discarded to scrappers. It seemed fitting that the new ship should be named *America*. She was to be operated by United States Lines. Ordered from the famous Newport News Shipbuilding & Drydock Co.'s yard in Virginia, she was named by Eleanor Roosevelt, the wife of President Franklin D. Roosevelt, on August 31st, 1939, just one day before Hitler's forces invaded Poland and started World War II. When the *America* was completed in the summer of 1940, trans-Atlantic crossings were no longer considered safe and she was used briefly for cruising. Thereafter, she was made over as the troopship *West Point*. By the time she was returned to her owners in 1946, she had carried over 450,000 troops on long, crowded voyages.

She was in many ways a prototype to the larger *United States*, the World's fastest liner and the last of the true Blue Riband holders, which sailed from 1952 until 1969. But the *America*, though smaller and slower, was preferred by many loyal passengers on account of her comfortable atmosphere.

She was retired from US-flag service in 1964 and sold to Greek owners, Chandris Lines, becoming their *Australis*. With her passenger number greatly enlarged, she became one of the most successful ships on the migrant run from Europe to Australia. Under various owners, she briefly reverted to *America* in 1978, then *Italis*, *Noga*, *Alferdoss* and finally *American Star*. It was under that last name that she reached the end of her long career. While under tow from Greece to Thailand, so as to become a hotel ship at Bangkok, she went aground off the Canary Islands on January 18th, 1994, was abandoned and broke in two.

(Photograph: CA/ME)

The giant hull of the *Queen Elizabeth* takes shape on the slipway of John Brown & Co. at Clydebank. The building contract was signed on October 6th, 1936 and her keel was laid three months later. *(CA/ME)*

QUEEN ELIZABETH (83,673 grt; 1940 - 1972)

The Cunard Line's brilliant scheme to instigate the first two-ship trans-Atlantic express service with a weekly sailing in each direction produced the most famous pair of liners ever built. The *Queen Mary* came first and, because of this and also her record-breaking, Blue Riband-winning speed, she was always preferred by many passengers and certainly had one of the most glistening maritime careers ever. She came into service in the spring of 1936, in the great age of the Atlantic superliner, rivalling such ships as the *Bremen*, *Rex* and *Normandie*. She had a spectacular maiden voyage that received worldwide press attention and immediately established her reputation, prompting the boast that "every school child on both continents has heard of the *Queen Mary*." The second partner in this extraordinary team, known almost everywhere as 'the Queens', did not experience any of this initial celebrity. In fact, she arrived quietly and almost immediately went into war service.

She was quite different from the *Queen Mary*, which, in fact, was an updated version of the classic *Aquitania* of 1914. The *Queen Elizabeth* looked more modern, with two instead of three funnels, and the upper decks were clear of the ventilators and other apparatus which seemed to crowd the topmost areas of the older ship. She had just twelve boilers as against the *Mary*'s twenty-four. One of Cunard's technical engineers, disguised as a grocery clerk, had made a trip on the rival *Normandie* and his findings were influential in the design of the *Elizabeth*. As a result, there was quite a difference between Cunard's first and second express liners. Launched on September 27th, 1938 by Her Majesty Queen Elizabeth, later the Queen Mother, the huge new liner (which remained the largest passenger ship ever built until the debut of the *Carnival Destiny* in 1996) was scheduled to enter service in April, 1940. Instead, during the fall of 1939, as the European political situation worsened, her completion was no longer considered a high priority. Many of the work gangs at the John Brown yard were re-assigned to warships. The *Elizabeth*'s interiors were left unfinished, vast and shell-like, and only essential electrical and plumbing work was completed. It was even suggested that she should be sold to the US government.

The unfinished ship was thought to be a huge target for the Luftwaffe and, in February, 1940, Winston Churchill, then First Lord of the Admiralty, ordered her away from British shores. New York was selected as the haven where she could berth alongside the temporarily laid-up *Queen Mary*. This was, of course, a top-secret decision. The crew heard rumors of Halifax as the *Elizabeth*'s destination but the big graving dock at Southampton was alerted that she would be arriving there for final outfitting. It was all part of a scheme by British Intelligence to mislead the Nazis. Obviously, it worked. On the very day that the new 'Queen' was due at Southampton, enemy bombers were circling over the Channel, waiting for her. But the liner, with some shipyard workers still onboard, was speeding out into the Atlantic and darting to the safety of American waters. Berlin was furious.

The *Queen Elizabeth* finally reached Manhattan's Pier 90 on March 7th. Months later, in November, she was sent off to war – one of the most important Allied troopships. First assigned to Indian Ocean duties, by 1942 she was returned to the North Atlantic, to the famed "G.I. shuttle". Carrying 15,000-plus service personnel on each crossing (to Gourock in Scotland), she was paired with the equally powerful *Queen Mary*, but in a far different relay from the luxurious express service which Cunard and their designers had anticipated.

Both of these big Cunarders were changed extensively during their urgent, highly secretive war years. They were, for example, given 'standee' bunks that were stretcher-like contraptions made of canvas slung between poles. These required a minimum of space and were arranged as many as six high. Consequently, a former two-berth stateroom could hold ten times that number. These standees were also placed in the former lounges and other public rooms, with only two dining rooms and a pair of saloons being retained as open spaces.

Both 'Queens' were meticulously guarded during the War. Their crewmembers were often handpicked and 750 guards were stationed at the Cunard New York terminal. Nevertheless, bottle caps were once found stuck in the nozzles of fire hoses onboard the *Elizabeth* and, later, holes were discovered in several lifeboats, which sank when lowered. Two unexploded bombs were found in a pile of blankets in April, 1943 and were immediately thrown overboard. But overall, both the *Elizabeth* and the *Mary* gave impeccable and unsurpassable wartime service. Miraculously, they survived just about undamaged.

The *Elizabeth*, selected to be the first to be restored, entered service in October, 1946. She was joined by the *Mary* in the following summer and the two-ship weekly Atlantic service, a Cunard dream since the late 'Twenties, finally came into operation. The 'Queens' were the most spectacularly profitable pair of Atlantic superliners ever built and headed the great Cunard-White Star passenger

CLOUDS OF WAR

Dwarfing several destroyers being built for the Brazilian government, the mighty *Queen Elizabeth* is seen at the John Brown yard on September 5th, 1938. Later that month, on the 27th, she was due to be launched by H.M. Queen Elizabeth. (CA/ME)

fleet. The line was said to be carrying one-third of all North Atlantic sea-going travellers in the 'Fifties and at one point, during 1958, had twelve passenger ships in service to the United States and Canada.

However, by the early 'Sixties, as the jet aircraft was succeeding in its takeover, both 'Queens' began to show increasing deficits. Even a special, costly upgrading of the *Elizabeth*, given in the winter of 1965-66 and intended to make her more suitable for tropical cruising, was of little help. When it was decided to retire the *Mary* in September, 1967, the decision was extended to include her running-mate as well. Originally intended to sail until as late as 1975, the *Elizabeth* came off the Atlantic trade in October, 1968. Following somewhat in the *Queen Mary*'s wake (she went to Long Beach, California to become a hotel and museum ship), the *Elizabeth* was sent to Port Everglades, Florida for similar purposes. But, amidst deepening financial and start-up problems, the 2,238-passenger liner sat for two years – rusting, sunscorched, mostly neglected. Finally, placed on the auction block in September 1970, she was sold to the Taiwanese shipping tycoon, C. Y. Tung. His plan was to refit her as a floating university-cruiseship touring the World. Renamed *Seawise University* and placed under the

QUEEN ELIZABETH

This photograph, taken at John Brown's yard on February 27th, 1940 was not released to the newspapers until March 6th. By then, the still incomplete *Queen Elizabeth*, the World's largest liner, had safely 'escaped' to New York. Several of the spectators in this picture were members of the wartime armed forces. *(CA/ME)*

Bahamas flag, she voyaged out to Hong Kong via the Caribbean and South Africa – but it was a tedious affair, marred by breakdowns. A year or so later, on January 9th 1972, the former *Queen Elizabeth* was just about ready. She had undergone $6,000,000 worth of refitting and was lying in Hong Kong harbor, shortly to sail for Japan, where she would be drydocked, and then to start her maiden voyage. She was due to call at New York that fall during a World cruise. But fires suspiciously broke out and spread rapidly throughout the ship. Fireboats and other craft poured vast amounts of water onto her, but with the same reckless miscalculation that had ruined the *Normandie* nearly thirty years earlier. The next morning, the *Seawise University* turned on her side and capsized. She was a total loss. Talk of salvage and restoration was based more on optimism than reality. In the end, the only hope was scrapping where she lay. A Japanese firm took charge and removed the remains. Today, a container-port built on landfill occupies the spot. At New York, her memory endures. In Lower Manhattan, along Water Street, near to the South Street Seaport Museum and in front of the C. Y. Tung Building, there is a sculpture in tribute to the former Cunarder. Her record was one of the greatest of all trans-Atlantic liners.

Contrasts of War: the Queen Elizabeth, *painted in war time grey, rests at Pier 90, where she arrived on March 7th, 1940. The Italian Line's* Rex, *by now among the very last liners connecting Europe to America, is leaving for her 100th eastbound crossing, which will prove to be her penultimate voyage. The date is April 13th, 1940.* (Todd Neitring Collection)

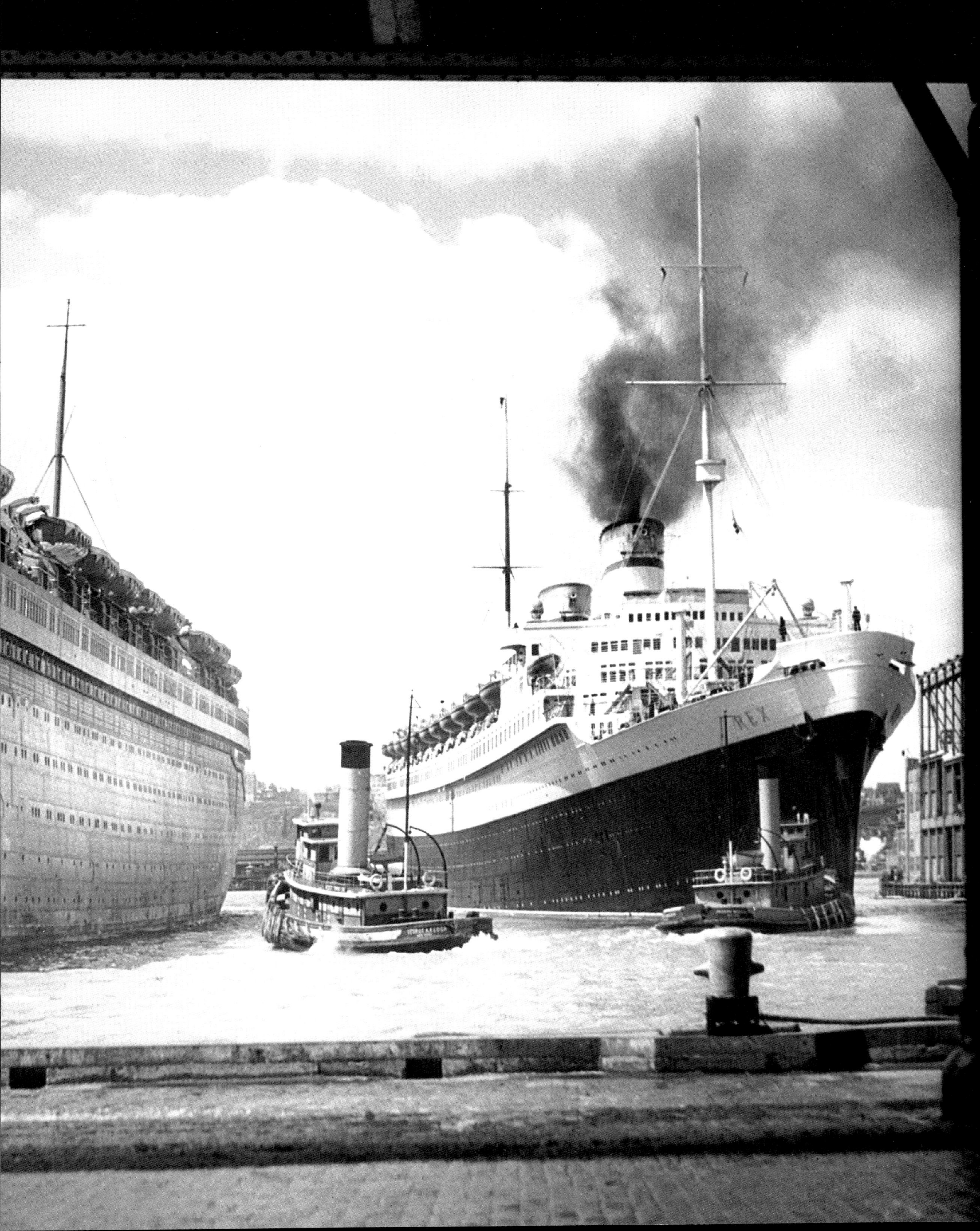
REX

AFTERWORD

The story of the *Liners of the Golden Age*, does not quite end with the *Queen Elizabeth*. Several other liners were being built when the War broke out. Some, such as the *Maréchal Pétain* entered service once the conflict was over. Others, such as the *Stockholm* were lost. But the real finale to our story has yet to come. There is still one glorious survivor. Several years ago – some thirty or so after she made her last departure from "Luxury Liner Row" at Manhattan – I spent a few nights on the *Hotel Queen Mary*, once the great speed champion *Queen Mary* and now permanently moored at Long Beach, California. What a link to the 'Thirties, to that grand and busy era for passenger ships on all the seas!

We arrived after dark (it is a 30-minute ride from Los Angeles airport) and so the first impression was one of radiance: twinkling lights strung from end to end; the three enormous, floodlit funnels; those outer and upper decks all lighted and aglow; and seemingly hundreds of portholes and windows, all sparkling. An elevator carried us to a large gangway that in turn fed into the lobby on A Deck. Immediately, we were drawn back to yesterday, yesteryear, to the 'Thirties. It reminded me of a set from that Hollywood immortal, *Grand Hotel*, or perhaps from some of those lush musicals. There were swirls and large floral patterns in the carpets. There were polished woods, oversized chairs and sofas and trumpet lamps. There were also mounted photographs of onetime celebrity passengers: the Churchills, the Windsors, Bob Hope and Cary Grant, Joan Crawford and Greta Garbo. As a hotel guest, you now join their ranks – well, sort of. I too was a "passenger" on the great *Queen Mary*.

A sense of good care prevailed as I walked along the seven foot-wide corridors. There was a tone of deliberate order, even serenity. There was none of that crowded, busy-as-you-go atmosphere of some big hotels, for example. Happily, I was assigned to one of the so-called Royalty Staterooms, number 145 on Main Deck. It measured an impressive 420 square feet and was priced at $140 per day, double occupancy, at the time. It was certainly reminiscent of glamorous shipboard luxury: a full bath, a second sink, a dressing area,

The Messageries Maritimes liner *La Marseillaise*, was launched on June 10th, 1942 with the name of *Maréchal Pétain*. Sunk as a block ship at Port Bouc by the Germans during their retreat from Southern France, she was recovered and put into service in 1949, ten years after she had been ordered.

AFTERWORD

The *Stockholm* was the only ocean liner to be launched twice. Solemnly sent down the slipway by H.R.H. Princess Margret of Sweden on May 29th, 1938 at the Italian yard of Monfalcone (as shown in the picture), she was later destroyed by a fire, partly dismantled, re-hauled on the slipway and launched again on March 10th, 1940. She was destroyed by British bombers while laid up near Trieste in 1944.

large double-door closets, an electric fireplace (there was air-conditioning as well), television (that amenity was barely known aboard ships when the *Mary* last sailed in the mid-'Sixties) and even a mounted electric fan (no longer in use, but an ornamental reminder of the devices that used to help cool down the 81,200-ton ship on steamy summertime voyages.)

But then, of course, the *Queen Mary* is more than just a hotel. She is a museum as well, the largest maritime facility anywhere. Although she has long since been classed officially as a "building" – since she is powerless and receives all her needs from shore – she actually remains one of the largest passenger ships afloat, only recently exceeded by the new cruiseships of 100,000 tons and more. The museum re-creations, the order of them all and the sense of detail, were superb. An engine room visit, for instance, included a sound and light show. Dramatic voice overlays added to the excitement. Then there were also re-creations of restaurant table settings, the radio room, the hospital, the beauty salon and even of wartime conditions when the *Mary* sailed as an Allied trooper, carrying over 15,000 on many voyages. And, of course, memorabilia abounded: mounted photos and log books, china and silverware, menu cards and some prized steamship posters.

As I departed two nights later, a young bellman said that he hoped I would return. Indeed, I intend to – a stay on the *Queen Mary* is a fantastic treat, a journey through Time on one of the greatest *Liners of the Golden Age*.

FLEET LIST by Maurizio Eliseo and Anthony Cooke

New York's famous luxury liner row in the 1930s. (CA/ME)

Key to the Fleet List

The name of the vessel is the first she had in the period covered by this book (1930 – 1940) and it corresponds to the title of the relevant chapter with the history of the ship. Previous and subsequent names are to be found in the text of the fleet list.

There is then the name of the Owners, followed, where applicable, by the acronym and the English name of the company and the place where they were headquartered at the time.

The name of the Builders and the place where the ship was built come next, followed by the yard number. Dimensional data given include the gross tonnage (1 ton = 100 cubic feet), i.e. the inside volume of the vessel, excluding the double bottom. For ships registered in Panama (duly indicated in the fleet list), the gross tonnage is instead a figure calculated on the basis of a formula taking into consideration linear measurement and other factors. Significant changes of gross tonnage are reported (if, for instance an open air veranda was enclosed during a refitting, the net tonnage and the gross tonnage were then increased by this new extra enclosed volume.)

The power of the propulsion plant is given in hp (1 hp = 0.746 kW); for reciprocating steam engines is expressed in indicated horse power ('ihp'), obtained from the steam pressure developed inside the cylinders; for turbines, the unit of measure is the shaft horse power, the actual power measured on the shaft; while for oil engines the brake horse power ('bhp'), i.e. the power measured on the crankshaft, is used. Turbines on early vessels were directly coupled to the shafts, while after World War I, more efficient sets of turbines, geared to the shaft, were introduced (often, each set was made of three turbines, one of low, one of medium and one of high pressure).

Turbo-electric or Diesel-electric propulsion means that turbines or oil engines were coupled to electric generators supplying the electricity to drive the electric propulsion motors. When the propulsion plant of the vessel was not manufactured by the Builders, the name of the manufacturer is given. The speed is the maximum attained on sea trials.

In order to make the research of the ship easier, the fleet list is in alphabetical order.

ALBERT BALLIN

Hamburg-Amerika Linie (HAPAG, Hamburg America Line), Hamburg
Blohm & Voss, Hamburg, yard no. 403
20,815 grt; 627x73 ft
Two sets of geared steam turbines; 13,500 shp; twin screw; 16 kn
Passengers: 251 first class; 340 second class; 960 third class; crew 415
Sister ships: *Deutschland*, *Hamburg* and *New York*

1922, December 16th: launched.
1923, July 4th: maiden voyage, Hamburg – New York.
1930: refit by Blohm & Voss, including new boilers and turbines; 29,000 shp; 19.5 kn.
1934: further refit by Blohm & Voss with new bow; 677 ft; 21 kn; passengers: 204 first class; 361 tourist class; 400 third class.
1935, October: renamed *Hansa*; Albert Ballin was Jewish and it was not acceptable in Nazi Germany to have a ship which was named in his memory.
1940: taken up as an accommodation ship by the German Navy.
1945, March 6th: struck a mine and sank off Warnemünde while evacuating German refugees from East Prussia.
1949: raised by the Soviets and converted at Antwerp and Warnemünde.
1953: the still uncompleted ship was renamed *Sovietsky Soyuz*.
1954: damaged by explosion and fire.
1955, September: after six years, the ship was finally delivered to Sovtorgflot, who placed her in service out of Vladivostock; 23,009 grt; now had a single funnel instead of the original two.
1971: overhauled at Taikoo Dockyard, Hong Kong.
1984: scrapped.

ALCANTARA

Royal Mail Steam Packet Co., Ltd., London
Harland & Wolff, Belfast; yard no. 586
22,181 grt; 656x78 ft
Two Burmeister & Wain oil engines; 15,000 bhp; twin screw; 17 kn
Passengers: 432 first class; 223 second class; 775 third class
Sister ship: *Asturias*

1926, September 23rd: launched.
1927, March 4th: maiden voyage Southampton – Buenos Aires.
1931: collapse of the parent Kylsant group; Royal Mail Steam Packet Co. later reconstructed as Royal Mail Lines, Ltd.
1934, November: returned to Harland & Wolff for rebuilding; 22,209 grt; two sets of geared steam turbines; 22,000 shp; 19 kn; length o.a. 666 ft; passengers: 331 first class; 220 second class; 768 third class.
1935, May 4th: re-entered service.
1939, September 27th: armed merchant cruiser; forward funnel removed.
1940, July 28th: damaged during a battle with the German auxiliary cruiser *Thor* in the South Atlantic.
1944: converted to troop transport by Cammell Laird at Birkenhead.
1948, October 8th: first post-War commercial voyage Southampton – Buenos Aires after restoration; 22,608 grt; passengers: 221 first class; 185 second class; 470 third class; still only had one funnel.
1958, May: sold to Japanese shipbreakers.

AMERICA

United Sates Lines, New York
Newport News Shipbuilding & Dry Dock Co., Newport News, Virginia, yard no. 369
26,454 grt; 723x93 ft
Two sets of Parsons geared steam turbines; 37,400 shp; twin screw; 24 kn
Passengers: 543 cabin class; 418 tourist class; 241 third class; crew: 643

1939, August 31st: launched
1940, August 10th: maiden cruise to the West Indies; her intended transatlantic service was no longer possible.
1941, July: taken over by the U.S. Navy as the troopship *U.S.S. Westpoint*.
1946, July 22nd: released by the Navy and refitted to resume service as *America*; 26,314 grt; passengers: 516 first class, 371 cabin class, 159 tourist class.
1946, November 14th: first commercial transatlantic crossing, New York – Southampton and Le Havre.
1949, November: 33,532 grt.
1951: with the S.S. *United States* soon to enter service, it was possible to extend the route to Bremerhaven.
1960: refit; 33,961 grt; cabin and tourist class combined.
1964, November: sold to Chandris Lines, Piraeus; refitted as *Australis*; 26,485 grt; 2,258 single class passengers.
1965, August 20th: maiden voyage, Piraeus – Sydney, subsequently Southampton – Sydney, outward via Suez, returning via Panama; later, outward via the Cape.
1977, November: began the final voyage under the Australian migrant scheme; laid up at Timaru, New Zealand.
1978, June: sold to Venture Cruise Lines, who renamed her *America* and used her for an unsuccessful cruise programme out of New York.
1978, August 28th: re-purchased at auction by Chandris; later laid up in Perama Bay as the *Italis*, now with a single funnel instead of two.
1979, July: briefly used for Mediterranean cruises.
1979, September: laid up.
1980: sold to Compagnie Noga d'Importation et Exportation; now called *Noga* but still laid up.
1984: sold to Silver Moon Ferries, who renamed her *Alferdoss*; still inactive.
1994, January 18th: while in tow from Greece to Bangkok with the name *American Star* to be transformed into a floating hotel, she went ashore on a rocky coast off the Canary Islands. Broken in two, the last remains of the ship are being slowly washed away by the sea.

ANCON

Panama Railroad Company, Inc. (Panama Line), New York
Bethlehem Steel Co., Quincy, Massachusetts, yard nos. 1468
10,021 grt; 493x64 ft
Two sets of geared steam turbines; 9,150 shp; twin screw; 18.5 kn
Passengers: 202 first class
Sister ship: *Cristobal*, *Panama*

1939, February 25th: launched.
1939, June 22nd: maiden voyage New York – Cristobal.
1942, January 11th: became a U.S. Army transport; 1942, August: transferred to the U.S. Navy (*U.S.S. Ancon* – AP66); later became Amphibious Force command ship AGC4.
1946, February 25th: returned to her owners; refitted for civilian service.
1951: Panama Line became a division of the Panama Canal Company.
1961, April 1st: government-owned Panama Line was directed by President John F. Kennedy to cease all commercial operations.
1961, June: laid up.
1962, January 8th: sale of the vessel to the Maine Maritime Academy through the U.S. Department of Commerce announced.
1962, June 29th: re-entered service as the training ship *State of Maine*.
1973, May: broken up at Wilmington, Delaware.

ANDES

Royal Mail Lines, Ltd., London
Harland & Wolff, Ltd., Belfast, yard no. 1005
25,689 grt; 669x83 ft
Two sets of geared steam turbines; 30,000 shp; twin screw; 21 kn
Passengers: 403 first class; 204 second class; crew: 451

1939, March 7th: launched.
1939, September: maiden voyage to Buenos Aires, planned for the 26th, cancelled owing to the outbreak of the Second World War; converted into a troopship.
1945, May: carried the Norwegian government-in-exile to Oslo.
1948, January 22nd: maiden commercial voyage Southampton – Buenos Aires after refit; passengers: 324 first class, 204 second class.
1960, June 10th: became a full-time cruise ship after rebuilding at Vlissingen; 25,895 grt; passengers: 480 first class.
1971, May 7th: arrived at Ghent, Belgium, to be broken up.

AORANGI

Union Steamship Co. of New Zealand (P&O Group), London
Fairfield Shipbuilding and Engineering Co., Ltd., Glasgow, yard no. 603
17,491 grt; 600x72 ft
Four Sulzer oil engines; 13,000 bhp; quadruple screw; 18.2 kn
Passengers: 436 first class; 284 second class; 227 third class; crew 328

1924, June 17th: launched.
1925, January 2nd: maiden voyage Southampton – Vancouver; then placed on the Vancouver to New Zealand and Australia route.
1931, August: transferred to Canadian Australasian Line, a joint-venture between Union Steamship and Canadian Pacific.
1938: refitted; passengers 248 first class; 266 cabin class; 125 third class.
1940, February: troop transport.
1944: accommodation and depot ship in various Pacific ports.
1946: returned to her owners and refitted; passengers 212 first class; 170 cabin class; 104 third class.
1948, August 19th: first post-War voyage from Sydney to Vancouver.
1953, July 25th: arrived at Dalmuir, Glasgow for breaking up.

AQUITANIA

Cunard Steam Ship Co. Ltd., Liverpool
John Brown & Co., Ltd., Clydebank; yard no. 409
45,647 grt; 901x97 ft
Four direct driven steam turbines; 62,000 shp; quadruple screw; 24.3 kn
Passengers: 618 first class; 614 second class; 1998 third class; crew 972

1913, April 21st: launched.
1914, May 30th: maiden voyage Liverpool – New York.
1914, August: taken over by the Royal Navy and converted into an auxiliary cruiser.
1915: troop transport, then hospital ship.
1919, June 14th: first post-War civilian voyage Southampton-New York; November: converted to oil-firing.
1926, January 28th: forced to quit Quarantine Island by a gale, she smashed the pier while docking.
1926: refurbished; passengers: 610 first class; 950 second class; 640 tourist class.
1939, November 21st: troop transport.
1948, May: 1st voyage Southampton – Halifax; one-class ship.
1950, February 21st: arrived at Faslane for breaking up.

ARANDORA

Blue Star Line, Ltd., London
Cammell Laird & Co., Ltd., Birkenhead; yard no. 921
12.847 grt; 535x68 ft
Two sets of geared steam turbines; 8,400 shp; twin screw; 16 kn
Passengers: 164 first class
Sister ships: *Almeda, Andalucia, Avila* and *Avalona*

1927, January 4th: launched.
1927, May: entered service London – Buenos Aires.
1929: became a full-time cruise ship following a refit by Fairfield Shipbuilding & Engineering Co., Ltd.; 14,694 grt; passengers: 354 first class; renamed *Arandora Star*.
1934, December: re-entered service after a further refit; 15,305 grt.
1936: further rebuilt; 15,501 grt.
1939, December: taken up by the Royal Navy for experiments with anti-torpedo nets.
1940, May: troop transport.
1940, July 2nd: torpedoed and sunk by *U 47* while crossing the Atlantic with 1178 Italian and Germans prisoners of war and 430 crew; 761 lives were lost.

ARUNDEL CASTLE

Union-Castle Line, London
Harland & Wolff Ltd., Belfast; yard no. 455
18,980 grt; 661x73 ft
Two sets of geared steam turbines; 15,000 shp; twin screw; 18 kn
Passengers: 234 first class; 362 second class; 274 third class; 300 steerage; crew 440
Sister ship: *Windsor Castle*

1915: laid down with the intended name of *Amroth Castle*; work suspended owing to the War.
1919, September 11th: launched.
1921, April 22nd: maiden voyage Southampton – Cape Town.
1937: rebuilt by Harland & Wolff with new raked bow and two funnels instead of four and new turbines; 19,118 grt; length o.a. 686 ft; passengers: 219 first class; 167 second class; 194 tourist class.
1939: troop transport.
1950, September: re-entered civilian service after overhaul and refit by Harland & Wolff; 19,216 grt; passengers: 164 first class; 371 tourist class.
1958, December: left Southampton on her last voyage to the breakers in Kowloon.

ASAMA MARU

Nippon Yusen Kaisha (NYK Line), Tokyo
Mitsubishi Shipbuilding, Nagasaki, yard no. 450
16,975 grt; 583x72 ft
Four Sulzer oil engines; 19,000 bhp; quadruple screw; 21 kn
Passengers: 222 first class; 96 second class; 504 third class; crew 330
Sister ship: *Tatsuta Maru*

1928, October 30th: launched.
1929, October 10th: maiden voyage Yokohama – San Francisco.
1937, September 2nd: blown ashore in a hurricane at Saiwan Bay, Hong Kong.
1938, March: refloated after being partly dismantled; two of her four engines had to be removed in order to lighten her.
1938, September 15th: resumed service.
1941: taken over by the Japanese Navy for use as a troop transport.
1944, November 1st: sunk by the U.S. submarine *Atule* in the China Sea.

ATHOS II

Messageries Maritimes, Marseilles
AG 'Weser', Bremen
15,275 grt; 566x66 ft
Two sets of geared steam turbines; 9,500 shp; twin screw; 16 kn
Passengers: 165 first class; 155 second class; 100 third class; crew: 350
Sister ship: *D'Artagnan*

1925, November 12th: launched.
1927, March 25th: maiden voyage Marseilles – Far East.
1938: two additional turbines added; 16,000 shp; 18.5 kn; passengers: 84 first class; 108 second class; 113 third class.
1939, August: laid up in Algiers.
1940: laid up at Marseilles except for a single repatriation voyage from Alexandria to Marseilles in July 1940.
1942, December: taken over as a troop transport by the Allies.
1946, July 17th: first post-War voyage Marseilles-Saigon.
1959, August 3rd: arrived at La Spezia for breaking up.

AUGUSTUS

Navigazione Generale Italiana (NGI), Genoa
Ansaldo S.A., Genoa Sestri, yard no. 282
32,650 grt; 711x83 ft
Four MAN-Ansaldo oil engines; 28,000 bhp; quadruple screw; 20.5 kn
Passengers: 302 first class; 504 second class; 1,404 third class; crew: 500
Sister ship: *Roma*.

1926, December 13th: launched.
1927, November 27th: maiden voyage Genoa-Buenos Aires; occasionally employed on the Genoa-New York route.
1932, January 2nd: transferred to the new company 'Italia Flotte Riunite', together with all the NGI fleet.
1939: Italian Line announced that the vessel and her sister ship *Roma* would be laid up at the end of the year to be converted into two modern trans-Atlantic motor liners for both the North and South American run. The plan foresaw re-engining by new Fiat oil engines (eventually built and fitted after the War on the new *Giulio Cesare* and *Augustus*), the fitting of a new stem and stern, the whole rebuilding of upperworks (with a single funnel) and hotel areas, designed in modern style by *Conte di Savoia*'s interior archtect Gustavo Finaly Pulitzer.
1939, December 2nd: transferred to the Genoa–Valparaiso route.
1940, May 23rd: laid up in Trieste at the end of a Mediterranean cruise.
1940, July 9th: arrived in Genoa, laid up.
1942, July 7th: taken over by the Italian Navy to be converted into an aircraft carrier; renamed *Sparviero*.
1943, September: after the Italian Armistice the work on the vessel was suspended; at this time she was a gutted hull waiting to be rebuilt.
1944, September 25th: the Germans sank the *Sparviero* to block the Genoa port entrance.
1948: IRDES of Genoa (a company specializing in underwater salvage) dismantled the hulk on the spot.

AWATEA

Union Steam Ship Company of New Zealand, Ltd., Wellington
Vickers-Armstrongs, Ltd., Barrow-in-Furness, yard no. 707
13,480 grt; 545x74 ft
Two sets of geared steam turbines; 22,500 shp; twin screw; 23.3 kn
Passengers: 377 first class; 151 tourist class; 38 third class.

1936, February 25th: launched.
1936, August 5th: left Birkenhead for her delivery voyage to Wellington.
1936, September 5th: maiden voyage Wellington-Auckland-Sydney
1937, October: trans-Tasman record crossing between Auckland and Sydney at an average speed of 23.1 knots.
1941, August 11th: last call at Auckland; then requisitioned and transformed for trooping.
1942, November 7th: bombed and set afire by German raiders while engaged in the Allied landings 'Operation Torch', off Bougie, Algeria. Abandoned one mile off the port breakwater.
1942, November 11th: the smouldering hulk, still afloat, was torpedoed and sunk together with the British auxiliary cruiser *Tynwald* by the Italian submarine *Argo*.

BATORY

Gdynia-Ameryka Linje (Gdynia-America Line), Gdynia
Cantieri Riuniti dell'Adriatico, Monfalcone, yard no. 1127
Twi Sulzer-CRDA oil engines; 14,000 shp; twin screw; 20 kn
Passengers: 370 tourist class; 400 third class; crew: 260
Sister ship: *Pilsudski*

1935. July 3rd: launched.
1936, May 18th: maiden voyage, Gdynia – New York.
1939, September: laid up at New York at the outbreak of the Second World War but handed over to the British government; used as a landing ship and a troopship, still with a largely Polish crew; managed by Lamport & Holt. Took part in the Norwegian campaign of 1940, the evacuation from France and the North African and Sicilian landings.
1946: handed back to her owners; during a refit at Antwerp she was damaged by fire but was repaired; passengers: 412 first class; 420 tourist class.
1947, April 1st: first post-War commercial voyage, Southanpton – New York; subsequently resumed her Gdynia – New York service.
1950: Gdynia-Ameryka became Polish Ocean Lines.
1951, April: *Batory* denied berthing rights at New York following a series of incidents including the smuggling of an East German spy out of America. August: commenced a new Gdynia – Bombay – Karachi service following a refit on the Tyne.
1953: her captain asked for political asylum in Britain.
1957, August 26th: commenced a new Gdynia – Montreal service after a further refit, this time at Bremerhaven; passengers: 76 first class, 740 tourist class.
1968, December: replaced on the Atlantic run by the newly-acquired *Stefan Batory* (ex-*Maasdam*).
1969, June: sold to Gdansk city for use as a floating hotel.
1971, May 11th: arrived at Hong Kong for breaking up.

BELGENLAND

Red Star Line, Antwerp
Harland & Wolff Ltd., Belfast, yard no. 391
27,132 grt; 697x79 ft
Two triple expansion steam engines plus low pressure turbine; 18,500 ihp; triple screw; 18 kn
Passengers: 500 first class; 600 second class; 1500 third class

1914, December 31st: launched and laid up in incomplete state.
1917, June 21st: completed as the 2-funnelled freighter *Belgic* (24,547 grt) for operation by the White Star Line.
1918: fitted out as troop transport.
1921, April: laid up.
1923, April 4th: maiden voyage Antwerp – New York after completion as the three-funnelled passenger liner *Belgenland* as originally planned for the Red Star Line.

1933, March: laid up, except for occasional cruises.
1935, February 16th: first voyage New York to Havana, via Miami and Nassau after she had been transferred to the Atlantic Transport Line and renamed *Columbia* (24,578 grt) for use in the Panama Pacific Line New York – California service and cruising.
1935, May 18th: National Tours chartered the ship to make four thirteen-day cruises to South America and the West Indies during Summer.
1935, September: laid up in New York.
1936, March 26th: sold to Douglas & Ramsey of Glasgow for scrap.
1936, May 4th: arrived Bo'ness to be broken up.

BERENGARIA

Cunard Steam Ship Co., Ltd., Liverpool
Vulcan, Hamburg; yard no. 314
52,117 grt; 909 x 98 ft
Four direct driven steam turbines; 74,000 shp; quadruple screw; 24 kn
Passengers: 908 first class; 972 second class; 942 third class; 1772 steerage; crew 1180
Sister ships: *Vaterland* and *Bismarck*

1912, May 23rd: launched as *Imperator* by the German Kaiser; originally intended to be named *Europa*.
1914, June 10th: maiden voyage Cuxhaven-New York.
1914, August: laid up in Hamburg for the duration of the War.
1919, April 27th: taken over by the U.S. Shipping Controller; sailed to New York, where became a US Navy transport.
1920, February 21st: first voyage Liverpool-New York under charter to Cunard.
1921, February: sold to Cunard Line and renamed *Berengaria*.
1922, May: first voyage after extensive refit in Newcastle; oil burning; 52,226 grt; passengers: 972 first class; 630 second class; 515 Tourist class; 606 third class.
1938, March 3rd: damaged by fire while in New York; returned to Southampton by her own means but without passengers; laid up.
1938, December 6th: left Southampton to be broken up at Jarrow; the lower part of the hull was towed to Rosyth in 1946 and broken up.

BERGENSFJORD

Den Norske Amerikalinje (Norwegian America Line), Kristiania (Oslo)
Cammell, Laird & Co., Birkenhead; yard no. 787
10,666 grt; 530 x 61 ft
Two quadruple expansion steam engines; 8500 ihp; twin screw; 17 kn
Passengers: 105 first class; 216 second class; 760 third class.
Sister ship: *Kristianiafjord*

1913, April 8th: launched.
1913, September 27th: maiden voyage Oslo-New York.
1931: refitted by AG 'Weser' of Bremen; central propeller driven by a low pressure turbine added; maximum speed increased to 18 kn; passengers 90 Cabin class, 573 third class.
1940, December: transformed in New York to Allied troop transport, managed by Furness, Withy & Co. with Norwegian crew.
1946, February: returned to her Norwegian owners; sold in November to Home Lines, renamed *Argentina*; passengers: 32 first class; 969 tourist class.
1947, January 13th: first voyage for Home Lines Genoa-Central America; occasionally used on the Genoa-New York route.
1953, February: sold to Zim Israel Line, Haifa, renamed *Jerusalem*.
1953, April 29th: first voyage Haifa-New York; later used on the Haifa-Marseilles route.
1957: renamed *Aliya*.
1959, August 13th: arrived in La Spezia to be broken up.

BERLIN

Norddeutscher Lloyd (NDL, North German Lloyd), Bremen
Bremer Vulkan, Vegesack, yard no. 614
15,286 grt; 572x69ft
Two triple expansion steam engines; 12,000 ihp; twin screw; 16.0 kn
Passengers: 220 first class; 284 second class; 618 third class; crew 326

1925, March 24th: launched.
1925, September 26th: maiden voyage Bremerhaven – New York.
1928, November 15th: took part in the rescue of passengers and crew from the British liner *Vestris* which had sunk the previous day in a gale.
1929: passengers: 257 cabin class; 261 tourist class; 361 third class.
1938, October 17th: laid up at Bremerhaven.
1939, May: re-activated for two cruises for the KdF organisation.
1939, July 17th: damaged by boiler explosion at Swinemünde killing 17. Later repaired and fitted out as naval hospital ship.
1944: accommodation ship at Gdynia.
1945, February 1st: sunk by a mine off Swinemünde.
1949: raised by the Russians, towed to Warnemünde; renamed *Admiral Nachimov*.
1957, May 2nd: entered Black Sea service after lengthy rebuilding at Rostock; 17,053 grt; 870 passengers.
1986, August 31st: collided with the Russian freighter *Pyotr Vasev* near Novorossiysk and sank; 423 lives lost out of 1234 on board.

BERMUDA

Furness Withy & Co., Ltd., London
Workman, Clark & Co., Ltd., Belfast; yard no. 490
19,086 grt; 547x74 ft
Four Doxford oil engines; 14,500 bhp; quadruple screw; 18.2 kn
Passengers: 616 first class; 75 second class

1927, July 28th: launched.
1928, January 14th: maiden voyage New York – Hamilton, Bermuda.
1931, June 16th: partially destroyed by fire at Hamilton; towed to her builders in Belfast for restoration.
1931, November 19th: when the work was almost completed, she was again burnt out by a further fire; total loss.
1931, December 24th: hulk raised.
1932, May: bought by Workman, Clark & Co., Ltd.; engines salvaged; hull towed to Rosyth for breaking but ran aground off the coast of Scotland and abandoned.

BREMEN

Norddeutscher Lloyd (NDL, North German Lloyd), Bremen
Deschimag A.G. 'Weser', Bremen, yard no. 872
51,656 grt; 938x102 ft
Four sets of geared steam turbines; 135,000 shp; quadruple screw; 28.5 kn
Passengers: 800 first class; 500 second class; 300 tourist class; 600 third class; crew 990
Sister ship: *Europa*

1928, August 16th: launched.
1929, July 16th: maiden voyage Bremerhaven – New York taking the Blue Riband from the *Mauretania* by crossing at an average speed of 27.83 knots; return eastbound crossing was at 27.92 knots.
1930, March 25th: lost the Blue Riband to her sister *Europa*.
1933, June: made a record eastbound crossing at 28.51 knots after improve-

ments to her machinery, but this obviously did not qualify her for the Blue Riband which is for westbound crossings only.
1939, August 30th: owing to the imminence of War, she made a delayed departure from New York without passengers, sailing for Bremerhaven via Murmansk and arriving safely on December 13th.
1940: naval accommodation ship at Bremerhaven; there was a proposal to convert her for use as a landing ship in the invasion of Britain but this never materialised.
1941, March 16th: destroyed by fire after arson by a disgruntled crew member; scrapped at the end of the hostilities.
1946, April 1st: the final remains of the hull were towed up the Weser river and deliberately stranded opposite Nordenham, where they can still been seen at low tide.

BRITANNIC

White Star Line, Liverpool
Harland & Wolff, Ltd., Belfast (yard no. 807)
26,943 grt; 712x82 ft
Two Burmeister & Wain - H&W oil engines; 20,000 shp; twin screw; 18 kn
Passengers: 504 cabin class; 551 tourist class; 493 third class; crew: 500.
Sister ship: *Georgic*

1929, August 6th: launched.
1930, June 28th: maiden voyage, Liverpool – New York. The largest motor ship in the British merchant navy until the advent of her sister, *Georgic*.
1934, June 19th: the assets of the White Star Line, including *Britannic*, were transferred to the new Cunard-White Star, Ltd.
1935, April 19th: transferred to the London – New York service.
1939, August 29th: taken over by the British government for conversion to a troop transport.
1947, March: returned to Cunard-White Star Line.
1948, May 22nd: first post-War voyage, Liverpool – New York. (27,666 grt; passengers: 429 first class; 564 tourist class.) also became a popular cruise ship.
1960, May: several transatlantic voyages cancelled as a result of a damaged crankshaft in one of her engines.
1960, December 4th: arrived at Liverpool at the end of her last transatlantic voyage.
1960, December 19th: arrived at Inverkeithing for scrapping.

CABO SAN AUGUSTIN

Ybarra & Compañía, Seville
Soc. Española de Construcción Naval, Bilbao (yard no.38)
11,868 grt; 500x63 ft
Two MAN oil engines; 9,200 bhp; twin screw; 16 kn
Passengers: 12 second class; 500 third class; crew: 112
Sister ship: *Cabo Santo Tomé*

1931, May: launched.
1931, September 25th: maiden voyage Genoa – Marseilles – Buenos Aires. Some later voyages called at Barcelona.
1934: refitted with more second class accommodation; 12,589 grt.
1936, July: with the outbreak of the Spanish Civil War, the Ybarra service to South America was suspended. *Cabo San Augustin* served as a transport for the Republican government, bringing munitions from the Russian Black Sea ports.
1939, March-April: at the end of the Civil War, *Cabo San Augustin* was one of four Spanish transports in Russian waters. All were seized by the Soviet authorities. She was renamed *Dnyepr* and used as a troop transport.
1941, October 3rd: torpedoed and sunk by a German aircraft off Anapa on the Crimean coast.

CALEDONIA

Anchor Line, Glasgow
Alexander Stephen & Son, Ltd., Linthouse, Glasgow, yard no. 495
17,046 grt; 552x70ft
Two sets of geared steam turbines; 13,500 shp; twin screw; 17 kn
Passengers: 205 first class; 403 second class; 800 third class
Sister ship: *Transylvania*

1925, April 21st: launched.
1925, October 3rd: maiden voyage Glasgow – New York.
1939, September: taken up as armed merchant cruiser, renamed H.M.S. *Scotstoun*.
1940, June 13th: torpedoed and sunk by U 25 200 miles West of the Irish coast.

CANADA

Ostasiatiske Kompagni (East Asiatic Company), Copenhagen
Nakskov Skibsvaerft, Nakskov (a subsidiary of the ship's owners), yard no. 62
11,108 grt; 493x64 ft
One Burmeister & Wain oil engine; 8,300 bhp; single screw; 17 kn
Passengers: 55 first class
Sister ships: *Amerika* and *Europa*

1935, May 16th: launched.
1935, August 7th: maiden voyage Copenhagen – Vancouver.
1939, November 3rd: struck a mine while nearing Hull on a voyage from Vancouver; sank the following day.

CAP ARCONA

Hamburg Sud Amerika Linie, Hamburg
Blohm & Voss, Hamburg; yard no. 476
27,560 grt; 676x84 ft
Two sets of geared steam turbines; 28,000 shp; twin screw; 21 kn
Passengers: 575 first class; 275 second class; 465 third class; crew 630

1927, May 14th: launched.
1927, November 19th: maiden voyage Hamburg – Buenos Aires.
1940, November 29th: German Navy accommodation ship at Gotenhafen (Gdynia).
1945: carried a total of 26,000 refugees from the Eastern territories; on May 3rd she was attacked by British planes near Lübeck and sank with the loss of approximately 5000 lives (owing to the lack of records, the exact number is not known); wreck broken up later on the spot.

CATHAY

Peninsular & Oriental Steam Navigation Co., Ltd. (P&O Line), London
Barclay, Curle & Co., Ltd., Glasgow, yard no. 602
15,104 grt; 545x70ft
Two quadruple expansion steam engines; 13,000 ihp; twin screw; 17.5 kn
Passengers: 203 first class; 103 second class
Sister ships: *Chitral* and *Comorin*

1924, October 31st: launched.
1925, March 27th: maiden voyage London – Sydney.
1939, October 11th: British armed merchant cruiser.
1942: troop transport; November 11th: bombed and sunk by German planes off Bougie, Algeria.

CHAMPLAIN

Compagnie Générale Transatlantique (French Line), Le Havre
Chantiers & Ateliers de St. Nazaire, Penhoët, yard no.Y6
28,094 grt, 641x83 ft
Two sets of geared steam turbines; 25,500 shp; twin screw; 21 kn
Passengers: 623 cabin class; 308 tourist class; 122 third class; crew 575

1931, August 15th: launched.
1932, February 1st: works suspended after the bankruptcy of the owners; the building was resumed five days later, after the French State assured the financing of the ship and announced a rescue plan for the French Line.
1932, June 18th: maiden voyage Le Havre – New York.
1936: refitted; 28,124 grt; funnel heightened; 635 cabin class; 317 tourist class; 134 third.
1936, May 21st: the vessel made headlines docking in New York for having on board $3 million worth of rough uncut Russian diamonds, claimed to be at the time the largest import of precious gems in the United States.
1937, January 22nd: stranded off Ambrose but was able to free herself without significant damage.
1940, June 6th: left New York bound for Le Havre with passengers.
1940, June 12th: sailed from Le Havre, while the port was being bombed by the Germans, bound for North Africa with refugees; on the 17th, while approaching the bay of La Pallice to embark members of the French government and their families, struck a magnetic mine; 12 people lost their lives; on the 21st the German submarine *U65* finished off the half sunken ship with a torpedo.
1941: the Italian company Serra was entrusted with the salvage of the liner but three of its divers lost their lives and the attempt was shelved.
1960 - 1964: the remains of the wreck were slowly recovered and scrapped.

CHITRAL

Peninsular & Oriental Steam Navigation Co., Ltd. (P&O Line), London
Alexander Stephen & Son, Ltd., Linthouse, Glasgow, yard no. 504
15,248 grt; 548x70 ft
Two quadruple expansion steam engines; 13,000 ihp; twin screw; 17 kn
Passengers: 199 first class; 135 second class
Sister ship: *Cathay* and *Comorin*

1925, January 27th: launched.
1925, July 3rd: maiden voyage London – Sydney.
1930: low pressure exhaust steam turbine added; 18 knots.
1939, October: armed merchant cruiser.
1944: troop transport.
1947: returned to owners and refitted as emigrant ship; 15,555 grt.
1948, December 30th: first post-War voyage London – Sydney under charter to the British government.
1953, April: scrapped at Dalmuir.

COLOMBIE

Compagnie Générale Transatlantique (CGT, the French Line), Le Havre
Ateliers & Chantiers de France, Dunkerque, yard no. 144
13,391 grt; 509x66 ft
Two sets of geared steam turbines built at Penhoët; 9,000 shp; twin screw; 17 kn
Passengers: 201 first class; 146 second class; 144 third class; crew: 251

1931, July 31st: launched.
1931, November 1st: maiden voyage, Le Havre – French Antilles; later also cruising.
1940: laid up at Fort de France, Martinique but was later reactivated.

1942, December: seized by American forces at Casablanca and converted into a troopship at New York.
1945, April: re-entered service after conversion into the hospital ship *USS Aleda E. Lutz*.
1946, April 11th: returned to the French Line and assumed her original name; used as a French government hospital ship on the Indo-China run.
1948: sent to the De Schelde yard at Vlissingen for restoration as a passenger liner. 13,803 grt; single funnel instead of the original two. Passengers:192 first class; 140 cabin class; 246 tourist class.
1950, November: returned to her pre-War service to the West Indies.
1963: full time cruise ship.
1964, March: sold to Typaldos Bros., Piraeus; re-named *Atlantic*, later *Atlantica*; cruising.
1967: laid up at Perama.
1970: partially scrapped.
1974: the remaining hull towed to Spain and broken up at Barcelona.

COLUMBUS

Norddeutscher Lloyd (NDL, North German Lloyd), Bremen
F. Schichau, Danzig, yard no. 929
32,354 grt; 775x83 ft
Two triple expansion steam engines; 32,000 ihp; twin screw; 19 kn
Passengers: 513 first class; 574 second class; 705 third class; crew 733
Sister ship: *Homeric*

1922, August 12th: launched after a previous attempt on June 17th had failed; the vessel had been laid down in 1914 with the intended name of *Hindenburg*.
1924, April 22nd: maiden voyage Bremerhaven – New York.
1927, August 2nd: a propeller shaft failure destroyed one of the engines; a less powerful unit was transferred from an NDL freighter reducing the speed to 17.5 knots.
1929, December: delivered after being re-engined at Blohm & Voss, Hamburg with two new sets of geared turbines to make her a more compatible running-mate for the *Bremen* and *Europa*; funnels replaced, more in the style of the new ships.
1939, August: owing to the imminence of War, a Caribbean cruise was abandoned and the passengers were abruptly landed at Havana; the ship went to Vera Cruz for safety.
1939, December 14th: sailed from Vera Cruz in an attempt to reach Germany.
1939, December 19th: scuttled by the crew 320 miles East of Cape Hatteras after being intercepted by the British destroyer *Hyperion*.

CONTE BIANCAMANO

Lloyd Sabaudo, Genoa
William Beardmore & Co., Ltd., Dalmuir, Glasgow; yard no. 640
24,416 grt; 653x76 ft
Two sets of geared steam turbines; 24,000 shp; twin screw; 21 kn
Passengers: 280 first class; 420 second class; 390 third class; 660 steerage; crew 500
Sister ship: *Conte Grande*.

1925, April 23rd: launched.
1925, November 20th: maiden voyage Genoa – New York.
1932, January 2nd: transferred to the newly formed Italia Flotte Riunite, into which Lloyd Sabaudo was merged; transferred in September to Genoa – Buenos Aires service.
1935, February 24th: first of twelve trooping voyages to Massawa.
1937, January 2nd: transferred to Lloyd Triestino; 23,255 grt; passengers: 230 first class; 481 second class; 704 third class.
1937, April 16th: first voyage Genoa to Far East.

1940, January 21st: rescued 316 survivors from the *Orazio* which had been destroyed by fire off Marseilles.
1940, February 23rd: first voyage Genoa – Valparaiso under charter to the Italian Line as a replacement for the *Orazio*. 1940, June 10th: laid up at Balboa, C.Z. on Italy's entry into the War.
1941, March 21st: seized by the U.S. government.
1942, August 14th: commissioned as the troop transport *U.S.S. Hermitage*.
1947, January 11th: it was announced that during his state visit to Washington seeking for further U.S. help for the post-War reconstruction of his country, Italian Prime Minister Alcide De Gasperi obtained the return to Italy of the vessel, together with her sister *Conte Grande*.
1947, August 18th: returned to Italian government and renamed *Conte Biancamano*; the vessel, however, maintained American ownership, being chartered to Italy at the symbolic cost of $1 per year.
1949, November 10th: first post-War voyage for Italian Line Genoa – Buenos Aires after extensive rebuilding at Monfalcone; 23,562 grt; length o.a. 665 ft; passengers: 215 first class; 333 cabin class; 1030 tourist class; used on both North and South Atlantic routes.
1960, August 16th: arrived at La Spezia from lay-up in Naples to be broken up; forward part of the superstructure has been preserved and can now be seen at the Science Museum in Milan.

CONTE DI SAVOIA

Italia Flotte Riunite (Italian Line), Genoa
San Marco, Trieste; yard no. 783
48.502 grt; 815 x 96 ft
Four sets of geared steam turbines; 125.000 shp; quadruple screw; 29.4 knots
Passengers: 500 first class; 366 special class, 412 tourist class; 912 third class; crew: 786

1931, October 28th: launched by H.R.H. Maria José of Savoy, crown princess.
1932, January 2nd: Lloyd Sabaudo, which had ordered the ship, merged into Italia Flotte Riunite; the vessel never bore Lloyd Sabaudo's colours on her funnels.
1932, October 14th: speed trials in the Gulf of Genoa; at an average speed of 29.43 the vessel proved to be the fastest liner yet built.
1932, November 30th: maiden voyage Genoa–New York; first liner fitted with a stabilizing plant (three Sperry gyros).
1933, March: failed attempt to gain the Blue Riband.
1934: modifications to the underwater part of the stern to solve yawing problems.
1936: revamping of the hotel areas, with merging of special and tourist class; passengers: 360 first class, 778 tourist class, 922 third class.
1940, June 2nd: arrived in Genoa at the end of her last commercial crossing from New York.
1940, June 8th: arrived in Malamocco, Venice lagoon; laid up.
1943, September 11th: bombed and set afire by German warplanes by mistake, in the confusion following the Italian armistice announced three days before.
1945, October 10th: refloated after the demolition of the burnt out upperworks; plan to convert her into an emigrant carrier for the South American route and discussions with the French Line and the Holland America Line to put her back in line service are shelved.
1950, April 24th: arrived in tow at Monfalcone yard to be scrapped.

CONTE GRANDE

Lloyd Sabaudo, Genoa
Stabilimento Tecnico Triestino, Trieste; yard no. 764
25,661 grt; 655x76 ft
Two sets of geared steam turbines; 26,000 shp; twin screw; 21.8 kn
Passengers: 578 first class; 420 second class; 720 third class; crew 532
Sister ship: *Conte Biancamano*.

1927, June 29th: launched.
1928, April 3rd: maiden voyage Genoa – New York.
1932, January 2nd: transferred to the newly formed Italia Flotte Riunite, into which Lloyd Sabaudo was merged; employed on both North and South Atlantic service.
1940, June 9th: laid up at Santos on Italy's entry into the War.
1941, August 22nd: seized by the Brazilian government; managed by Lloyd Brasileiro.
1942, March 10th: sold to the U.S. government.
1942, November 2nd: entered service as troop transport *U.S.S. Monticello*.
1947, January 11th: it was announced that during his state visit to Washington seeking for further U.S. help for the post-War reconstruction of his country, Italian Prime Minister Alcide De Gasperi obtained the return to Italy of the vessel, together with her sister *Conte Biancamano*.
1947, March 29th: returned to Italian government and renamed *Conte Grande*; the vessel, however, maintained American ownership, being chartered to Italy at the symbolic cost of $1 per year.
1949, July 15th: first post-War voyage Genoa – Buenos Aires for the Italian Line after being rebuilt at Genoa; 23,841 grt; length o.a. 667 ft; passengers: 215 first class; 333 cabin class; 950 tourist class; also used in the New York service.
1960, December 15th: one voyage Genoa – Sydney for Lloyd Triestino.
1961, September 7th: arrived at La Spezia for demolition after lay-up at Genoa.

CONTE ROSSO

Lloyd Sabaudo, Genoa
William Beardmore & Co., Ltd., Dalmuir, Glasgow; yard no. 611
18,017 grt; 588 x 74 ft
Two sets of geared steam turbines; 22.000 shp; double screw; 21.3 knots
Passengers: 208 first class; 268 second class; 1890 third class; crew: 442
Sister ship: *Conte Verde*

1914, March 26th: building contract signed. Construction halted after the outbreak of World War I. On October 6th, 1916 the British Admiralty bought the vessel for £127,288 and ordered her completion as the aircraft carrier *H.M.S. Argus*, launched as such on December 2nd, 1917.
1920, January 16th: the keels of a new *Conte Rosso*, and of a sister ship, the *Conte Verde*, are laid by Beardmore.
1921, January 26th: stuck on the slipway during the launching ceremony; successfully launched only on the following February, 10th.
1922, March 29th: maiden voyage Genoa-South America.
1922, May 15th: transferred to the Genoa-New York service.
1928, April 19th: back on the South America line.
1932, February 11th: first voyage Genoa–Shanghai after being transferred to Lloyd Triestino and revamped; open air swimming pool and lido added; 17.856 grt; passengers: 250 first class, 170 second class, 220 third class.
1936: re-engined; new experimental high pressure boilers of the Loeffler-type and two new high pressure turbines fitted; speed increased by two knots.
1940, June: transformed into troop transport after Italy's entry into the War.
1941, May 24th: torpedoed by the British submarine *Upholder* while in convoy, en-route from Naples to Tripoli loaded with soldiers; 1291 deaths.

CONTE VERDE

Lloyd Sabaudo, Genoa
William Beardmore & Co., Ltd., Dalmuir, Glasgow; yard no. 612
18,765 grt; 592 x 74 ft
Two sets of geared steam turbines; 22.000 shp; twin screw; 21 knots

Passengers: 230 first class; 290 second class; 1880 third class; crew 440
Sister ship: *Conte Rosso*

1920, January 16th: keel laid.
1922, October 21st: launched.
1923, April 4th: Maiden voyage from Genoa to Rio de Janeiro, Santos and Buenos Aires.
1932, January 2nd: transferred to Italia-Flotte Riunite; used for three Summer cruises in the Mediterranean from Venice but no line service.
1932, October 5th: first voyage Trieste–Shanghai for Lloyd Triestino; passengers: 250 first class, 170 second class, 220 third class.
1937, September 2nd: adrift owing to a gale while sailing in the China Sea; driven ashore by the strong winds on the coast nearby. Refloated 20 days later and dry-docked for repairs before resuming service.
1940, June 3rd: interned at Shanghai in the imminence of the entry of Italy into the War,
1942: chartered to the Japanese and converted into a hospital ship for the exchange of wounded prisoners of war with China; Italian crew.
1943, September 9th: scuttled by the crew to prevent the Japanese seizing her following the Italian armistice. Later refloated and towed by the Japanese to the Maizuru yard, Honshu to be repaired; renamed *Kotobuki Maru*.
1944, December: seriously damaged by U.S. Air Force bombers; repaired and transformed into troop transport.
1945, May 8th: U.S. warplanes sank the ship in the Bay of Nakata.
1949, June: refloated after having been given back to the Italians.
1951, September 3rd: sold for scrap to a Japanese yard.

CRISTOBAL

Panama Railroad Company, Inc. (Panama Line), New York
Bethlehem Steel Co., Quincy, Massachusetts, yard no. 1469
10,021 grt; 493x64 ft
Two sets of geared steam turbines; 9,150 shp; twin screw; 18.5 kn
Passengers: 202 first class
Sister ships: *Ancon* and *Panama*

1939, March 4th: launched.
1939, August 17th: maiden voyage, New York – Cristobal.
1942, January: became U.S. Army transport.
1946, June 14th: returned to her owners; refitted for civilian service.
1951: Panama Line became a division of the Panama Canal Company.
1961: Commercial service ceased; Panama Line now carried freight and passengers only for the government and for the canal.
1981, December: broken up at Brownsville, Texas.

DE GRASSE

Compagnie Générale Transatlantique (French Line), Le Havre.
Cammell Laird & Co., Ltd., Birkenhead, yard no. 886
17,707 grt; 574x71 ft
Two sets of geared steam turbines; 13,000 shp; twin screw; 16 kn
Passengers: 399 cabin class; 1712 third class

1924, February 23rd: launched, having been laid down in 1920 as the *Suffren*. Fitting out completed at St.Nazaire owing to a strike at Birkenhead.
1924, August 21st: maiden voyage Le Havre – New York.
1932: refitted; 18,435 grt; passengers: 536 cabin class; 410 third class.
1940: laid up at Bordeaux; later became an accommodation ship for German forces.
1944, August 30th: sunk by the retreating German army.
1945, August 30th: raised; taken to St. Nazaire for repair and refit; given a single, larger funnel instead of the original two; 18,435 grt; passengers: 500 cabin class; 470 tourist class.
1947, July 12th: first post-War voyage, Le Havre – New York.
1951: further refit; 19,918 grt.
1952, April: transferred to Le Havre – West Indies route.
1953, March 26: Sold to Canadian Pacific, who renamed her *Empress of Australia*.; 19,379 grt; passengers: 220 first class; 444 tourist class.
1953, April 28th: first voyage, Liverpool – Quebec.
1956, February: sold to Sicula Oceanica (SIOSA Line), Palermo and renamed *Venezuela*; 18,567 grt; Naples – La Guaira service.
1960: refitted at Genoa with new raked bow; 18,769 grt; length o.a. 614 ft. Passengers: 180 first class; 500 tourist class; 800 third class.
1962, March 17th: ripped herself open on a rock off Cannes.
1962, August 26th: sold to shipbreakers at La Spezia after having been refloated.

DEMPO

Rotterdamsche Lloyd, Rotterdam
Koninklijke Mij. 'De Schelde', Vlissingen; yard no. 189
16,979 grt; 573x70 ft
Two Sulzer oil engines; 14,000 bhp; twin screw; 18.5 kn
Passengers: 236 first class; 280 second class; 70 third class; 48 fourth class; crew: 335
Sister ship: *Baloeran*

1930, July 26th: launched, construction having been delayed by a fire.
1931, March 18th: maiden voyage, Rotterdam – Batavia and Surabaya.
1932, July 6th: serious fire in a cargo hold while lying at Tandjong Priok.
1940, March 1st: laid up at Surabaya.
1940: following the invasion of The Netherlands, she made several voyages between the Dutch East Indies and New York, on one of which she carried the government's gold reserves.
1941, January: chartered to the British government for conversion to a troopship. Managed by P&O.
1944, March 17th: torpedoed and sunk by the German submarine *U-371* off the Algerian coast.

DILWARA

British India Steam Navigation Co., Ltd., London
Barclay, Curle & Co., Ltd., Glasgow, yard no. 654
11,080 grt; 517x63 ft
Two Doxford oil engines; 6,500 bhp; twin screw; 16 kn
Passengers: 104 officers and families; 100 second class; 1,150 troops.
Sister ships: *Dunera*, *Ettrick* (P&O) and *Devonshire* (Bibby Line)

1935, October 17th: launched.
1936: entered service as a troopship.
1952: refitted; 12,555 grt; passengers: 125 first class; 96 second class; 104 third class; 705 troops.
1960: sold to China Navigation Co., Ltd., London (John Swire & Sons, Ltd.); refitted as a dual-purpose ship for pilgrim service (243 first class; 1,669 others) and for cruising (200 passengers); renamed *Kuala Lumpur*.
1971, December 1st: arrived at Kaohsiung for scrapping.

DOMINION MONARCH

Shaw, Savill & Albion, Ltd., London
Swan, Hunter & Wigham Richardson, Ltd., Newcastle-upon-Tyne, yard no. 1547

27,155 grt; 682x85 ft
Four Doxford oil engines; 32,000 bhp; quadruple screw; 21 kn
Passengers: 517 first class; crew: 385

1938, July 27th: launched.
1939, February 17th: maiden voyage, Southampton – Wellington via Cape Town and Sydney.
1940, August: taken up as a troop transport.
1948: re-entered civilian service after a lengthy refit; 26,463 grt; 508 first class passengers.
1961, December 30th: final sailing on the Southampton – Wellington route.
1962, June: acted as a floating hotel at Seattle.
1962, November 25th: arrived at Osaka under the name *Domonion Monarch Manu*, having been sold to Japanese buyers for scrapping.

DUCHESS OF ATHOLL

Canadian Pacific Steamships, Ltd., London
William Beardmore & Co., Ltd., Dalmuir, Glasgow, yard no. 648
20,119 grt; 601x75 ft
Two sets of geared steam turbines; 21,200 shp; twin screw; 18 kn
Passengers: 573 cabin class; 480 tourist class; 510 third class; crew 518
Sister ships: *Duchess of Bedford*, *Duchess of Richmond* and *Duchess of York*.

1927, November 23rd: launched.
1928, July 7th: preliminary cruise.
1928, July 13th: maiden voyage Liverpool – Montreal.
1935, December: lost her rudder during an Atlantic storm.
1939, December: taken up by the British government as a troop transport.
1942, October 10th: torpedoed and sunk by German submarine *U 178* in the South Atlantic.

DUILIO

Navigazione Generale Italiana (NGI), Genoa
Ansaldo S.A., Genoa Sestri, yard no. 175
24,281 grt; 635x76 ft
Four direct driven steam turbines; 22,000 shp; quadruple screw; 20.5 kn
Passengers: 280 first class; 670 second class; 600 third class; crew 480
Sister ship: *Giulio Cesare*

1916, January 9th: launched; she had been laid down in May 1914 but construction was halted owing to the War.
1923, October 31st: maiden voyage Genoa – New York.
1928, August: transferred to the South American service.
1932, January 2nd: NGI merged into the newly formed Italia Flotte Riunite (Italian Line).
1934, March 6th: first voyage Genoa – Cape Town after the Italian Line won a mail contract from the South African Government, much to the consternation of the Union-Castle Line; refitted in Genoa; hull painted all-white; funnels shortened; 23,635 grt; passengers: 170 first class; 170 second class; 395 tourist class.
1937, January 2nd: transferred to Lloyd Triestino; continued in South African service.
1939, November 7th: laid up in Genoa after a single trooping voyage from Cadiz.
1942, March: chartered to the International Red Cross for three round repatriation voyages of civilians from Italian colonies in East Africa.
1944, July 10th: sunk by Allied bombers while laid up in Zaule Bay, Trieste.
1948, February 11th: demolition commenced at the nearby San Rocco yard after the hulk was refloated by Tripcovich Salvage Co. of Trieste.

EMPRESS OF AUSTRALIA

Canadian Pacific Steamships, Ltd., London
'Vulcan', Stettin, yard no. 333
21,498 grt; 615x75 ft
Two sets of steam turbines with hydraulic gearing; 17,000 shp; twin screw; 17 kn
Passengers: 370 first class; 190 second class; 415 third class; 1000 steerage; crew 500
Sister ships: *Resolute* and *Reliance*.

1913, December 20th: launched as *Admiral von Tirpitz* for HAPAG, Hamburg-Amerika Linie, (Hamburg-America Line), Hamburg.
1914, February: name changed to *Tirpitz*. August: construction halted.
1920, December 1st: completed and handed over to Great Britain as war reparations for use as a troop transport under the management of P&O.
1921, July: sold to Canadian Pacific and renamed *Empress of China*.
1922, June 16th: after overhaul and modification by the 'Vulcan' and John Brown yards, delivery voyage from Glasgow to Vancouver; now named *Empress of Australia*, entered service Vancouver – Yokohama.
1923, September 1st: rescued over 1000 people after the great Tokyo earthquake.
1927, June: first voyage Southampton – Quebec after fitting of new Parsons turbines by Fairfield Shipbuilding and Engineering Co., Ltd., Glasgow. 18,000 shp; 20 kn. Passengers 400 first class; 150 second class; 630 third class.
1939, May 6th: carried King George VI and Queen Elizabeth to Quebec at the start of their North American tour.
1939, September: became troop transport; never re-entered civilian service.
1952, May: arrived at Inverkeithing for breaking up.

EMPRESS OF BRITAIN

Canadian Pacific Steamships, Ltd., London
John Brown & Co., Ltd., Clydebank, yard no. 530
42,348 grt; 760x97 ft
Four sets of geared steam turbines; 66,500 shp; quadruple screw; 25.5 kn
Passengers: 465 first class; 260 tourist class; 470 third class; crew 740

1930, June 11th: launched.
1931, May 27th: maiden voyage Southampton – Quebec; world cruising in the winter months.
1939, June 15th: brought King George VI and Queen Elizabeth back from Canada after their North American tour.
1939, November 25th: taken up by the British government as a troopship.
1940, October 26th: set on fire by a German bomber when nearing the coast of Ireland; taken in tow by the Polish destroyer *Burza* but torpedoed and sunk by *U-32* two days later.

EMPRESS OF JAPAN

Canadian Pacific Steamships, Ltd., London
Fairfield Shipbuilding & Engineering Co., Ltd., Glasgow (yard no. 634)
26,030 grt; 666x84 ft
Two sets of geared steam turbines; 34,000 shp; twin screw; 23 kn
Passengers: 399 first class; 164 second class; 100 third class; 510 steerage; crew 579

1929, December 17th: launched.
1930, June 14th: maiden voyage Liverpool – Quebec, then made her way via the Panama Canal to Vancouver, from whence she sailed to Yokohama on August 7th. The transpacific express route from Vancouver was her regular service.
1939, November 26th: taken up as a troop transport.

1942, October 16th: with Japan now an enemy, the *Empress of Japan* was renamed *Empress of Scotland*.
1948, May 3rd: finally returned to her owners. Refitted for the company's Liverpool – Canada service, which she entered on May 5th, 1950. (26,313 grt; passengers: 458 first class; 250 tourist class.)
1958, January: sold to the new Hamburg-Atlantik Line and renamed *Hanseatic*. (30,030 grt; 673 ft. long; now two funnels instead of her previous three; passengers: 85 first class; 1167 tourist class.) July 21st: maiden voyage for her new owners, Cuxhaven – New York.
1966, September 7th: damaged by fire while lying at New York. Towed to Hamburg, which she reached safely despite breaking loose from her tugs in mid-Atlantic. Laid up.
1966, December: sold for scrapping at Hamburg.

EUROPA

Norddeutscher Lloyd (NDL, North German Lloyd), Bremen
Blohm & Voss, Hamburg; yard no. 479
49,746 grt; 941x102 ft
Four sets of geared steam turbines; 130,000 shp; quadruple screw; 28.5 kn
Passengers: 687 first class; 524 second class; 306 tourist class; 507 third class; crew 970
Sister ship: *Bremen*

1928, August 15th: launched.
1929, March 26th: badly damaged by fire while being fitted out.
1930, March 19th: maiden voyage, Bremerhaven to New York, during which she took the Blue Riband from her Bremen-built sister with an average speed of 27.91 knots on the crossing from Cherbourg to the Ambrose Light.
1931: funnels lengthened to reduce the smoke nuisance on the after decks.
1933, June: The *Bremen* regained the record with a crossing at 28.51 knots, only to lose it two months later to the Italian *Rex*.
1936, March: first class became cabin class.
1939, September: laid up at Bremerhaven, later becoming an accommodation ship for the German Navy.
1940: plans to convert her in readiness for the invasion of Britain were abandoned.
1942: plans for her conversion into an aircraft carrier were also dropped.
1945, May: seized by the U.S. Navy and used to transport as many as 6,000 troops per voyage across the Atlantic.
1946, June: awarded to France and allotted to CGT (the French Line) as the replacement for the lost *Normandie*. Renamed *Liberté*.
1946, December 8th: sank during a storm at Le Havre after breaking loose from her moorings and colliding with the sunken wreck of the *Paris*.
1947, April 15th: raised and towed to St. Nazaire for rebuilding.
1949, October: work was severely delayed by a fire which destroyed part of the passenger accommodation.
1950, August 17th: joined the *Ile de France* in the French Line's express Le Havre – New York service. (51,839 grt. Passengers: 569 first class; 562 cabin class; 382 tourist class.)
1962, January 30th: arrived at La Spezia for demolition.

FÉLIX ROUSSEL

Messageries Maritimes, Marseilles
Ateliers & Chantiers de la Loire, St. Nazaire; yard no. A444 E
16,753 grt; 568x68 ft
Two Sulzer oil engines by Cie des Constructions Mécaniques; 11,000 bhp; twin screw; 16 kn
Passengers: 196 first class; 113 second class; 89 third class; crew: 268
Sister ships: *Georges Philippar* and *Aramis*

1929, December 17th: launched. Named after a former president of Messageries Maritimes.
1930, December: maiden voyage, Marseilles – Indo-China, China and Japan.
1935: lengthened and re-engined (17,083 grt; 600x68 ft; 14,700 bhp; 18 kn.)
1940, July: taken over by the British and used as a troopship under Bibby Line management.
1947: returned to owners. A lengthy refurbishment included the replacement of the two square funnels by a single stack of oval section.
1950, September 22nd: first post-War commercial voyage, Marseilles – Far East.
1955, April: sold to Compañía Internaciónal Transportadora (Arosa Line), registered at Panama and renamed *Arosa Sun*. Refitted at Trieste. (20,126 grt; passengers: 60 first class; 890 tourist class.)
1955, July 7th: maiden Arosa Line voyage, Trieste – New York and Quebec; subsequently Bremerhaven - Quebec service and cruising.
1958, October 8th: laid up at Bremerhaven prior to a proposed refit; but arrested for debt in December on the collapse of the Arosa Line.
1960: bought by Hoogoven, the Dutch steelmakers, for use as a workers' accommodation ship at Ijmuiden.
1974: scrapped at Bilbao.

FRANCE

Compagnie Générale Transatlantique (French Line), Le Havre
Chantiers et Ateliers de Saint Nazaire, Penhoët; yard no. 55
23,666 grt; 713 x 76 ft
Four direct driven steam turbines; 45,000 shp; quadruple screw; 25 kn
Passengers: 534 first class, 442 second class, 250 third class, 800 steerage; crew 500

1910, September 20th: launched with the name *France* (keel laid as *La Picardie*).
1912, April 20th: maiden voyage Le Havre-New York.
1914, August: requisitioned and used during the War as auxiliary cruiser, troop transport and hospital ship.
1919, August 6th: first post-War commercial voyage Le Havre-New York.
1920, October: on the westbound leg of a regular crossing to New York a boiler explosion killed nine crew members; after disembarking their bodies in Brest she continued her course to New York.
1923: refitted; oil burning; passengers: 517 first class, 444 second class, 510 third class, 152 steerage; 23,769 grt.
1932, September: laid up in Le Havre.
1935, April 15th: arrived in Dunkirk to be broken up.

GEORGE WASHINGTON

United States Lines, New York
Vulcan, Stettin; yard no. 286
25,570 grt; 723 x 73 ft
Two quadruple expansion steam engines; 22,000 ihp; twin screw; 20 kn
Passengers: 652 first class, 286 second class, 216 third class, 1842 steerage; crew 593
Sister ships: *Amerika* and *Kaiserin Auguste Victoria*

1908, November 10th: launched as *George Washington*.
1909, June 12th: maiden voyage Bremerhaven-New York.
1914, August: remained in New York at the outbreak of the First World War; interned.
1917, April 6th: seized by the U.S. government; converted into U.S. Navy troop transport; name unchanged.
1919: transferred to the U.S. Army.
1920, January: transferred to the U.S. Shipping Board; laid up.
1920, October: chartered to the U.S. Mail Line; refitted; 23,788 grt.
1921, August 3rd: first voyage New York-Bremen; collapse of the U.S. Mail Line;

transferred to United States Lines; still in the New York-Bremen service via the Channel ports.
1931, November: laid up in Patuxent River.
1940, August: reactivated as U.S. Navy transport.
1941: renamed *Catlin*; made available to the British Ministry of War transport once again under the name *George Washington*; managed by the Anchor Line.
1942, February: serious boiler problems; returned to the Americans.
1942, June: refitted at New York; new oil-fired boilers installed; resumed service as a U.S. Army troop transport.
1947, March: damaged by fire at New York; laid up.
1951, June 17th: further fire which left the ship a total loss; scrapped.

GIULIO CESARE

Navigazione Generale Italiana (NGI), Genoa
Swan, Hunter & Wigham Richardson, Ltd., Newcastle-upon-Tyne, yard no. 267
21,848 grt; 634x76 ft
Four geared steam turbines by Wallsend Slipway & Engineering Co., Ltd.; 21,900 shp; quadruple screw; 20.5 kn
Passengers: 243 first class; 306 second class; 1824 third class; crew 542
Sister ship: *Duilio*

1920, February 7th: launched; she had been laid down in December 1913 but construction was halted owing to the War.
1922, May 4th: maiden voyage Genoa – Buenos Aires; originally intended for the New York service, she made only occasional voyages on that route.
1932, January 2nd: NGI merged into the newly formed Italia Flotte Riunite (Italian Line).
1934, February 4th: first voyage Genoa – Cape Town after the Italian Line won a mail contract from the South African Government, much to the consternation of the Union-Castle Line; refitted in Genoa; hull painted all-white; funnels shortened; 21,782 grt; passengers: 170 first class; 170 second class; 300 tourist class.
1937, January 2nd: transferred to Lloyd Triestino; continued in South African service.
1939, April 20th: first voyage Genoa – Shanghai; October 14th: laid up in Genoa.
1942, March: chartered to the International Red Cross for three round repatriation voyages of civilians from Italian colonies in East Africa.
1944, September 11th: sunk by Allied bombers while laid up in Zaule bay, Trieste.
1949: raised and scrapped in Muggia, near Trieste.

GRIPSHOLM

Svenska Amerika Linien (Swedish American Line), Gothenburg
Armstrong, Whitworth & Co., Ltd., Newcastle-upon-Tyne, yard no. 999
17,993 grt; 573x75ft
Two Burmeister & Wain oil engines; 13,500 bhp; twin screw; 17 kn
Passengers: 127 first class; 482 second class; 948 third class; crew 360

1924, November 26th: launched.
1925, November 21st: maiden voyage Gothenburg – New York.
1940 - 1946: voyages under charter to the International Red Cross for the repatriation of prisoners of war.
1946, March: first post-War voyage.
1950: re-entered service after rebuilding at the Howaldtwerke, Kiel; 19,105 grt; length o.a. 590 ft; passengers: 210 first class; 610 tourist class.
1954, February 1st: first voyage after transfer to the new Bremen-America Line, a joint-venture by Swedish American Line and North German Lloyd.
1955, January 7th: taken over by North German Lloyd and renamed *Berlin*; 18,600 grt; passengers: 98 first class; 878 tourist class.
1966, November 26th: arrived at La Spezia to be broken up.

HIGHLAND BRIGADE

Nelson Line, London
Harland & Wolff, Ltd., Belfast, yard no. 812
14,131 grt; 544x69 ft
Two Burmeister & Wain oil engines; 10,000 bhp; twin screw; 15 kn
Passengers: 135 first class; 66 second class; 500 third class
Sister ships: *Highland Monarch, Highland Chieftain, Highland Hope, Highland Princess* and *Highland Patriot*

1928, November 1st: launched.
1929, May: entered service London – Buenos Aires.
1932: reorganisation of the parent Royal Mail group; Nelson Line absorbed by Royal Mail Lines.
1940: taken over by the British government as a troopship.
1946, January 18th: damaged by a mine near Singapore.
1947, November: resumed London – Buenos Aires service; passengers: 104 first class; 335 third class.
1959: sold to John S. Latsis and converted into a pilgrim carrier; one of her two funnels removed; renamed *Henrietta*; seasonal service, mainly North Africa to Jeddah.
1960: renamed *Marianna*.
1965, June 6th: arrived at Kaoshiung for scrapping.

HOMERIC

White Star Line, Liverpool
F. Schichau, Danzig, yard no. 891
34,351 grt; 774x82 ft
Two triple expansion steam engines; 32,000 ihp; twin screw; 19 kn
Passengers: 529 first class; 487 second class; 1750 third class; crew 730
Sister ship: *Columbus*

1913, December 17th: launched as *Columbus* for North German Lloyd, Bremen.
1914, August: construction halted owing to the outbreak of the War.
1919: allotted to Britain. Eventually bought by White Star Line and renamed *Homeric*.
1922, February 15th: maiden voyage Southampton – New York.
1923 - 1924: refitted and converted to oil-firing. 19.5 knots.
1934, February: Cunard and White Star merged.
1935, September: laid up at Southampton.
1936, February: sold for breaking up at Inverkeithing.

ILE DE FRANCE

Compagnie Générale Transatlantique (CGT, French Line), Le Havre
Chantiers et Ateliers de St. Nazaire (Penhoët), St. Nazaire, yard no. R5
43,153 grt; 792x92 ft
Four direct driven steam turbines; 60,000 shp; quadruple screw; 23.5 kn
Passengers: 537 first class; 603 second class; 646 third class; crew 800

1926, March 14th: launched.
1927, June 22nd: maiden voyage Le Havre - New York.
1929: catapult fitted for launching a mail flying boat; removed in 1931.
1932, November: major refit lasting six months; stern reinforced to reduce vibrations; interior revamped and telephones installed in all first class cabins;

passengers: 670 first class; 408 second class; 508 third class.
1939, September: laid up in New York.
1940: troop transport for French Government.
1940, July: taken over by British government after French capitulation; at first, managed by P&O, later by Cunard-White Star.
1945, September: handed back to French government, still used for trooping.
1946, February 3rd: returned to CGT; re-entered civilian service in October.
1947, April: start of complete refitting at Saint Nazaire; now had two funnels instead of three and furnished with some of the fittings from the *Normandie*; passengers: 541 first class; 577 second class; 227 tourist class.
1949, July 21st: re-entered the Le Havre – New York service.
1956, July 26th: rescued 753 people from the sinking *Andrea Doria* off the coast of Nantucket.
1957, February: ran aground off Martinique.
1958, November 1st: final voyage Le Havre – New York; arrived back in Le Havre on the 17th; laid up.
1959, February 26th: left Le Havre under the name *Furanzu Maru* having been sold to Japanese breakers; however, before being scrapped she was chartered by the breakers to an American film company to play the part of the fictional *Claridon* in the film 'The Last Voyage'; during the shooting of the film, the forward funnel was demolished and the ship was sunk in shallow water; she was subsequently raised and scrapped at Osaka.

JOHAN VAN OLDENBARNEVELT

Stoomvaart Mij. 'Nederland' (Nederland Line), Amsterdam
Nederlandsche Scheepsbouw Mij., Amsterdam; yard no. 194
19,040 grt; 608x75 ft
Two Sulzer diesel engines; 14,000 bhp; twin screw; 19 kn
Passengers: 366 first class; 280 second class; 64 third class; 60 fourth class; crew 360
Sister ship: *Marnix van St. Aldegonde*

1929, August 3rd: launched.
1930, May 7th: embarked on her maiden voyage from Amsterdam to Batavia but was involved in a collision and had to return to Amsterdam, eventually departing some days later.
1939, August 30th: single voyage Amsterdam to New York under charter to the Holland America Line.
1940, May: following the invasion of The Netherlands, the *Johan van Oldenbarnevelt* was handed over to the British who, after having her converted by Harland & Wolff at Belfast, used her as a troopship, still with a mainly Dutch crew.
1945, October: handed back to the Nederland Line.
1946, July: resumed her pre-War service to the East Indies.
1950, September 5th: switched to Amsterdam – Sydney emigrant service, returning via Djakarta to embark returning Dutch nationals.
1952, January 23rd: re-entered service after an extensive refit (19,787 grt; 1414 passengers in a single class).
1954 - 1958: occasional transatlantic emigrant and student voyages out of Rotterdam under charter to the Netherlands government.
1959, April 3rd: first voyage in a new round-the-World service by way of Australia and New Zealand, outward via Suez and home via Panama. 20,314 grt; 1210 single class passengers.
1962, November: hotel ship at Fremantle during the Commonwealth Games.
1963, March: handed over to the Greek Line (managers: Goulandris Bros.), who had bought her some months earlier. Refitted at Genoa and renamed *Lakonia*.
1963, April 24th: left Southampton on her first Greek Line cruise, which took her to the Canary Islands.
1963, December 22nd: Caught fire while off Madeira. 128 dead. Taken in tow but sank on the 29th.

KANIMBLA

McIlwraith, McEacharn, Ltd., Melbourne
Harland & Wolff, Ltd., Belfast, yard no. 955
10,985 grt; 484x66 ft
Two Burmeister & Wain oil engines; 8,500 bhp; twin screw; 17 kn
Passengers: 203 first class; 250 second class; crew: 160

1935, December 12th: launched.
1936, June 10th: maiden voyage, Sydney – Adelaide; mainly sailed between Sydney and Fremantle but Melbourne – Cairns in winter months.
1939, August 27th: taken up by the Royal Australian Navy for conversion into an armed merchant cruiser.
1943: converted into a L.S.(I) - landing ship (infantry); took part in many Pacific campaigns.
1945: still in government service, she repatriated troops and prisoners-of-war.
1949: one voyage carrying migrants from London to Sydney.
1950, December 13th: resumed her owners' service; passengers: 231 first class; 125 second class.
1952, June 14th: ran aground in Moreton Bay, suffering severe bottom damage
1958: started making cruises.
1961, January: sold to the Pacific Transport Co., Panama; re-named *Oriental Queen* and used for pilgrim voyages from Indonesia to Jeddah.
1964: chartered to Toyo Yusen Kaisha, Tokyo for cruises out of Australian ports; bought outright by Toyo Yusen Kaisha in 1967 for Yokohama – Guam service and for student cruises.
1973, December 7th: arrived at Kaohsiung for scrapping.

KUNGSHOLM

Svenska Amerika Linien (Swedish American Line), Gothenburg
Blohm & Voss, Hamburg, yard no. 477
20,223 grt; 609x78 ft
Two Burmeister &Wain oil engines; 17,000 bhp; twin screw; 18 kn
Passengers: 115 first class; 490 second class; 970 third class; crew 340

1928, March 17th: launched.
1928, November 24th: maiden voyage Gothenburg – New York.
1939, September: cruising from New York.
1942, January 2nd: sold to U.S. War Shipping Administration and converted to troop transport *John Ericsson*, managed by United States Lines.
1947, March: damaged by fire.
1947, July: re-purchased by the Swedish American Line but sold to South Atlantic Line, one of the constituents of the Home Lines in December; repaired and refitted in Genoa; renamed *Italia*.
1948, July 27th: first voyage Genoa – Buenos Aires.
1949, June: transferred to the Genoa – New York route.
1952, March: transferred to a Hamburg – New York service; passengers: 213 first class; 1106 tourist class.
1961: New York – Bahamas service and cruising.
1964: sold to Freeport Bahamas Enterprises, becoming an unsuccessful floating hotel, the *Imperial Bahama*.
1965, September: arrived Bilbao for scrapping.

LAFAYETTE

Compagnie Générale Transatlantique (CGT, French Line), Le Havre
Chantiers & Ateliers de St. Nazaire, Penhoët, yard no. J6
25,178 grt; 613x77 ft
Four MAN oil engines (two built by Penhoët); 18,000 bhp; twin screw; 18 kn
Passengers: 583 cabin class; 388 tourist class; 108 third class; crew: 472

1928, May: keel laid.
1929, May 9th: launched.
1930, May 17th: maiden voyage, Le Havre – New York.
1934, March 19th: limped into Plymouth late and damaged owing to a gale.
1935, January 18th: damaged in a collision with a tug while leaving Le Havre.
1938, May 4th: caught fire while in dry dock at Le Havre; scrapped at Rotterdam.

L'ATLANTIQUE

Compagnie de Navigation Sud Atlantique, Bordeaux
Chantiers & Ateliers de St. Nazaire, Penhoët, yard no. P6
42,512 grt; 744x92 ft
Four sets of geared steam turbines; 50,000 shp; quadruple screw; 23.8 kn
Passengers: 414 first class; 158 second class; 584 third class; crew 663

1930, April 15th: launched.
1931, September 29th: maiden voyage Bordeaux – Buenos Aires.
1933, January 4th: caught fire while sailing towards Le Havre, fortunately without passengers; drifted for over two days, then towed to Cherbourg; a legal dispute between the company and the insurance underwriters led to the abandoned hulk lying at Cherbourg for over three years.
1936, February: towed to Port Glasgow for scrapping.

LEVIATHAN

United States lines, New York
Blohm & Voss, Hamburg, yard no. 212
54,282 grt; 948 x 100 ft
Four direct driven steam turbines; 90,400 shp; quadruple screw; 25.8 kn
Passengers: 752 first class; 535 second class; 850 third class, 1772 steerage; crew 1234
Sister ships: *Imperator* and *Bismarck*

1913, April 3rd: launched as the *Vaterland*.
1914, May 14th: maiden voyage Cuxhaven-New York.
1914, August: laid up in New York.
1917, April 4th: seized by the U.S.A.
1917, July 25th: entered service as U.S. Navy troop transport. Renamed *Leviathan* on September 6th.
1919, September: laid up.
1923, July 4th: maiden voyage for the U.S. Lines' New York-Southampton service after a 16 months refit in Newport News; 59,956 grt; 110,000 shp; 27.5 knots; passengers: 970 first class, 666 tourist class, 1402 third class.
1931: tonnage reduced to 48,932 grt to save harbour dues.
1932: laid up; briefly reactivated in 1934 for four additional transatlantic voyages.
1938, February 14th, arrived at Rosyth, Scotland, from New York to be broken up.

MAJESTIC

White Star Line, Liverpool
Blohm & Voss, Hamburg, yard no. 214
56,551 grt; 956x100 ft
Four direct drive steam turbines; 86,000 shp; quadruple screw; 24.7 kn
Passengers: 750 first class; 545 second class; 850 third class; crew 1000
Sister ships: *Berengaria*, *Leviathan*

1914, June 20th: launched as *Bismarck* for HAPAG, Hamburg-America Line of Hamburg; work suspended with the outbreak of War.
1919: vessel assigned to Britain; building resumed under British supervision.
1920, October 5th: fire delayed completion.
1922, April: renamed *Majestic* for the White Star Line; she was 'de facto' the largest liner in the World until the advent of the *Normandie* in 1935. Indeed, according to N.R.P. Bonsor, if she had been measured by the same rules as those used for the *Leviathan*, her gross tonnage would have been 62,000 tons.
1922, March 22nd: arrived at Southampton for the first time.
1922, May 10th: maiden voyage Southampton – New York.
1934, February: Cunard and White Star merged.
1936, February: laid up in Southampton.
1936, May: purchased for breaking up by T.W. Ward but re-sold to the British Admiralty for conversion at Southampton to the training ship *Caledonia*. Funnels and masts reduced in order to pass under the Forth Bridge.
1937, April: permanently berthed at Rosyth.
1939, September 29th: destroyed by a fire and sank.
1940, March: breaking up started on the spot.
1943, July: the remainder of the wreck towed to Inverkeithing.

MALOJA

Peninsular & Oriental Steam Navigation Co., Ltd. (P&O Line), London.
Harland & Wolff, Ltd., Belfast. yard no. 588
20,837 grt; 625x73 ft
Two quadruple expansion steam engines; 16,000 ihp; twin screw. 16 kn
Passengers: 327 first class; 329 second class
Sister ship: *Mooltan*

1923, April 19th: launched.
1923, November: maiden voyage London – Bombay, later used on the London-Australia run.
1929: fitted with two auxiliary low-pressure steam turbines; 17.5 kn.
1939, October: entered naval service as an armed merchant cruiser.
1941: converted to troop transport.
1947: overhauled and refitted by Silley Weir & Co., London.
1948, June 10th: re-entered passenger service as an emigrant-carrier; passengers: 1030 tourist class.
1954, April: sailed for Inverkeithing to be broken up.

MALOLO

Matson Navigation Co., San Francisco
William Cramp & Co., Philadelphia, yard no. 509
17,232 grt; 582 x 83 ft
Two sets of geared steam turbines; 25,000 shp; twin screw; 22 kn
Passengers: 693 first class

1926, June 26th: launched.
1927, May 25th: during delivery voyage collided with the Norwegian freighter *Jacob Christensen* and almost sank.
1927, November 16th: after repairs, maiden voyage San Francisco – Honolulu.
1937: refitted and renamed *Matsonia*; 17,226 grt.
1942, February: U.S. Navy troop transport.
1946, May 22nd: first peacetime voyage San Francisco – Honolulu.
1948: sold to Mediterranean Lines (the Home Lines) and refitted at Genoa; renamed *Atlantic*; 15,602 grt; passengers: 349 first class; 203 cabin class; 626 tourist class.
1949, May 14th: first voyage Genoa - New York.
1952, February 29th: initiated new Southampton to Canada service; 20,553 grt.
1954, December: renamed *Queen Frederica* for the new Home Lines Greek-flag subsidiary National Hellenic American Line; Piraeus – New York service.
1961: refitted at Genoa; 21,329 grt; passengers: 174 first class; 1500 tourist class.

1965, November: National Hellenic American Line taken over by Chandris Lines; the ship now mainly used for emigrant voyages to Australia and for cruising.
1971, September 22nd: laid up in the River Dart, England.
1972, June: laid up in Piraeus.
1973: a few further cruises then returned to lay-up.
1977: sold for scrap; during the demolition a fire gutted the remains.

MANHATTAN

United States Lines, New York
New York Shipbuilding Co., Camden, N.J.
24,289 grt, 705x86 ft
Two sets of geared steam turbines; 36,620 shp; twin screw; 22.7 kn
Passengers: 582 cabin class; 461 tourist class; 196 third class; crew 478
Sister ship: *Washington*

1931, December 5th: launched.
1932, August 10th: maiden voyage New York – Hamburg via the Channel ports.
1939, December 30th: precluded by the Neutrality Act from trading with belligerent nations, was diverted to a New York – Genoa service, Italy still being officially neutral.
1940, June: cruising and intercoastal voyages.
1941, January 12th: aground for three weeks at West Palm Beach.
1941, June: became the U.S. Navy transport *U.S.S. Wakefield*.
1942, September 3rd: caught fire while crossing the Atlantic in convoy; taken in tow, reaching Halifax; repaired at Boston.
1946, May: laid up in the Hudson River.
1965, March 6th: arrived at Kearny, N.J. for scrapping.

MARIPOSA

Oceanic Steamship Company (subsidiary of Matson Navigation Co.), San Francisco)
Bethlehem Shipbuilding Corporation, Quincy, Mass., yard no. 1440
18,017 grt; 632x79 ft
Two sets of geared steam turbines; 28,000 shp; twin screw; 22.8 kn
Passengers: 475 first class; 230 cabin class; crew 359
Sister ships: *Monterey* and *Lurline*

1931, July 18th: launched.
1932, February 2nd: maiden voyage San Francisco – Sydney via Honolulu.
1941, December: taken over by the War Shipping Administration as a troopship.
1946, September: refit commenced in preparation for commercial service for the Matson Line; work ceased because of the costs involved; laid up at Alameda, CA.
1953, December: sold to the Home Lines; refitted at Trieste and renamed *Homeric*; 18,563 grt; length overall: 641 ft.; passengers: 147 first class, 1,096 tourist class.
1955, January 24th: first Home Lines voyage, Venice – New York; then placed in Southampton – New York and later Southampton – Canada service.
1956, July: averaged 22.02 kn between Quebec and Le Havre, the fastest post-War eastbound crossing between Canada and Europe.
1963, October: cruising, mainly between New York and Bermuda and the Bahamas.
1973, July 1st: seriously damaged by fire when off Cape May, N.J.; she was laid up at Genoa.
1974, January: arrived at Kaohsiung for scrapping; turbines sold to Chandris Lines for transfer to their *Ellinis* (ex-*Lurline*).

MAURETANIA [1]

Cunard Steam Ship Co., Ltd., Liverpool
Swan, Hunter & Wigham Richardson, Wallsend-on-Tyne; yard no. 735
Four direct driven Parsons steam turbines; 78,000 shp; quadruple screw; 27 kn
Wallsend Slipway & Engineering, Co., Wallsend-on-Tyne
31,938 grt; 790 x 88 ft
Passengers: 560 first class, 475 second class, 1300 third class; crew 812
Sister ship: *Lusitania*

1906, September 20th: launched.
1907, November 16th: maiden voyage Liverpool – New York. At the time the largest ship in the World.
1909, September: averaged 26.06 knots on a westbound crossing, winning the Blue Riband from her sister *Lusitania* and holding it for an unprecedented 20 years.
1915, June: troop transport and hospital ship during WWI.
1919, June 27th: first post war voyage Southampton – New York.
1922, March: refitting after a fire completed; oil burning; passengers 589 first class, 400 second class, 767 third class; 30,696 grt.
1929, August: having lost the Blue Riband to the new German challenger *Bremen*, the *Mauretania* responded with a westbound crossing at 26.9 knots and an eastbound one at 27.22 knots. Although she failed to regain the record, this was a remarkable performance for an ageing and dated liner.
1933, May: hull painted white with green boot top and band; used as a cruise ship.
1935, July 4th: arrived in Rosyth, Scotland to be broken up.

MAURETANIA [2]

Cunard-White Star Line, Ltd., Liverpool
Cammell Laird & Co., Ltd., Birkenhead, yard no. 1029
35,738 grt; 772x90 ft
Two sets of geared steam turbines; 42,000 shp; twin screw; 23 kn
Passengers: 440 cabin class; 450 second class; 470 third class; crew: 780

1938, July 28th: launched.
1939, June 17th: maiden voyage, Liverpool – New York; later used on London–New York service.
1939, December: laid up in New York.
1940, March: troop transport.
1947, April 26th: returned to civilian service after a refit by her builders; 35,677 grt; 475 first class; 390 cabin class; 300 tourist class.
1962, December: used increasingly for cruise service and for a few New York–Naples voyages; 406 first class; 364 cabin class; 357 tourist class.
1965, November 23rd: arrived at Inverkeithing for breaking up.

MILWAUKEE

Hamburg-Amerika Linie, (HAPAG, Hamburg-America Line), Hamburg.
Blohm & Voss, Hamburg, yard no. 483
16,699 grt; 565x72 ft
Two MAN oil engines; 12,600 bhp; twin screw; 16.5 kn
Passengers: 270 cabin class; 259 tourist class; 428 third class; crew 335
Sister ship: *St. Louis*.

1929, February 20th: launched.
1929, June 18th: maiden voyage Hamburg – New York.
1936: conversion to cruise ship; passengers: 559 first class.
1940: taken up by the German Navy for use as an accommodation ship at Kiel.
1945, May: seized by the British; intended for use as a troop transport

under the name *Empire Waveney*.
1946, March 1st: caught fire and sank while being refitted at Liverpool.
1946, May: salvaged; towed to Glasgow for breaking; remains of the hull later towed to Troon for final scrapping.

MINNEWASKA

Atlantic Transport Line, London
Harland & Wolff, Ltd., Belfast, yard no. 613
21,716 grt; 626x80 ft
Two sets of geared steam turbines; 16,000 shp; twin screw; 17.8 kn
Passengers: 369 first class
Sister ship: *Minnetonka*

1923, March 22nd: launched.
1923, September 1st: maiden voyage, London – New York.
1931, December: Atlantic Transport Line put in liquidation; vessels laid up.
1932: transferred to Red Star Line; Antwerp – New York service.
1933, October: laid up.
1934: broken up at Port Glasgow.

MONTCALM

Canadian Pacific Steamships, Ltd., London
John Brown & Co., Ltd., Clydebank, yard no. 464
16,418 grt; 575x70 ft
Two sets of geared steam turbines; 14,000 shp; twin screw; 17.5 kn
Passengers: 542 cabin class; 1268 third class; crew 390
Sister ships: *Montrose, Montclair*.

1920, July 3rd: launched.
1922, January 17th: maiden voyage Liverpool – St. John; St. Laurence service in the summer months.
1929, March 16th: first voyage Southampton – St. John after fitting of new geared turbines by Harland & Wolff.
1939, October 17th: entered service as the armed merchant cruiser *Wolfe*. Later used as troop transport and submarine depot ship.
1942, May 22nd: sold to the British Admiralty.
1950: laid up.
1952, November: arrived at Faslane for breaking up.

MONTE SARMIENTO

Hamburg Süd Amerika Linie (Hamburg South America Line), Hamburg
Blohm & Voss, Hamburg, yard no. 407
13,625 grt; 524x66 ft
Two geared MAN oil engines; 6,800 bhp; twin screw; 14.5 kn
Passengers: 1328 third class; 1142 steerage; crew 280
Sister ships: *Monte Olivia, Monte Cervantes, Monte Pascoal, Monte Rosa*.

1924, July 31st: launched.
1924, November 15th: maiden voyage Hamburg – Buenos Aires; often used for cheap cruises, sometimes on charter to KdF.
1939, December 21st: accommodation ship for German Navy at Kiel.
1942, February 26th: sunk during an air raid.
1943: raised and towed to Hamburg for scrapping.

MORRO CASTLE

New York & Cuba Mail Steamship Company, Inc. (Ward Line), New York
Newport News Shipbuilding & Dry Dock Co., Inc., Newport News, Virginia; yard no. 337
11,520 grt; 531x70 ft
Two steam turbines driving General Electric generators and motors; 18,100 shp; twin screw; 21 kn
Passengers: 430 first class; 100 tourist class; crew 220
Sister ship: *Oriente*

1930, March 5th: launched.
1930, August 23rd: maiden voyage New York – Havana.
1934, September 8th: captain found dead in his cabin. Shortly afterwards, several fires were discovered and the ship was soon ablaze. 133 lives out of 546 were lost. The hulk drifted ashore at Asbury Park, New Jersey.
1935: wreck broken up at Baltimore. It has since been established that the fires were probably set by the ship's radio officer.

NEW YORK

Hamburg-Amerika Linie, (HAPAG, Hamburg-America Line), Hamburg
Blohm & Voss, Hamburg; yard no. 474
22,181 grt; 656x78 ft
Two Burmeister & Wain oil engines; 15,000 bhp; twin screw; 17 kn
Passengers: 432 first class; 223 second class; 775 third class
Sister ships: *Albert Ballin, Deutschland* and *Hamburg*.

1926, October 20th: launched.
1927, April 1st: maiden voyage Hamburg – New York.
1930, April: re-entered service after refit at Blohm & Voss; 21,867 grt; 2 new sets of geared turbines; 19,000 shp; 21.9 knots.
1934, March: further refit; 22,337 grt; length o.a. 677 ft; 23.9 kn; passengers 210 first class; 350 tourist class; 400 third class.
1934, December 18th: rescued the crew of the Norwegian freighter *Sisto*, sinking in a hurricane.
1936, May 7th: collided with the Dutch freighter *Alphard*, which sank; the *New York* rescued the crew.
1939, August 28th: left New York without passengers and, owing to the subsequent outbreak of War, crossed via Murmansk, finally arriving in Hamburg on December 13th.
1940: naval accommodation ship at Kiel.
1945, April 3rd: bombed and wrecked.
1949, March: wreck raised and scrapped.

NIEUW AMSTERDAM

Nederlandsche-Amerikaansche Stoomvaart Mij (Holland Amerika Lijn; Holland America Line), Rotterdam
Rotterdamsche Droogdok Mij, Rotterdam, yard no. 200
36,287 grt; 759x88 ft
Two sets of geared steam turbines by Koninklijke Mij. 'De Schelde'; 35,100 shp; twin screw; 23 kn
Passengers: 556 first class; 455 cabin class; 209 third class; crew: 694.

1937, April 10th: launched.
1938, May 10th: maiden voyage, Rotterdam – New York via Channel ports.
1939, October: cruising from New York following the outbreak of war.
1940, May 14th: laid up in New York after the invasion of The Netherlands; handed over to the British government; September: converted to troopship at Halifax; placed under Cunard-White Star management.

1946, April 10th: triumphant return to Rotterdam after sailing over half-a-million miles in trooping service.
1947, October 29th: first post-War commercial voyage, Rotterdam – New York, after refit; 36,667 grt; passengers: 552 first class, 426 cabin class, 209 tourist class.
1960: refit; 36,982 grt; passengers: 574 first class, 583 tourist class; re-entered service 18th January, 1962.
1967: re-boilered by Wilton-Fijenoord, Schiedam.
1971: used almost entirely for cruising.
1972: transferred to the Netherlands Antilles flag.
1973, December 12th: arrived at Port Everglades at the end of her final cruise.
1974, March 2nd: arrived at Kaohsiung for scrapping.

NIEUW HOLLAND

Koninklijke Paketvaart Mij (KPM), Batavia
Nederlandsche Scheepsbouw Mij, Amsterdam, yard no. 187
10,903 grt; 527x62 ft
Two sets of geared steam turbines; 8,000 shp; twin screw; 15 kn
Passengers: 123 first class; 50 third class; crew 199
Sister ship: *Nieuw Zeeland*.

1927, December 17th: launched.
1928: Dutch East Indies to Australia service.
1940: troop transport.
1947: KPM merged into the new Koninklijke Java-China Paketvaart Lijnen of Amsterdam; 11,215 grt; passengers: 155 first class.
1959, February: sold for breaking up at Hong Kong.

NIEUW ZEELAND

Koninklijke Paketvaart Mij (KPM), Batavia
Rotterdamsche Droogdok Mij, Rotterdam, yard no. 142C
10,906 grt; 527x62 ft
Two sets of geared steam turbines; 8,000 shp; twin screw; 15 kn
Passengers: 123 first class; 50 third class; crew 200
Sister ship: *Nieuw Holland*.

1928, January 6th: launched.
1928: Dutch East Indies to Australia service.
1935, December: new turbines fitted by Fijenoord, Rotterdam.
1940: troop transport.
1942, November 11th: torpedoed and sunk by *U-407* in the Mediterranean.

NOORDAM

Nederlandsche-Amerikaansche Stoomvaart Mij (Holland Amerika Lijn; Holland America Line), Rotterdam
Machinefabrik en Scheepswerf van P. Smit, Jr., Rotterdam, yard no. 515
10,704 grt; 502x64 ft
Two Burmeister & Wain oil engines; 13,000 bhp; twin screw; 19 kn
Passengers: 125 tourist class
Sister ship: *Zaandam*; *Westerdam* and *Zuiderdam* near-sisters

1938, April 9th: launched.
1938, September 28th: maiden voyage, Rotterdam – New York.
1940, March 14th: first voyage, New York – Batavia via Cape Town.
1942, April: taken over as an American troopship.
1946, July: first post-War voyage Rotterdam – New York, following a refit; 10,276 grt; 148 first class passengers.

1963: sold to Cielomar SA, Panama, who renamed her *Océanien* for charter to Messageries Maritimes.
1963, August 2nd: first voyage Marseilles – Sydney.
1967, February 14th: arrived at Split for breaking up.

NORMANDIE

Compagnie Générale Transatlantique (CGT, French Line), Le Havre
Chantiers & Ateliers de St. Nazaire, Penhoët, yard no. T6
79,280 grt, 1030x118 ft
Four turbo-electric units from Société Générale de Construction Electrique & Mécanique Alsthom; 165,000 shp; quadruple screw; 32 kn
Passengers: 848 first class; 670 tourist class; 454 third class; crew 1345

1930, October 29th: building contract signed.
1931, January 26th: keel laid and construction of the hull started.
1931, December 11th: first massive strike of 5000 yard workers out of a total of 5700 working on the ship fighting against the intention of reducing their salaries.
1932, February 1st: following the bankruptcy of the French Line, work on the *Normandie* and the *Champlain* was suspended. On the 6th work was resumed after the French State rescued the Owners and took over the building contracts of the two liners.
1932, October 18th: a press release by the French Line announced that hull 'T6' was to be christened *Normandie* by the wife of the French President Albert Lebrun.
1932, October 29th: launched.
1933, July 25th: a special law is passed in France recognising the vessel as a National Icon and as such to be fully financed and run by the State.
1935, May 5th: first outing at sea of the vessel for sea trials on the measured mile of Glénans, during which the *Normandie* reached 32 knots, despite unforeseen strong vibrations at the stern.
1935, May 29th: maiden voyage Le Havre – New York, during which she seized the Blue Riband from the *Rex* with a crossing at an average speed of 29.98 kn. Mme. Lebrun, wife of the President of France, was a passenger on the voyage.
1936, March: some reconstruction to reduce vibration, including the fitting of new propellers. 83,423 grt, further emphasising that she was bigger than the new *Queen Mary*.
1936, August: lost the Blue Riband to the *Queen Mary* but regained it in July, 1937 (30.58 kn in the westernly direction); *Queen Mary* clinched matters in August, 1938 with a westbound crossing at 30.99 kn.
1938, February 5th: the vessel sailed from New York for the first of her two long cruises to Rio de Janeiro.
1939, August 28th: with war about to break out in Europe, was laid up at her pier in New York.
1941, December 12th: seized by the U.S. Maritime Commission; transferred to the U.S. Navy later that month and renamed *U.S.S. Lafayette*; conversion into a troop transport commenced.
1942, February 9th: a fire started by a welder's torch spread along the ship; she capsized the following day owing to the amount of water pumped into her.
1943, August 7th: refloated after lengthy operations to pump her out and to lighten her by removing funnels, mast and superstructure; November 3rd: laid up at Brooklyn.
1945, October 11th: after the abandonment of tentative plans to convert her into an aircraft carrier, the *Lafayette* was stricken from the Navy List.
1946, November: the hull was towed to Port Newark, N.J. for scrapping.

OCEANIA

Cosulich Line (Italia Flotte Riunite), Trieste
Cantieri Riuniti dell'Adriatico, Monfalcone; yard no. 253

19,507 grt, 590 x 78 ft
Four Fiat-Grandi Motori (Turin) oil engines; 24.000 bhp; quadruple screw; 22.5 knots
Passengers: 885 one-class; 500 steerage; crew: 253
Sister ship: *Neptunia*

1932, September 29th: launched.
1933, July 8th: sailed from Trieste for the first of three Summer introductory cruises in the Mediterranean.
1933, September 21st: maiden trans-Atlantic voyage Trieste-South America.
1935, September: single trooping voyage to Eastern Africa for the Abyssinian campaign.
1940, June 2nd: placed in lay-up in Trieste. At this time, one of the very first fire-fighting automated sprinkler systems was fitted on board.
1941, May 26th: first voyage Naples-Tripoli as troop transport.
1941, September 18th: torpedoed and sunk together with her sister *Neptunia* by the British submarine *Upholder* off the Libyan coast.

OLYMPIC

White Star Line, Liverpool
Harland & Wolff, Ltd., Belfast; yard no. 400
45,324 grt; 882 x 92 ft
Two triple expansion engines and one low pressure steam turbine; 51,000 ihp; triple screw; 23.5 kn
Passengers: 1054 first class, 510 second class, 1020 third class; crew 860
Sister ships: *Titanic* and *Britannic*

1910, October 20th: launched.
1911, June 14th: maiden voyage Southampton-New York.
1912, October 9th: at her builders for an extensive refurbishment, mainly to improve her safety, after the sinking of her sister ship *Titanic*.
1913, April 2nd: back in transatlantic service; 46,439 grt; passengers: 735 first class, 675 second class, 1030 third class.
1915, September: troop transport.
1918, May 12th: while approaching the French coast fully laden with troops, managed to avoid the torpedoes fired by the *U-103* and to ram and sink the German submarine.
1920, July 21st: first post-War voyage after refitting; oil burning; passengers: 750 first class, 500 second class, 1150 third class.
1927 - 1928: progressive enlargement of tourist class using spaces previously allocated to the second class and part of the third class; passengers: 618 first class, 561 tourist class, 382 third class.
1935, April 12th: laid up in Southampton.
1935, October 13th: arrived in Jarrow to be broken up.
1937, September: remaining lower part of the hull re-sold to shipbreakers in Inverkeithing and towed there to be dismantled.

ORAMA

Orient Steam Navigation Co., Ltd., London
Vickers, Ltd., Barrow-in-Furness, yard no. 598
19,777 grt; 659x75 ft
Two sets of geared steam turbines; 20,000 shp; twin screw; 20.0 kn
Passengers: 592 first class; 1244 third class
Sister ships: *Oronsay, Otranto, Orford* and *Orontes*

1924, May 20th: launched as *Orama* although originally laid down as *Oriana*.
1924, November 15th: maiden voyage London – Brisbane.
1939, June 16th: sailed from London on her last commercial voyage to Sydney.
1939, August 10th: sailed from Sydney to London; while cruising the Indian Ocean off Minocoy, she received orders via telegraph to head for Cape Town awaiting further orders; on 2nd Septembers sailed from Cape Town for London.
1939, December 12th: sailed from London for Halifax to embark 900 Canadian troops which she then disembarked at Greenock on Christmas eve.
1940, June 8th: attacked in the North Sea by the German cruiser *Admiral Hipper* and set afire; sunk by a torpedo fired from the *Hans Lody*.

ORANJE

Stoomvaart Mij. 'Nederland', Amsterdam
Nederlandsche Scheepsbouw Mij., Amsterdam, yard no. 270
20,016 grt; 656x84 ft
Two Sulzer oil engines; 37,500 bhp; twin screw; 22 kn
Passengers: 283 first class; 283 second class; 92 third class; 82 fourth class.

1938, September 8th: launched by Her Majesty Queen Wilhelmina.
1939, August 4th: maiden cruise to Madeira.
1939, September 4th: maiden voyage Amsterdam – Batavia via Cape Town; war had already broken out but The Netherlands remained neutral until the country was invaded in May, 1940.
1939, December: laid up at Sourabaya.
1941, February: re-activated and handed over to the Royal Australian Navy, becoming a hospital ship in July, but still under the Netherlands flag.
1946, July 19th: returned to her owners; refitted.
1947: Amsterdam – Batavia service via Suez.
1953, January 6th: collided in the Red Sea with her great rival, Royal Rotterdam Lloyd's *Willem Ruys*; repaired, fitted with a completely new bow section.
1959, January: re-entered service after being refitted by her builders; 20,551 grt; passengers: 323 first class; 626 tourist class.
1960, 7th September: first voyage in a new round-the-World service to Australia and New Zealand.
1962: acted as a royal yacht for a cruise to celebrate the Silver Wedding of Queen Juliana.
1964, September 4th: sold to Achille Lauro, Naples; greatly rebuilt at Genoa as the *Angelina Lauro*; 24,377 grt; lengthened to 674 ft. Passengers: 189 first class; 377 interchangeable; 1050 tourist class.
1966, March 6th: finally entered Lauro service, Bremerhaven or Southampton to Australian ports; her début had been delayed by a serious fire on August 24th, 1965.
1972, November 23rd: transferred to a joint venture between Costa and Lauro Lines and switched to full-time cruising to the West Indies and South America; subsequently advertised as *Angelina*, although registered name remained *Angelina Lauro*; the hull maintained the blue livery of Lauro, while the funnel adopted the Costa logo.
1979, 31st March: destroyed by fire at St. Thomas, Virgin Islands.
1980 September 24th: heeled over and sank while in tow to Taiwan to be scrapped.

ORION

Orient Steam Navigation Co., Ltd., London
Vickers-Armstrongs, Ltd., Barrow-in-Furness, yard no. 697
23,371 grt, 665x82 ft
Two sets of geared steam turbines; 24,000 shp; twin screw; 21 kn
Passengers: 486 first class; 653 tourist class; crew: 466
Sister ship: *Orcades*

1934, December 7th: launched.
1935, August 14th: maiden voyage, a Mediterranean cruise from Southampton,

during which she took on board 528 passengers and crew from the Cunard-White Star *Doric* which had been involved in a collision; September 29th: first voyage on her regular London – Australia route via Suez.
1939, September: taken up as a troop transport.
1941, September: collided with the battleship *H.M.S. Revenge*.
1947, February 25th: first post-War commercial voyage on the Australian route, after being refitted by her builders; 23,696 grt; passengers: 546 first class, 706 tourist class.
1958: refitted; passengers: 342 cabin class; 722 tourist class.
1960, May: passed to P&O-Orient Lines, which combined the two companies' Australian and Pacific services; *Orion* was transferred to the one-class tourist and migrant service; passengers: 1,691.
1963, May: used as a hotel ship at Hamburg, where a large exhibition was being staged.
1963, October: arrived at Tamise, in Belgium, to be broken up.

OSLOFJORD

Den Norske Amerikalinje (Norwegian America Line)
Deschimag AG 'Weser', Bremen, yard no. 932
18,673 grt; 590x73 ft
Two MAN oil engines; 17,600 bhp; twin-screw; 20 kn
Passengers: 152 cabin class; 307 tourist class; 401 third class; crew: 310

1937, December 29th: launched.
1938, May 10th: maiden voyage, Oslo – New York.
1939: following the outbreak of the Second World War, placed in cruise service out of New York.
1940, April: laid up in New York following the invasion of Norway; handed over to the British government for conversion into a troopship.
1940, December 13th: hit a mine off the mouth of the Tyne and sank.

PARIS

Compagnie Générale Transatlantique (CGT, French Line), Le Havre
Chantiers et Ateliers de St. Nazaire (Penhoët), St. Nazaire, yard no. 68
34,569 grt; 764x85 ft
Four direct driven steam turbines; 45,000 shp; quadruple screw; 22.4 kn
Passengers: 561 first class; 468 second class; 2210 third class; crew 657

1916, September 12th: launched, after delay owing to the First World War. Hull towed to safety at Quiberon Bay, Brittany.
1921, June 15th: maiden voyage Le Havre – New York.
1925: refitted; passengers: 563 first class; 460 second class; 1092 third class; crew 645.
1929, August: a serious fire destroyed most of the passenger accommodation. Refitted; passengers: 560 first class; 530 second class; 844 third class.
1937: it was announced that she would be transformed into a full time cruise ship and advertisements were published showing the vessel with a white hull, but the plan never materialised.
1939, April 18th: caught fire again while at Le Havre loading artworks from the Louvre for the New York World's Fair, which were fortunately saved and dispatched later by the *Champlain*. On the 19th, when the fire was extinguished two other fires broke out; the same day the vessel heeled over owing to the volume of water which had been pumped into her.
1946, December 8th: the *Liberté*, ex *Europa*, broke her mooring during a storm and collided with the wreck of the *Paris*.
1947: wreck scrapped on the spot.

PASTEUR

Compagnie de Navigation Sud Atlantique, Bordeaux
Chantiers & Ateliers de St. Nazaire, Penhoët, yard no. R8
29,253 grt; 697x 88 ft
Four sets of geared steam turbines; 60, 000 shp; quadruple screw; 25.5 kn
Passengers: 287 first class; 126 second class; 338 third class; crew: 540

1938, February 15th: launched.
1939: maiden voyage from Bordeaux to Buenos Aires, due to start on September 10th, was cancelled due to the recent outbreak of the Second World War.
1940, June 2nd: sailed from Brest to Halifax, carrying the French gold reserves to safety.
1940, August: became a troopship under Cunard-White Star Line management.
1945, June: handed over to the French government who used her as a troopship under Sud Atlantique management.
1948: refitted; 30,447 grt.
1957, January 25th: laid up.
1957, September 18th: sold to Norddeutscher Lloyd (North German Lloyd); rebuilt by Bremer Vulkan and re-named *Bremen*; 32,236 grt; 216 first class; 906 tourist class.
1959, July 9th: first voyage for her new owners, Bremerhaven – New York.
1966: refitted; 32,360 grt.
1970, September 1st: Norddeutscher Lloyd amalgamated with Hamburg-America Line to form HAPAG-Lloyd.
1971: sold to Chandris Cruises, Piraeus and re-named *Regina Magna*; 23,801 grt.
1972, May: cruising from European ports and in the Caribbean.
1974: Chandris Cruises merged with Chandris Lines; *Regina Magna* laid up at Perama Bay.
1977: sold to Philippine Singapore Ports Corporation for use as the accommodation ship for 3,500 construction workers at Jeddah under the name *Saudi Phil I*.
1978, March: became *Filipinas Saudi I*.
1980, June 6th: sank while under tow to Kaohsiung for scrapping.

PENNSYLVANIA

American Line (International Mercantile Marine), New York
Newport News Shipbuilding & Dry Dock Co., Newport News, Virginia; yard no. 329
20,526 grt; 613x80 ft
Two sets of turbo-electric machinery by General Electric Co.; 17,000 shp; twin screw; 18.5 kn
Passengers: 385 first class; 365 tourist class; crew 350
Sister ships: *California* and *Virginia*

1929, July 10th: launched.
1929, October 19th: maiden voyage New York – San Francisco in the Panama Pacific Line service.
1938, April: laid up in New York and sold to the U.S. Maritime Commission who allotted her to the American Republics Line (Moore & McCormack management) and renamed her *Argentina*.
1938, November 5th: first voyage New York – Buenos Aires after extensive refit; one funnel instead of two; 20,614 grt.
1942: taken over by the U.S. War Shipping Administration for trooping.
1948, January 15th: resumed New York – Buenos Aires civilian service, now for Moore-McCormack Lines; 20,707 grt.
1958: laid up in the James River.
1964, October: broken up at Kearny, New Jersey.

PRESIDENT HOOVER

Dollar Steamship Line, San Francisco
Newport News Shipbuilding & Dry Dock Co., Newport News, VA., yard no. 339
21,936 grt; 654x81 ft
2 General Electric turbo-electric units; 32,800 shp; twin screw; 22 kn
Passengers: 307 first class; 133 tourist class; 378 steerage; crew 385
Sister ship: *President Coolidge*

1930, December 9th: launched.
1931, August 13th: maiden voyage New York – San Francisco. Then placed in service between San Francisco and the Far East.
1937, December 10th: diverted from her normal course by the war in China, she ran aground off the southern coast of Taiwan; several attempts to refloat her failed.
1938: broken up on the spot by a Japanese company.

PRETORIA

Deutsche Ost-Afrika Linie (DOAL; German East Africa Line), Hamburg
Blohm & Voss, Hamburg, yard no. 506
16,662 grt; 577x73 ft
2 sets of geared steam turbines; 14,200 shp; twin screw; 18 kn
Passengers: 152 first class; 338 tourist class; crew: 263
Sister ship: *Windhuk* (Woermann Line)

1936, July 16th: launched.
1936, December 19th: maiden voyage, Hamburg – Cape Town.
1939, November 29th: German Navy accommodation ship at Pillau.
1945, February 22nd: hospital ship.
1945, May: seized by the British as a war prize; October: placed under the management of the Orient Line as the troopship *Empire Doon*.
1949: became *Empire Orwell* after a refit which included removing two turbine units, this reducing output to 10,000 shp; 18,036 grt.
1958: chartered to the Pan Islamic Steamship Co. of Karachi for use as a pilgrim ship, Karachi – Jeddah.
1958, November: sold to the Blue Funnel Line (Alfred Holt & Co., Ltd.), Liverpool for conversion into a full-time pilgrim ship; 17,891 grt; 106 first class; 2,000 third class.
1959, March: entered service as the *Gunung Djati*, carrying pilgrims from Indonesia.
1962: taken over by the Indonesian government; still named *Gunung Djati*.
1964: sold to Pelajaran 'Sang Saka', Djakarta; still in pilgrim service.
1966: sold to Pelarajan 'Arafat', Djakarta.
1973, October: re-entered service after a refit at Hong Kong; steam turbines replaced by two MAN diesel engines; 12,000 bhp.
1979: taken over by the Indonesian Navy and used as the accommodation ship *Tanjung Pandan*.
1987: scrapped.

QUEEN ELIZABETH

Cunard-White Star Line, Liverpool
John Brown & Co., Ltd., Clydebank, yard no. 552
4 sets of geared steam turbines; 200,000 shp; quadruple screw; 32 kn
Passengers: 823 first class; 662 cabin class; 798 tourist class; crew: 1,296

1938, September 27th: launched by Her Majesty Queen Elizabeth.
1940, March 2nd: left the Clyde, apparently for Southampton but actually for New York, where she arrived on March 7th; laid up.
1940, November: left New York for Sydney, where she was converted into a troop transport.
1946, March 6th: handed over to Cunard-White Star and refitted for passenger service.
1946, October 16th: maiden commercial voyage, Southampton – New York.
1968, November 4th: arrived at Southampton at the end of her last voyage in the transatlantic service.
1968, December 8th: sailed for Port Everglades; a concern called the Elizabeth Corporation (later Queen, Ltd.) ran her as a hotel and tourist centre; unsuccessful.
1970: bought at auction by C.Y.Tung, Hong Kong.
1971, July 16th: arrived at Hong Kong after a troubled five months-long voyage; registered in the name of Seawise Foundation; renamed *Seawise University*; refitted as a floating university intended for round-the-World voyages.
1972, January 9th: when the refit was almost complete, the ship caught fire, capsizing on the 10th.
1974: removal of much of the remains of the ship.

QUEEN OF BERMUDA

Furness, Withy & Co., Ltd., London
Vickers-Armstrongs, Ltd., Barrow-in-Furness; yard no. 681
22,575 grt, 580x76 ft
4 turbo-electric units from General Electric; 20,000 shp; quadruple screw; 21kn
Passengers: 700 first class; 31 second class; crew 410

1932, September 1st: launched.
1933, February 21st: maiden voyage Liverpool – New York; then regular New York – Bermuda service.
1936, July 10th: struck in fog by the 72-ton American fishing ship *Bejamin W. Latham*, 8 miles south-east of Ambrose lightship, which reported heavy damage.
1939, October 28th: taken over by the Royal Navy; converted into an armed merchant cruiser; third funnel, a dummy, removed.
1943: became a troop transport.
1947: returned to her owners.
1949, February: resumed New York – Bermuda service after extensive renovation, including the restoration of the third funnel.
1962, April 7th: resumed service after a five month reconstruction at Harland & Wolff, Belfast, now with a single streamlined funnel, remodelled bow and lengthened stern.; length overall: 591 ft; 22,552 grt.
1966, December 6th: arrived at Faslane for scrapping.

QUEEN MARY

Cunard-White Star Line, Liverpool.
John Brown & Co., Ltd., Clydebank, yard no. 534
80,774 grt; 1,019x118 ft
4 sets of geared steam turbines; 200,000 shp; quadruple screw; 32 kn
Passengers: 776 cabin class; 784 tourist class; 579 third class; crew: 1,101

1930, December 27th: laid down, but building ceased a year later owing to the financial effects of the Great Depression.
1934, April 3rd: work resumed.
1934, September 26th: launched.
1936, May 27th: maiden voyage, Southampton – New York.
1936, July 26th: a plane with reporters on board crashed near the vessel, after circling her to take pictures off Nantucket lightship; out of nine people on the plane, Edward Ramsdell, the Boston Post photographer, lost his life.
1936, August: gained the Blue Riband from the *Normandie* with a westbound

crossing at an average speed of 30.14 kn; *Normandie* regained the record temporarily in July, 1937.
1938, August: *Queen Mary* took back the Blue Riband with a decisive westbound crossing at 30.99 kn; she retained it until 1952, when the S.S. *United States* seized it.
1939, September: laid up in New York.
1940, March: taken over by the British government for trooping duties.
1942, October 2nd: collided with the escorting cruiser *H.M.S. Curacoa* while nearing the Irish coast. The cruiser sank with the loss of 338 lives.
1947, July 31st: first post-War commercial voyage, Southampton – New York, after a major refit; 81,237 grt; passengers: 711 first class; 707 cabin class; 577 tourist class.
1958: stabilisers fitted.
1967, September 22nd: final departure from New York.
1967, October: sold to the City of Long Beach, CA and left Southampton for her new home on October 31st.
1971, May 10th: opened to the public as a hotel and tourist attraction.

RAJULA

British India Steam Navigation Co., Ltd., London
Barclay, Curle & Co., Ltd., Glasgow; yard no. 614
8,478 grt; 477x62 ft
Two triple expansion steam engines; 5,200 ihp; twin screw; 15 kn
Passengers: 30 first class; 30 second class; 92 third class; 5,113 deck class
Sister ship: *Rohna*

1926, September 22nd: launched.
1926, November 26th: delivered for service between Madras, Nagatpatam, Penang and Singapore, but introduction delayed by charter for trooping.
1927, June: entered service.
1938, September and 1939, November: briefly taken up by the British government for trooping.
1940, May: requisitioned for trooping.
1943: landing ship during the Mediterranean campaign.
1946: resumed commercial service; passengers 37 first class; 133 second class; 1600 deck class.
1962: refitted by Mitsubishi at Kobe.
1966, November 3rd: survived a tropical cyclone during which she was driven along the coast for 30 miles by the winds. Her passengers held a service of thanksgiving for the ship when they finally disembarked.
1973: transferred to the parent P&O company but remained on the same route; October 10th: sold the Shipping Corporation of India becoming their *Rangat*, Calcutta – Andaman Islands service.
1976: broken up at Bombay.

RELIANCE

Koninklijke Hollandsche Lloyd (Royal Holland Lloyd), Amsterdam
J.C. Tecklenborg AG, Geestemünde, yard no. 256
19,980 grt; 615x72 ft
Two triple expansion steam engines plus low pressure turbine; 17,000 ihp; triple screw; 17 kn
Passengers: 315 first class; 302 second class; 850 third class; crew 480
Sister ships: *Resolute* and *Tirpitz*

1914, February 10th: launched as *Johann Heinrich Burchard*.
1915, November: completed.
1916, June: sold to Royal Holland Lloyd for delivery at the end of the War.
1920, February 3rd: left Bremerhaven as the *Limburgia* for delivery to the Dutch; the Allies did not recognise the sale but she was able to evade interception by a British destroyer, arriving safely in Amsterdam two days later.
1920, May 19th: maiden voyage Amsterdam-Buenos Aires.
1922: sold to United American Lines, registered at New York as *Reliance*; 19,582 grt; passengers: 290 first class; 320 second class; 400 third class.
1922, May 2nd: first voyage Hamburg - New York after a refit in Germany.
1922, December: transferred to Panamanian flag, re-measured at 16,798 grt.
1926, July 27th: bought back by HAPAG; 19,527 grt.
1928: converted to full-time cruise ship.
1937: refitted at Blohm & Voss, Hamburg; passengers: 633 first class; 186 second class.
1938, August 7th: caught fire at Hamburg, total loss.
1941: broken up at Bremerhaven.

REX

Italia Flotte Riunite (Italian Line), Genoa
Ansaldo S.A., Genoa; yard no. 296
51,062 grt; 880 x 97 ft
Four sets of geared steam turbines; 136.000 shp; quadruple screw; 29.6 knots
Passengers: 378 first class; 378 special class; 410 tourist class; 860 thirs class; crew: 880

1930, April 27th: keel laid.
1931, August 1st: launched by Margherita of Savoy, Queen of Italy.
1932, January 2nd: Navigazione Generale Italiana, who had ordered the ship, merged into Italia Flotte Riunite; *Rex* never bore N.G.I.'s colours on her funnels.
1932, September 27th: sailed from Genoa on her maiden voyage to New York, but two days later, while off Gibraltar, was compelled to make a three day stopover owing to the failure of the turbo-generator plant caused by a water infiltration in the engine room.
1933, August 16th: arrived in New York after winning the Blue Riband with a record crossing at an average speed of 28.92 knots; the Rex was the first liner in history to fly the pennant of the Blue Riband, 29-metre long, one for each knot of the record; two years later she was also the first liner to be presented with the North Atlantic Blue Riband Challenge Trophy, known also as Hales Trophy, from the name of its British sponsor, Sir Harold K. Hales, M.P.
1938, February: the American tour operator American Express chartered the vessel for a four weeks cruise to Rio, to compete with a similar cruise offered by Raymond Whitcomb with the *Normandie*.
1940, May 18th: arrived in Genoa at the end of her last trans-Atlantic voyage from New York.
1940, June 6th: arrived in Pula, Istria, to be used as accommodation ship for workers of the local navy shipyard.
1940, August 15th: arrived in Trieste and laid up; after the Italian armistice the majority of the vessel's furnishing and fittings were removed by the occupying Nazi forces.
1944, September 5th: after the frequent Allied bombing of Trieste, which slightly damaged the ship, she was towed along the Istrian coast, between Capodistria and Isola, considered safer, but instead three days later R.A.F. and South African aircraft set her afire.
1947, August: despite the protests of the Allies, Jugoslavia began demolishing the vessel, lasting ten years, although numerous pieces are still in the mud, including one of the four giant bronze propellers.

ROMA

Navigazione Generale Italiana (NGI), Genoa
Ansaldo S.A., Genoa Sestri, yard no. 277
32,583 grt; 709x83 ft
Four sets of geared steam turbines; 44,000 shp; quadruple screw; 24.6 kn

Passengers: 375 first class; 500 second class; 700 third class; crew: 510
Sister ship: *Augustus* (oil engines)

1926, February 26th: launched after a failed attempt the day before. Boilers and turbines recovered from the battleship *Cristoforo Colombo*.
1926, September 21st: maiden voyage, Genoa - New York.
1932, January 2nd: transferred to Italia Flotte Riunite into which NGI had been merged.
1939: Italian Line announced that the vessel and her sister ship *Augustus* would be laid up at the end of the year to be converted into two modern trans-Atlantic motor liners for both the North and South American run. The plan foresaw re-engining by new Fiat oil engines (eventually built and fitted after the War on the new *Giulio Cesare* and *Augustus*), the fitting of a new stem and stern, the whole rebuilding of upperworks (with a single funnel) and hotel areas, designed in modern style by *Conte di Savoia*'s interior archtect Gustavo Pulitzer Finali.
1940, June 10th: on the very same day Italy entered the War, she arrived in Naples carrying 700 women and children evacuated from Tripoli and was subsequently laid up.
1941, July 12th: requisitioned in Genoa by the Navy and sent to O.A.R.N. works to be converted into an aircraft carrier. New sets of geared turbines fitted with a total output of 151.000 and 33 knots service speed.
1943, September 9th: following the Italian armistice there was a failed attempt to scuttle the ship by the yard workers; other further attempts to sink her, by either Partisans or Nazis failed and the vessel was found intact in Genoa at the end of the War.
1946: studies to reconvert her to a passenger liner proved the costs to be too high; the vessel was then delivered to the La Spezia scrapyards to be broken up.

RUYS

Koninklijke Paketvaart Mij. (KPM), Batavia
Koninklijke Mij. 'De Schelde', Vlissingen, yard no. 204
14,155 grt; 559x72 ft
Three Sulzer oil engines; 11,000 bhp; triple screw; 18 kn
Passengers: 82 first class; 82 second class; 500 steerage; crew: 221
Sister ships: *Boissevain* and *Tegelberg*

1937, September 21st: launched.
1938, April: entered service, Cape Town - Batavia - Kobe.
1940: troop transport.
1947: KPM merged with Java-China-Japan Line to become the Royal Interocean Lines, Amsterdam; Kobe - Cape Town - Buenos Aires.
1968, September 13th: arrived at Kaohsiung for scrapping.

SANTA PAULA

Grace Line, New York
Federal Shipbuilding & Drydock Co., Kearney, NJ; yard no. 122
9,135 grt; 508x72 ft
Two sets of geared steam turbines; twin screw; 4600 shp; 19 kn
Passengers: 225 first class; 65 third class
Sister ships: *Santa Rosa*, *Santa Lucia* and *Santa Elena*

1932, June 11th: launched.
1933, January 7th: maiden voyage New York - San Francisco - Seattle.
1938, January 14th: transferred to Caribbean service (New York - La Guaira).
1941, November: taken over by the American government's War Shipping Administration as a troopship.
1947, May 2nd: first post-War commercial voyage, New York - Caribbean.
1958, June: laid up at Hoboken, New Jersey.
1960: sold to Typaldos Bros. of Piraeus; refitted and renamed *Acropolis*.

1962: passengers: 450 first class; cruising.
1968: collapse of the Typaldos Line in the aftermath of the loss by fire of their ferry *Heraklion* in December 1966. *Acropolis* laid up at Perama.
1977: scrapped.

SATURNIA

Cosulich Line, Trieste
Cantieri Riuniti dell'Adriatico, Monfalcone, yard no. 160
23,940 grt; 632 x 80 ft
Two Burmeister & Wain (by Fabbrica Macchine S. Andrea, Trieste) oil engines; 20.000 bhp; double screw; 21 knots
Passengers: 279 first class; 257 second class; 309 third class; 1352 steerage; crew: 441
Sister ship: *Vulcania*

1925, December 29th: launched.
1927, September 21st: maiden voyage Trieste-South America.
1928, February 1st: first voyage Trieste-New York; used on both North and South Atlantic routes according to the seasonal needs.
1932, January 2nd: Cosulich Line merged into Italia Flotte Riunite and the company's ships assumed its livery; however, Cosulich maintained separate headquarters in Trieste.
1937, January 2nd: Cosulich Line put into liquidation; all company's activities transferred to the newly formed Italian Line (Società Anonima di Navigazione Italia), based in Genoa.
1935, May 8th: first voyage as troop transport for the Abyssinian campaign.
1935, December 24th: beginning of the re-engining works at the builder's yard at Monfalcone; two new Sulzer oil engines, developing 28.000 bhp, fitted; 22.5 knots; 24,470 grt; the vessel re-entered service in August 1936.
1942, March: after a long lay-up following Italy's entry into the War, chartered together with the sister ship *Vulcania* and the steamers *Duilio* and *Giulio Cesare* to the Interantional Red Cross for three voyages to East Africa for the repatriation of Italian civilians from the Italian colonies occupied by the Allied forces.
1943, September 9th: after the proclamation of the Italian armistice, managed to escape from Venice, avoiding capture by the Germans and heading towards Brindisi, already in Allied hands; the sister ship *Vulcania*, also in Venice, failed to escape and was interned by the Germans.
1944, June 26th: resumed service for the Americans as their hospital ship *Frances Y. Slanger*, named after the first U.S. Red Cross nurse victim of the War.
1946, November 15th: given back in New York to the Italian government, after a dispute with Greece, which wanted her and her sister ship as War reparations.
1948, April 16th: after being revamped, sailed from Genoa for the first post-War voyage Genoa-New York.
1955, November 8th: transferred to the Trieste-New York line.
1965, Aprile 10th: arrived in Trieste at the end of her last voyage; laid up and put up for sale.
1965, October 7th: arrived in La Spezia to be broken up.

SCHARNHORST

Norddeutscher Lloyd (NDL, North German Lloyd), Bremen
Deschimag AG 'Weser', Bremen, yard no. 891.
18,184 grt; 652x74 ft
Two sets of turbo-electric machinery; 32,000 bhp; twin screw; 23 kn
Passengers: 149 first class; 144 second class; crew: 281
Sister ship: *Gneisenau* (geared steam turbines)

1934, December 14th: launched.
1935, May 3rd: maiden voyage, Bremerhaven - Yokohama.
1939, September: laid up in Japan when war broke out.

1942, February 7th: sold to the Japanese for conversion into an aircraft carrier.
1943, December 15th: commissioned as the *Jinyo* for the Japanese Navy.
1944, November 17th: torpedoed and sunk by the U.S. submarine *Spadefish*.

SCYTHIA

Cunard Steam Ship Co., Ltd., Liverpool
Vickers Ltd., Barrow-in-Furness, yard no. 493
19,730 grt; 624x73 ft
Two sets of geared steam turbines; 14,500 shp; twin screw; 16 kn
Passengers: 337 first class; 331 second class; 1538 third class; crew 409
Sister ships: *Samaria, Laconia, Franconia* and *Carinthia*

1920, March 22nd: launched.
1921, August: completed at Lorient owing to a strike at Barrow. August 20th: maiden voyage Liverpool – New York.
1924: third class passengers reduced to 1100.
1934, February: Cunard and White Star merged.
1939, August: became a troop transport.
1942, November 23rd: damaged by aerial torpedoes at Algiers.
1943, September: repairs completed at Gibraltar and New York.
1948, October: returned to service for Cunard-White Star Line between Cuxhaven and Canadian ports carrying refugees and migrants.
1950, August 17th: first voyage to Quebec after refit; passengers: 248 first class; 630 tourist class; 19,930 grt.
1958, January 1st: left Southampton for delivery voyage to breakers at Inverkeithing.

STATENDAM

Nederlandsche Amerikaansche Stoomvaart Mij (Holland America Line), Rotterdam
Harland & Wolff, Ltd., Belfast, yard no. 612
29,511 grt; 697x81 ft
Two sets of geared steam turbines; 22,000 shp; twin screw; 20 kn
Passengers: 531 first class; 525 second class; 995 third class; crew 525

1919, January 29th: contract signed and keel laid in April 1920.
1924, September 11th: launched; construction had been delayed owing to the availability of two hulls on the stocks at Harland & Wolff in Glasgow; these became the *Volendam* and *Veendam*.
1927, April 20th: the uncompleted hull arrived safely under tow at the Wilton yard at Schiedam after running aground when leaving Belfast.
1929, April 11th: maiden voyage Rotterdam – New York.
1939, December 12th: sailed on final voyage from New York; laid up upon arrival at Rotterdam.
1940, May 11th: German paratroopers occupied the ship; she was hit by gunfire from Dutch troops and burned for four days.
1940, August: hulk towed to Hendrik Ido Ambacht for breaking up.

STAVANGERFJORD

Den Norske Amerikalinje (Norwegian America Line), Kristiania (Oslo)
Cammell Laird & Co., Ltd., Birkenhead, yard no. 821
12,977 grt; 553x64 ft
Two quadruple expansion steam engines; 9500 ihp; twin screw; 16 kn
Passengers: 88 first class; 318 second class; 823 third class; crew 225

1917, May 21st: launched but remained incomplete.
1918, April: transferred to New York to be completed.
1918, September 11th: maiden voyage New York – Oslo.
1924: refurbished and converted to oil firing.
1931, December: refitted at A.G. 'Weser', Bremen; 13,156 grt; two low pressure steam turbines added; 18.7 knots; passengers: 147 cabin class; 207 tourist class; 820 third class.
1939, December: laid up at Oslo; later used as accommodation ship for the German Navy.
1945, August: first post-War voyage Oslo – New York; passengers: 172 first class; 222 cabin class; 335 tourist class.
1953, December: while en route from New York to Norway, lost her rudder during a storm; after a failed attempt to take her in tow, she completed most of the rest of her voyage steering with her twin screws.
1964, February: arrived at Hong Kong for breaking up.

STIRLING CASTLE

Union-Castle Mail Steamship Co., Ltd., London
Harland & Wolff, Ltd., Belfast, yard no. 941
25,550 grt; 725x 82 ft
Two Burmeister & Wain oil engines; 24,000 bhp; twin screw; 20 kn
Passengers: 297 first class; 492 cabin class
Sister ships: *Athlone Castle* and *Capetown Castle*

1935, August 15th: launched.
1936, February 7th: maiden voyage, Southampton – Cape Town.
1936, September – October: broke the 43-year old record for the southbound passage and then took the northbound record also.
1940, October 19th: taken up by the British government as a troopship.
1947, October: resumed Southampton – Cape Town service after refit; passengers: 245 first class; 538 tourist class.
1966, March 3rd: arrived at Mihara, Japan for scrapping.

STRATHAIRD

Peninsular & Oriental Steam Navigation Co., Ltd. (P&O Line), London
Vickers-Armstrongs, Ltd., Barrow-in-Furness, yard no. 664
22,544 grt; 864x80 ft
Two BTH turbo-electric sets; 28,000 shp; twin screw; 23 kn
Passengers: 498 first class; 668 tourist class; crew 490
Sister ship: *Strathnaver*

1931, July 18th: launched.
1932, February 12th: maiden voyage London – Sydney.
1939: taken up by the British government as a troop transport.
1941, March 24th: left Liverpool for Cape Town, one of 23 ex-liners which formed the largest convoy of troopships to sail from Britain during the Second World War.
1946-1947: refitted by Vickers-Armstrongs, now with one funnel instead of three; passengers: 573 first class, 496 tourist class.
1948, January 22nd: first post-War voyage London – Sydney.
1954: refitted as an entirely tourist class ship; 1252 passengers.
1960, May: passed to P&O-Orient Lines, which combined the two company's Australian and Pacific services.
1961, July 24th: arrived at Hong Kong for breaking up.

STRATHEDEN

Peninsular & Oriental Steam Navigation Co., Ltd. (P&O Line), London
Vickers-Armstrongs, Ltd., Barrow-in-Furness, yard no. 722
23,722 grt; 664x82 ft

Two sets of geared steam turbines; 28,000 shp; twin screw; 22 kn
Passengers: 448 first class; 563 tourist class; crew: 563
Sister ship: *Strathallan*

1937, June 10th: launched.
1937, December 24th: maiden voyage, London – Sydney via Suez.
1939: taken up by the British government as a troopship.
1947, June: first post-War commercial voyage on the London – Sydney run, having been refitted at Barrow-in-Furness; passengers: 527 first class; 453 tourist class.
1950: chartered to the Cunard-White Star Line for Southampton – New York voyages; handed back to P&O later in the year.
1961: converted for single class service, still on the London – Sydney run; 1,200 passengers.
1963, December: briefly chartered to the Travel Savings Association for cruising.
1964: sold to John S. Latsis, Piraeus; converted into pilgrim ship; renamed *Henrietta Latsi*. She and her near-sister, *Marianna Latsi* (ex-*Strathmore*) were the largest ships ever employed in the pilgrim trades.
1966: re-named *Marianna Latsi*.
1969, May 19th: arrived at La Spezia to be broken up.

STRATHMORE

Peninsular & Oriental Steam Navigation Co., Ltd. (P&O Line), London
Vickers-Armstrongs, Ltd., Barrow-in-Furness, yard no. 698
23,428 grt; 665x82 ft
Two sets of geared steam turbines; 28,000 shp; twin screw; 22 kn
Passengers: 445 first class; 665 tourist class; crew 515

1935, April 4th: launched.
1935, September 27th: maiden voyage, a cruise; October 26th: first voyage on the London – Australia route.
1939, September: taken up as a troop transport.
1949, October 27th: re-entered civilian service after refit; now 23,580 grt; passengers: 497 first class; 487 tourist class.
1960, May: passed to P&O-Orient Lines.
1961, September: became a tourist class-only ship.
1963, November: sold to John S. Latsis, Piraeus for use as a pilgrim ship between West and North Africa and Jeddah; renamed *Marianna Latsi*.
1966: swapped names with *Henrietta Latsi* (formerly her near-sister *Stratheden*)
1967, April: laid up at Elefsis.
1969, May 27th: arrived at La Spezia for scrapping.

TATSUTA MARU

Nippon Yusen Kaisha (NYK Line), Tokyo
Mitsubishi Company, Nagasaki; yard no. 451
16,975 grt; 584x72 ft
Four Sulzer oil engines; 20,000 bhp; quadruple screw; 21 kn
Passengers: 220 first class; 96 second class; 504 third class; crew: 330
Sister ship: *Asama Maru*

1929, April 12th: launched.
1930, April 25th: maiden voyage, Yokohama – San Francisco.
1938: now known outside Japan as *Tatuta Maru*.
1941: requisitioned by the Japanese Navy as a transport.
1943, August: torpedoed and sunk by the American submarine *Tarpon*.

TRANSYLVANIA

Anchor Line, Glasgow
Fairfield Shipbuilding and Engineering Co., Ltd., Glasgow, yard no. 595
16,293 grt; 552x70 ft
Two sets of geared steam turbines; 13,500 shp; twin screw; 17 kn
Passengers: 279 first class; 344 second class; 800 third class
Sister ship: *Caledonia*

1925, March 11th: launched.
1925, September 12th: maiden voyage Glasgow – New York; also used for cruising and on the Anchor Line Indian service.
1926, August 2nd: the ship docked in Glasgow welcomed by a large crowd greeting 1300 Scottish-American clansmen.
1928, November 30th: arrived in New York 36 hours late owing to a gale; the liner took part to the rescue of the crew of the German freighter *Herrenwyk*, sunk by the storm 600 miles off the Irish coast.
1929, March 27th: ran aground in dense fog off Cape Hague; the following day she was able to free herself and make her way to Cherbourg harbor, guided through dangerous rocks and other sand bars by local fishing craft.
1939, September: taken up as armed merchant cruiser.
1940, August 10th: torpedoed and sunk by *U-96* off Malin Head.

VICTORIA

Lloyd Triestino, Trieste
Cantieri Riuniti dell' Adriatico, Trieste; yard no. 782
13,062 grt; 540x70 ft
4 Sulzer-type diesel engines; 18,660 bhp; quadruple screw; 23.3 kn
Passengers: 239 first class; 245 second class; 100 third class; 82 fourth class; crew: 254

1930, December 6th: launched.
1931, June: on trials she proved to be the fastest motor vessel in the World.
1931, June 27th: maiden voyage, Trieste – Alexandria.
1932, January 24th: switched to the Genoa – Bombay route.
1936, October: route extended beyond Bombay to Shanghai.
1940: became a troop transport.
1942, January 24th: torpedoed and sunk by British aircraft while carrying troops from Italy to Tripoli.

VIRGINIA

American Line (International Mercantile Marine), New York
Newport News Shipbuilding & Dry Dock Co., Newport News, Virginia; yard no. 326
20,773 grt; 613x80 ft
Two sets of turbo-electric machinery by General Electric Co.; 17,000 shp; twin screw; 18.5 kn
Passengers: 385 first class; 365 tourist class; crew 350
Sister ships: *California* and *Pennsylvania*

1928, October 18th: launched.
1928, December 6th: maiden voyage New York – San Francisco in the Panama Pacific Line service.
1929, September 13th: collided with the freighter *Hermion* off the Californian coast.
1938, April: laid up in New York and sold to the U.S. Maritime Commission who allotted her to the American Republics Line (Moore & McCormack management) and renamed her *Brazil*.
1938, October 8th: first voyage New York – Buenos Aires after extensive refit;

one funnel instead of two; 20,614 grt; passengers 234 first class; 185 tourist class.
1942: taken over by the U.S. War Shipping Administration for trooping.
1948, May: resumed New York – Buenos Aires civilian service, now for Moore-McCormack Lines.
1957, December: laid up in the James River.
1964, March: broken up at Kearny, New Jersey.

VOLENDAM

Nederlandsche Amerikaansche Stoomvaart Mij (Holland America Line), Rotterdam
Harland & Wolff, Ltd., Glasgow, yard no. 649
15,434 grt; 774x82 ft
Two sets of geared steam turbines; 8,000 shp; twin screw; 16 kn
Passengers: 263 first class; 435 second class; 1200 third class; crew 328
Sister ship: *Veendam*

1922, July 6th: launched, having been jointly ordered before the War for a proposed Canadian service by HAPAG, North German Lloyd, Red Star and Holland America.
1922, November 4th: maiden voyage Rotterdam – New York.
1928: refitted to take account of the reduction in emigrant traffic to the United States; passengers: 263 first class; 428 second class; 484 tourist class.
1940, May: taken over as a transport by the British government; managed by Cunard-White Star Line.
1940, August 30th: torpedoed by *U-59* and *U-60* during a transatlantic voyage (convoy B 205) 300 miles off the Irish coast but remained afloat; towed back to Britain by the salvage vessel *Ranger*. In Glasgow a further unexploded torpedo was found lodged in the hull. After temporary repairs sailed to Birkenhead for refit by Cammell Laird.
1941, July: returned to service.
1945, July 5th: returned to Holland America Line but chartered for further service to the British Ministry of Transport; later chartered to the Dutch government for repatriation of evacuees from the East Indies.
1947: one class emigrant ship for 1682 passengers on various routes.
1951, November 13th: laid up at Rotterdam.
1952, February 14th: sold for scrap at Hendrik Ido Ambacht.

VULCANIA

Cosulich Line, Trieste
Cantieri Riuniti dell'Adriatico, Monfalcone, yard no. 161
24,469 grt; 632 x 80 ft
Two Burmeister & Wain (by Fabbrica Macchine S. Andrea, Trieste) oil engines; 20.000 bhp; double screw; 21 kn
Passengers: 279 first class; 259 second class; 310 third class; 1350 steerage; crew: 532
Sister ship: *Saturnia*

1926, January 30th: with the intended name of *Urania*, laid down on the same slipway from which her sister *Saturnia* was launched one month earlier.
1926, December 18th: launched with the name *Vulcania*.
1928, December 19th: maiden voyage Trieste - New York.
1932, January 9th: first voyage Trieste - New York for the new state-controlled company Italia - Flotte Riunite.
1935, February 2nd: first of three trooping voyages for the Abyssinian campaign.
1935, December 21st: back in civilian service after being re-engined by her builders with two FIAT oil engines of 14,000 bhp each; 22.4 kn; passengers: 360 first class; 388 tourist class; 563 third class.
1939, November 29th: one voyage Genoa - New York.
1940, April 29th: transferred to the Trieste - South America line.
1940, June 14th: upon her arrival from South America, she was laid up in Naples after Italy's entry into the War.
1941, August 23rd: troop transport to North Africa until October 8th; then used to repatriate refugees from the former Italian colonies in East Africa.
1943, September 10th: fled from Venice - where she had arrived two days earlier from Trieste - in the early morning to avoid capture by the Germans. On the same day, intercepted off Pula, she was deliberately stranded by her captain on the shores of Brioni Island. Occupied by the Nazis, she was freed four days later and taken back to Venice. Used as accommodation ship and for occasional coastal voyages.
1945, March 21st: damaged during an air raid. Later, in May, seized by British Ministry forces, repaired and delivered to the U.S. administration.
1945, October 29th: arrived in Le Havre to be used for repatriation crossings of American soldiers to New York.
1946, November 15th: returned to Italy.
1947, July 27th: first post-War crossing Genoa - South America; then placed on the Genoa - New York service.
1955, October 29th: transferred to the the Trieste - New York line; passengers: 232 first class; 262 cabin class; 862 tourist class.
1965, November 2nd: sold to Fratelli Grimaldi's Sicula Oceanica (SIOSA Line) of Naples; renamed *Caribia* and refitted. Passengers: 337 first class; 368 cabin class; 732 tourist class.
1966, February 28th: first line voyage Southampton - West Indies; later transferred to full time cruising in the Mediterranean.
1972, September 23rd: grounded off Nice. Refloated and sold to La Spezia shipbreakers.
1973, September 18th: arrived in Barcelona after being sold to Spanish shipbreakers.
1974, July: arrived in tow in Kaohsiung after being bought by the Taiwanese breakers Kudos Marine, Ltd.; dismantled.

WILHELM GUSTLOFF

Deutsche Arbeitsfront (German Labour Front; 'Kraft durch Freude'; KdF), managed by Hamburg-Südamerikanische Linien, Hamburg
Blohm & Voss, Hamburg, yard no. 511
25,484 grt; 684x77 ft
Two MAN oil engines; 9,500 bhp; twin screw; 15.5 kn
Passengers: 1,463 in a single class; crew: 426
Sister ship: *Robert Ley*

1937, May 5th: launched.
1938, March 29th: visited by Adolf Hitler.
1938, April 2nd: maiden cruise, a three-day trip into the North Sea, during which she rescued the crew of a sinking British cargo ship; April 9th: left for Tilbury, to act as a floating polling station for German and Austrian citizens resident in Britain.
1938, April 20th: entered regular service as a workers' cruise ship.
1939, September 1st: taken over by the German Navy to act as a hospital ship.
1940, November 22nd: became an accommodation ship for submarine crews at Gdynia (renamed Gotenhafen during German occupation).
1945, January 30th: sailed from Gdynia crowded with civilian refugees and submarine crews escaping from the Russian advance; torpedoed and sunk by the Russian submarine *S-13* with a huge loss of life (although there are no official records, the number of deaths was in the region of 5200 souls).

BIBLIOGRAPHY

W. Armstrong, *Atlantic Highway*, The John Day Co., New York, 1962.

R.D. Ballard, S. Dunmore, *Lusitania*, Madison Press, Toronto, 1995.

B. Bernadac, C. Molteni de Villermont, *L'incendie de L'Atlantique*, Marines Editions, Nantes, 1997.

F.C. Bowen, A century of Atlantic travel, Little, Brown & Co., Boston, 1930.

N.R.P. Bonsor, *North Atlantic Seaway*, T. Stephenson & Sons, Ltd., Prescot, 1955.

F.O. Braynard, *Picture History of the Normandie*, Dover Publications, New York, 1987.

F.O. Braynard, *Berengaria, Leviathan & Majestic*, Patrick Stephens Ltd., Welingborough, 1990.

A. Cooke, *Emigrant Ships*, Carmania Press, London, 1991.

H.A. Dalkman, A. J. Schoonderbeek, *125 Years of Holland America Line*, The Pentland Press, Durham, 1998.

R.P. De Kerbrech, D.L. Williams, *Cunard White Star Liners of the 1930s*, Conway Maritime Press, London, 1988.

M. Eliseo, *Rex, Ships of Ships*, Tormena Editore, Genoa, 2003.

M. Eliseo, *Rex, Storia di un transatlantico*, Albertelli, Parma, 1992.

M. Eliseo, *The Sitmar Liners & the V Ships*, Carmania Press, London, 1996.

M. Eliseo, P. Piccione, *Transatlantici*, Tormena Editore, Genoa, 2001.

F.E. Emmons, *American Passenger Ships*, University of Delaware Press, Cranbury, NJ, 1985.

V. Garroni Carbonara (a cura di), *Transatlantici di Sogno*, catalogue of the exhibit, Genoa, 1996.

V. Grund, *Oranje Een Koninklijk Schip*, Van Soeren & Co., Amsterdam, 2001.

F. Haine, F. Lose, A. Kludas, *Die Grossen Passagierschiffe der Welt*, Kohler, Hamburg, 2002.

D. Howarth, S. Howarth, *The Story of P&O*, Weidenfeld and Nicolson, London, 1994.

A. Kludas, *Die Geschichte der Deutschen Passagierschiffahrt*, Vol. IV and V, Weltbild Verlag, Augsburg, 1994.

A. Kludas, *Great Passenger Ships of the World*, Vol. 3, Patrick Stephens Ltd., Welingborough, 1976.

A. Kludas, *Great Passenger Ships of the World*, Vol. 4, Patrick Stephens Ltd., Welingborough, 1977.

A. Kludas, *Record Breakers of the North Atlantic*, Chatam Publishing, London, 2000.

P.C. Kohler, *The Lido Fleet*, Seadragon Press, Alexandria, Virginia, 1998.

W.H. Miller, *American Passenger Ships*, Dover Publications, Mineola, New York, 2001.

W.H. Miller, *Passenger Liners American Style*, Carmania Press, London, 1999.

W.H. Miller, *Picture History of British Ocean Liners 1900 to the present*, Dover Publications, Mineola, New York, 2001.

W.H. Miller, *Picture History of the Queen Mary and Queen Elizabeth*, Dover Publications, Mineola, New York, 2004.

W.H. Miller, *Picture History of the United States*, Dover Publications, Mineola, New York, 2003.

P. Patarin, *Messageries Maritimes*, Editions Ouest –France, Rennes, 1997.

B. Peter, *Passenger Liners Scandinavian Style*, Carmania Press, London, 2004.

P. Piccione, *Genova città dei transatlantici*, Tormena, Genoa, 2004.

P. Plowman, *Emigrant Ships to Luxury Liners*, New South Wales University Press, Kensington, Australia, 1992.

R. Seamer, *The Floating Inferno*, Patrick Stephens Ltd., Welingborough, 1990.

A. Sproule, *Port Out Starboard Home*, Blandford Press, Poole, 1978.

J. Steele, *Queen Mary*, Phaidon, London, 1995.

E.C. Talbot-Booth, *Merchant Ships 1939*, Marston & Co., London, 1940.

J. Townsend Gibbons, *Palaces that went to Sea*, Nereus Publishing Co., Minneapolis, 1990.

G. Turner, *Empress of Britain*, Boston Mills Press, Toronto, 1992.

A. I. Tzamtzis, *The Greek Ocean Liners 1907 – 1977*, Militos Editions, Alimos, n.d.

C. R. Vernon, *British Passenger Liners of the Five Oceans*, Putnam, London, 1963.

D.L. Williams, R.P. De Kerbrech, *Damned by Destiny*, Teredo Books, Brighton, 1982.

D. Williams, *Liners in Battledress*, Conway Maritime Press, London, 1989.

STATISTICS

The 50 biggest liners
(gross tonnage as built)

QUEEN ELIZABETH	83,673
QUEEN MARY	80,774
NORMANDIE	79,280
MAJESTIC	56,551
LEVIATHAN	54,282
BERENGARIA	52,117
BREMEN	51,656
REX	51,062
EUROPA	49,746
CONTE DI SAVOIA	48,502
AQUITANIA	45,647
OLYMPIC	45,324
ILE DE FRANCE	43,153
L'ATLANTIQUE	42,512
EMPRESS OF BRITAIN	42,348
NIEUW AMSTERDAM	36,287
MAURETANIA	35,738
PARIS	34,569
HOMERIC	34,351
AUGUSTUS	32,650
ROMA	32,583
COLUMBUS	32,354
MAURETANIA	31,938
STATENDAM	29,511
PASTEUR	29,253
CHAMPLAIN	28,094
CAP ARCONA	27,560
DOMINION MONARCH	27,155
BELGENLAND	27,132
BRITANNIC	26,943
AMERICA	26,454
EMPRESS OF JAPAN	26,030
ANDES	25,689
CONTE GRANDE	25,661
GEORGE WASHINGTON	25,570
STIRLING CASTLE	25,550
WILHELM GUSTLOFF	25,484
LAFAYETTE	25,178
VULCANIA	24,469
CONTE BIANCAMANO	24,416
MANHATTAN	24,289
DUILIO	24,281
SATURNIA	23,940
FRANCE	23,666
STRATHMORE	23,428
ORION	23,371
QUEEN OF BERMUDA	22,575
STRATHAIRD	22,544
ALCANTARA	22,181
NEW YORK	22,181

The 50 most powerful liners *(horse power)*

QUEEN ELIZABETH	200,000
QUEEN MARY	200,000
NORMANDIE	165,000
REX	136,000
BREMEN	135,000
EUROPA	130,000
CONTE DI SAVOIA	128,000
LEVIATHAN	90,400
MAJESTIC	86,000
MAURETANIA	78,000
BERENGARIA	74,000
EMPRESS OF BRITAIN	66,500
AQUITANIA	62,000
ILE DE FRANCE	60,000
PASTEUR	60,000
OLYMPIC	51,000
L'ATLANTIQUE	50,000
PARIS	46,000
FRANCE	45,000
ROMA	44,000
MAURETANIA	42,000
ORANJE	37,500
AMERICA	37,400
MANHATTAN	36,600
NIEUW AMSTERDAM	35,100
EMPRESS OF JAPAN	34,000
PRESIDENT HOOVER	32,800
COLUMBUS	32,000
DOMINION MONARCH	32,000
HOMERIC	32,000
ANDES	30,000
CAP ARCONA	28,800
AUGUSTUS	28,000
MARIPOSA	28,000
STRATHAIRD	28,000
STRATHMORE	28,000
CONTE GRANDE	26,000
CHAMPLAIN	25,500
MALOLO	25,000
CONTE BIANCAMANO	24,000
ORION	24,000
OCEANIA	24,000
STIRLING CASTLE	24,000
CONTE ROSSO	22,000
CONTE VERDE	22,000
DUILIO	22,000
GEORGE WASHINGTON	22,000
STATENDAM	22,000
GIULIO CESARE	21,900
DUCHESS OF ATHOLL	21,200

The 50 longest-lived liners *(years)*

QUEEN MARY	68
BERLIN	61
ALBERT BALLIN	57
AMERICA	54
MALOLO	51
PRETORIA	51
BERGENSFJORD	46
VULCANIA	46
STAVANGERFJORD	45
FÉLIX ROUSSEL	44
GEORGE WASHINGTON	42
MARIPOSA	42
GRIPSHOLM	41
PASTEUR	41
ORANJE	40
SANTA PAULA	40
COLOMBIE	39
ARUNDEL CASTLE	38
DE GRASSE	38
SATURNIA	38
SCYTHIA	37
KUNGSHOLM	37
VIRGINIA	36
AQUITANIA	36
EMPRESS OF JAPAN	36
HIGHLAND BRIGADE	36
NIEUW AMSTERDAM	35
BATORY	35
CONTE BIANCAMANO	35
STRATHMORE	34
ANCON	34
CONTE GRANDE	33
EMPRESS OF AUSTRALIA	33
J. V. OLDENBARNEVELT	32
ANDES	32
ATHOS II	32
QUEEN OF BERMUDA	32
MANHATTAN	32
MONTCALM	31
ALCANTARA	31
ILE DE FRANCE	31
MALOJA	31
QUEEN ELIZABETH	31
NIEUW HOLLAND	31
EUROPA	30
BRITANNIC	30
RUYS	30
STIRLING CASTLE	30
AORANGI	30
VOLENDAM	29

SHIPS INDEX

ALBERT BALLIN	56	DILWARA	174	NOORDAM	182
ALCANTARA	81	DOMINION MONARCH	186	NORMANDIE	151
AMERICA	202	DUCHESS OF ATHOLL	98	OCEANIA	149
ANCON	192	DUILIO	48	OLYMPIC	21
ANDES	195	EMPRESS OF AUSTRALIA	36	ORAMA	66
AORANGI	60	EMPRESS OF BRITAIN	126	ORANJE	196
AQUITANIA	31	EMPRESS OF JAPAN	111	ORION	158
ARANDORA	83	EUROPA	107	OSLOFJORD	183
ARUNDEL CASTLE	41	FÉLIX ROUSSEL	114	PARIS	38
ASAMA MARU	102	FRANCE	22	PASTEUR	198
ATHOS II	80	GEORGE WASHINGTON	21	PENNSYLVANIA	98
AUGUSTUS	77	GIULIO CESARE	48	PRESIDENT HOOVER	130
AWATEA	172	GRIPSHOLM	72	PRETORIA	176
BATORY	162	HIGHLAND BRIGADE	101	QUEEN ELIZABETH	205
BELGENLAND	33	HOMERIC	44	QUEEN OF BERMUDA	146
BERENGARIA	24	ILE DE FRANCE	94	QUEEN MARY	165
BERGENSFJORD	24	J. V. OLDENBARNEVELT	109	RAJULA	75
BERLIN	71	KANIMBLA	170	RELIANCE	35
BERMUDA	83	KUNGSHOLM	96	REX	133
BREMEN	104	LAFAYETTE	119	ROMA	77
BRITANNIC	113	L'ATLANTIQUE	128	RUYS	176
CABO SAN AUGUSTIN	115	LEVIATHAN	28	SANTA PAULA	139
CALEDONIA	68	MAJESTIC	42	SATURNIA	92
CANADA	161	MALOJA	57	SCHARNHORST	160
CAP ARCONA	87	MALOLO	89	SCYTHIA	41
CATHAY	69	MANHATTAN	144	STATENDAM	100
CHAMPLAIN	142	MARIPOSA	140	STAVANGERFJORD	34
CHITRAL	69	MAURETANIA [1]	16	STIRLING CASTLE	170
COLOMBIE	124	MAURETANIA [2]	188	STRATHAIRD	130
COLUMBUS	63	MILWAUKEE	102	STRATHEDEN	178
CONTE BIANCAMANO	73	MINNEWASKA	58	STRATHMORE	162
CONTE DI SAVOIA	135	MONTCALM	38	TATSUTA MARU	118
CONTE GRANDE	73	MONTE SARMIENTO	64	TRANSYLVANIA	68
CONTE ROSSO	52	MORRO CASTLE	116	VICTORIA	122
CONTE VERDE	52	NEW YORK	86	VIRGINIA	98
CRISTOBAL	192	NIEUW AMSTERDAM	179	VOLENDAM	44
DE GRASSE	59	NIEUW HOLLAND	97	VULCANIA	92
DEMPO	121	NIEUW ZEELAND	97	WILHELM GUSTLOFF	183

Printed by
Tisak Zambelli, Rijeka
May 2005